A GEOLOGICAL EXCURSION GUIDE TO THE

NORTH-WEST HIGHLANDS

OF SCOTLAND

A Geological Excursion Guide to
RUM
The Paleocene Igneous Rocks of the
Isle of Rum, Inner Hebrides
C. H. Emeleus and V. R. Troll

A Geological Excursion Guide to the
MOINE
Geology of the Northern Highlands of Scotland
Rob Strachan, Ian Alsop, Clark Friend and Suzanne Miller

A GEOLOGICAL EXCURSION GUIDE TO THE
NORTH-WEST HIGHLANDS
OF SCOTLAND

Edited by

Kathryn M. Goodenough
and
Maarten Krabbendam

British Geological Survey
Murchison House
West Mains Road
Edinburgh EH9 3LA

Published in 2011 by
Edinburgh Geological Society

in association with
NMS Enterprises Limited – Publishing
a division of NMS Enterprises Limited
National Museums Scotland
Chambers Street
Edinburgh EH1 1JF

Publication format, text and images
© Edinburgh Geological Society 2011
(unless otherwise credited)

The rights of Kathryn M. Goodenough and
Maarten Krabbendam to be identified as the
authors of this book have been asserted by
them in accordance with the Copyright,
Designs and Patents Act 1988.

ISBN: 978 1 905267 53 8

Publication layout and design by
    NMS Enterprises Limited – Publishing.
Cover artwork by Mark Blackadder; photograph
    of A' Clach Thuill, the Split Rock, Bay of Stoer
    Formation (BGS photograph P661223, ©
    NERC). See also p. viii.
Printed and bound in China by Eurasia.

For a full listing of titles and related
merchandise, please contact:
www.nms.ac.uk/books
www.edinburghgeolsoc.org

Contents

Contributors

Rob W. H. Butler
Geology & Petroleum
  Geology
School of Geosciences
University of Aberdeen
Meston Building
Elphinstone Road
Aberdeen AB24 3UE

Clark R. L. Friend
45 Stanway Road
Risinghurst
Headington
Oxford OX3 8HU

Bob Holdsworth
Department of Earth
  Sciences
University of Durham
Science Labs
Durham DH1 3LE

Michael R. W. Johnson
Grant Institute of Earth
  Science
University of Edinburgh
West Mains Road
Edinburgh EH9 3JW

Rick Law
Department of
  Geosciences
Virginia Tech
Blacksburg
Virginia 24061, USA

A. Graham Leslie
British Geological Survey
West Mains Road
Edinburgh EH9 3LA

Ian Parsons
Grant Institute of Earth
  Science
University of Edinburgh
West Mains Road
Edinburgh EH9 3JW

Robert J. Raine
Lapworth Museum of
  Geology
University of Birmingham
Edgbaston
Birmingham B15 2TT

Present address:
Ichron Ltd
Century House
Gadbrook Business Centre
Northwich
Cheshire CW9 7TL

M. Paul Smith
Lapworth Museum of
  Geology
University of Birmingham
Edgbaston
Birmingham B15 2TT

Dr R. A. Strachan
School of Earth and
  Environmental Sciences
University of Portsmouth
Burnaby Road
Portsmouth PO1 3QL

Ruth Wightman
Midland Valley Exploration
  Ltd
144 West George Street
Glasgow G2 2HG

Robert Wilson
Department of Earth
  Sciences
University of Durham
Science Labs
Durham DH1 3LE

Acknowledgements

Work in the North-west Highlands, carried out by British Geological Survey (BGS) staff and collaborators, has been greatly helped by the support of the local people. Particular thanks are due to the staff and volunteers of the North West Highlands Geopark; to the many local landowners who assisted with access for fieldwork; to Scottish Natural Heritage staff in Ullapool; and to Chris Rix and all at Inchnadamph Lodge. The contributors have also benefited greatly from fruitful discussions with many people, too numerous to list here, during field excursions and conferences in the area. The majority of the figures in this excursion guide were drafted by Craig Woodward, BGS Edinburgh. This edition of the excursion guide owes much to Suzanne Miller, who gave us the impetus to start work on a new version of the Assynt guide that had been published in 1979.

Foreword

Michael Johnson and Ian Parsons

In the early 1880s, Charles Lapworth's discovery of the Moine Thrust in North-west Scotland and Marcel Bertrand's discovery of the Glarus Thrust in the Swiss Alps established thrust tectonics as a fundamental mechanism of crustal shortening in orogenic belts. The subsequent heroic phase of mapping of the North-west Highlands by the team of British Geological Survey geologists led by Ben Peach and John Horne (the 'investigator twins') established the region as classic, recognised as such around the world, not only for the clear display of the nature of thrust systems but also for the remarkable igneous, metamorphic and sedimentary geology. The Assynt area is famous because it encapsulates many characteristic features of North-west Highland geology and accordingly the Survey team devoted much effort in preparing a special map of it.

Obviously, a guide to the Assynt region was an imperative. The first edition (1937) of the Assynt guide was the work of two members of the British Geological Survey: Murray Macgregor, whose work was mainly in the Midland Valley, and James Phemister, who mapped parts of Sutherland. It contained excellent coloured maps.

The second edition (1979) was revised and extended by us and retained most of the locality descriptions and the coloured maps but added sketches of the structural phenomena, which are marvellously displayed on mountain sides. The timing was appropriate, coinciding as it did with a renewed attack on the problems of the Assynt region in the light of 'thin-skinned' thrust tectonics imported from the Appalachians and the Canadian Rockies. New maps of the major igneous intrusions at Borralan and Loch Ailsh were provided.

In the preparation of the present edition a large team has been assembled to provide up-to-date interpretations of the structural relationships, sedimentology, and metamorphic history. On the igneous front, the relationship between magmatism and thrusting is explored by expanding the discussion to include the minor intrusive rocks and the radiometric ages

1

obtained since 1979. The area covered by the guide now includes the thrust zone between Assynt and Eriboll (Lapworth's area) and more on the rocks of the foreland, which at the time of writing are the subject of intense study using methods such as zircon chronology.

The first two editions provided several generations of professional geologists, students and amateurs with access to the treasures of Assynt. The new expanded edition shows that this classic region continues to yield up its secrets!

Editorial Introduction

Kathryn Goodenough and Maarten Krabbendam

This guide describes the bedrock geology of the North-west Highlands from Ullapool northwards, including many classic localities in the Moine Thrust Zone and its foreland. The area described here also largely corresponds to the North West Highlands Geopark. The geology of the Moine Supergroup, lying east of the Moine Thrust, is discussed in a companion guide (*A Geological Excursion Guide to the Moine Geology of the Northern Highlands of Scotland*, published by the Edinburgh and Glasgow Geological Societies). The North-west Highlands are also of great interest for their Quaternary geomorphology, which is not discussed in this guide but is described in several other publications. These include *Classic Landforms of the Assynt and Coigach Area*, published by the Geographical Association, and two excursion guides published by the Quaternary Research Association.

This guide has been written for those with some knowledge of geology, whether students, interested amateurs, or professional geologists. Less technical introductions to the geology and landscape of the North-west Highlands are provided by *The Northwest Highlands: a Landscape Fashioned by Geology*, published by Scottish Natural Heritage; and *Exploring the Landscape of Assynt: A Walker's Guide and Map*, published by the British Geological Survey.

Access to the North-west Highlands has improved greatly since the earlier editions of this guide were written, with the construction of fast new roads and bridges such as that at Kylesku. Nonetheless, this remains a remote and mountainous area, with some of the most dramatic scenery in the British Isles. The excursions described here vary from roadside stops to challenging, full day mountain walks over extremely rough terrain. The weather in this area can change very rapidly, with sunny mornings giving way to pouring rain by lunchtime – and vice versa. Therefore, all parties following these excursions should be well equipped with warm and waterproof clothing, sturdy walking boots, and topographic maps of the area (a list of relevant maps is given below). From May to September, some form of midge repellent will also be essential. All localities are given with accurate grid references, and so the use of a GPS is recommended. At the time of writing, mobile phone coverage is reasonably good along the main roads and on the mountain-tops, but largely non-existent in the more remote glens.

Under the Land Reform (Scotland) Act 2003, access to the Scottish countryside is open to all, but these rights bring with them responsibilities. You should always keep dogs under control; leave gates as you find them; never leave litter; avoid damage to the local environment, whether animal, vegetable or mineral; and follow reasonable advice from land managers if management operations are going on. This last point is particularly important in the North-west Highlands, where deer-stalking can take place from July until February. Stalking is a crucial part of the sustainable management of deer populations and of the economy of this area, and should be respected by all visitors. During the stalking season, if you wish to follow excursions away from the road, please follow all requests made by estate staff, either in person or through signage. If at all possible, the relevant estate should be contacted in advance of the excursion. Estate contact details are not given here, because of the likelihood of these changing during the lifetime of this guide; useful information can be obtained from www.whoownsscotland.org.uk.

Many of the localities listed in this guide are Sites of Special Scientific Interest (SSSIs). Where this is the case, it is normally stated in the text. There should be no hammering or *in situ* sampling of any kind at these localities. If you have a genuine research reason for sample collection, you should first request permission from the local office of Scottish Natural Heritage [www.snh.org.uk]. At sites that are not SSSIs, hammering is allowed, but is rarely needed, since the field relationships are generally very clear. If you really want to collect samples, please consider the other visitors that will come after you; repeated hammering by generations of geologists has already destroyed geological and geomorphological evidence at some localities in this area.

Travel to the North-west Highlands is easiest by car; the journey to Ullapool from Inverness takes around one hour, with the total journey from Ullapool northwards to Durness taking a further two hours. The nearest train stations are at Dingwall and Lairg, which are both reached by a small number of trains a day from Inverness. Scheduled buses run from Dingwall and Inverness to Ullapool, and connect with buses to Lochinver. At the time of writing, a post-bus from Lairg serves Lochinver and Durness. Access to the majority of the excursions listed here will be difficult without some form of private transport. For larger parties, hired coaches may be useful and will have no problems with the main roads, but some of the localities described here are accessed by single-track roads that are not suitable for large vehicles.

The North-west Highlands are quite sparsely inhabited. Limited accommodation is available in a number of the towns and villages within the area of this guide, but booking in advance is always recommended, and indeed is essential in the summer. A choice of hotels, bed & breakfasts, self-catering accommodation and camping can be found in the larger centres of Ullapool, Lochinver and Durness. Individual hotels and/or hostels are situated in the villages of Achiltibuie, Achmelvich, Inchnadamph, Kylesku, Scourie, Rhiconich and Kinlochbervie.

Background Information

Topographic maps

The best maps to use for these excursions are the Ordnance Survey 1:50,000 scale Landranger or 1:25,000 scale Explorer maps. The excursions described in this guide lie on Landranger sheets 9 (Cape Wrath); 15 (Loch Assynt); 19 (Gairloch and Ullapool); and 20 (Beinn Dearg and Loch Broom). Ordnance Survey maps are available in a range of outlets across the North-west Highlands.

Geological maps

Geological maps are published by the British Geological Survey (BGS), and can be purchased online via www.bgs.ac.uk, at the BGS offices in Edinburgh and Keyworth (Nottingham), or at the Natural History Museum, London. An overview of the geology is given by the 1:625,000 scale Bedrock Geology: UK North map. More detailed information is provided by the 1:50,000 sheets, and Excursions 1 and 6–11 lie within the Assynt Special Sheet. The remainder of the excursions are spread across sheets 101E (Ullapool); 101W (Summer Isles); 107E (Loch Glencoul); 107W (Point of Stoer); 113 (Cape Wrath) and 114W (Loch Eriboll).

Background reading

A vast number of papers have been written about the geology of the North-west Highlands over the last 100 years; many of these are referenced in the text, and details are given in the reference list at the back of the guide. A few books are recommended as general background reading. The first two in the list below offer information about the geology of the area and

6

the history of research; both are written from a personal standpoint and do not require extensive geological knowledge to read. The second pair of books provide up-to-date, detailed reviews of the current state of scientific knowledge about the geology of Scotland.

OLDROYD, D. R. (1990): *The Highlands Controversy: Constructing Geological Knowledge through Fieldwork in Nineteenth-Century Britain* (Chicago: University of Chicago Press).

RIDER, M. H. (2005): *Hutton's Arse* (Rogart: Rider-French Consulting).

TREWIN, N. H. (ed.) (2002): *The Geology of Scotland* (London: The Geological Society).

WOODCOCK, N. and STRACHAN, R. A. (eds) (2000): *Geological History of Britain and Ireland* (Oxford: Blackwell Science).

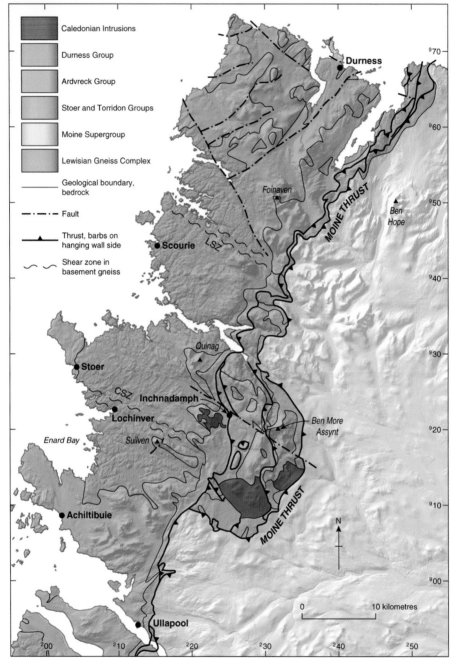

Fig. 1 Simplified geological map of the area covered by this excursion guide.
CSZ = Canisp Shear Zone; LSZ = Laxford Shear Zone

8

Geological Framework of the North-west Highlands

Michael Johnson, Ian Parsons, Paul Smith,
Robert Raine and Kathryn Goodenough

The North-west Highlands are internationally famous because they contain superb evidence for large-scale horizontal shortening of continental crust, as a result of the piling-up of thrust sheets along the Moine Thrust Zone during the Caledonian orogeny, in the early Silurian. The Moine Thrust Zone extends for around 200km, from Loch Eriboll to the Isle of Skye, and the total displacement along its component thrusts was at least 100km. This guide describes the northern part of the Moine Thrust Zone (Fig. 1). The thrust relationships are clearly displayed on the mountainsides, in one of the few parts of Britain in which the visitor can enjoy geological vistas that can truly be compared with the Alps. However, the thrust zone is just one of the important geological features of the North-west Highlands; the foreland succession, comprising an Archaean-Palaeoproterozoic gneiss complex overlain by Proterozoic and early Palaeozoic sedimentary rocks, has also been studied in significant detail. The area additionally contains a suite of alkaline igneous intrusions, which includes some of the most potassic igneous rocks in Britain.

The geology of the area was first extensively studied during the nineteenth century, and sparked some major scientific arguments, which have been described in detail elsewhere (e.g. Oldroyd, 1990). Although that period of debate concluded with the publication of the North-west Highlands memoir (Peach *et al.*, 1907), research into the rocks and structure of the region has continued throughout much of the last century (Butler, 2007; Law *et al.*, 2010a). Modern overviews of the geology are provided by Mendum *et al.* (2009), Trewin (2002), and Woodcock and Strachan (2000).

The stratigraphical succession in the North-west Highlands extends from the Archaean through to the Ordovician. The Archaean to Palaeoproterozoic tectonic history of Scotland is complex, but is steadily being unravelled with the application of modern geochronological techniques.

During much of the Proterozoic era, Scotland lay within a major super-continent called Rodinia. This continent broke up towards the end of the Neoproterozoic, and Scotland, together with Greenland and parts of North America, was then part of the continent of Laurentia, which existed for much of the Palaeozoic. Palaeomagnetic data show that Laurentia drifted from close to the South Pole in the late Neoproterozoic, to close to the equator in the Ordovician, thus experiencing a range of different climatic belts. During the Silurian, closure of an ocean called Iapetus led to the collision of Laurentia with the continents of Baltica and Avalonia, and the formation of the Moine Thrust Zone.

The rock units of the North-west Highlands record almost 3000 million years of this remarkable and diverse geological history, including two major Proterozoic unconformities. The area can be broadly divided into three distinct structural domains, each characterised by its different structures and lithologies (Fig. 1). These are:

(1) The unmoved region or foreland lying to the west of the lowest thrust (the Sole Thrust). The complete foreland stratigraphical succession is shown in Table A.
(2) The Moine Thrust Zone, which includes the Moine Thrust and the subsidiary thrusts occurring structurally below and to the west of it.
(3) The rocks of the Moine Supergroup lying to the east of, and structurally above, the Moine Thrust.

A variety of post-Cambrian igneous rocks occur within all three of these domains. They include two alkaline plutons, one of which represents the only silica-undersaturated major intrusion in the British Isles, and a suite of dykes and sills ranging from calc-alkaline to peralkaline in composition. Emplacement of these intrusions spanned the development of the Moine Thrust Zone, and therefore provides upper and lower age limits for thrusting.

A: The Structural Units

(1) The Foreland

The rocks of the foreland include the Archaean basement of the Lewisian Gneiss Complex, the overlying Meso- to Neoproterozoic sandstone-domi-

Table A			Thickness in metres	Age
DURNESS GROUP	**Durine Formation**	Light grey, fine-grained peritidal dolostones	≥ 130	**ORDOVICIAN**
	Croisaphuill Formation	Mid-grey, burrow-mottled limestones	≥ 350	
	Balnakeil Formation	Mid- to dark-grey dolostone and limestone	≥ 85	
	Sangomore Formation	Light grey and buff finely laminated dolostones and limestones	55	
	Sailmhor Formation	Dark grey mottled dolostones with cherts	115	
ARDVRECK GROUP	**Eilean Dubh Formation**	Very light grey dolostones, locally laminated, with stromatolites	≥ 135	**CAMBRIAN**
	Ghrudaidh Formation	Lead grey burrow-mottled or massive dolostones	65	
	An t-Sròn Formation	Salterella Grit Member; quartz arenite and thin siltstones	< 20	
		Fucoid Beds Member; dolomitic shales	12–27	
	Eriboll Formation	Pipe Rock Member; quartz arenite with vertical *Skolithos* worm-burrows	75–100	
		Basal Quartzite Member; cross-bedded quartz arenite with pebbly base	75–125	
	Unconformity: plane of marine erosion			
TORRIDON GROUP	**Aultbea Formation**	Fine–medium-grained red sandstones, lacking pebbles, commonly with contorted bedding	~ 2000	**NEOPROTEROZOIC**
	Applecross Formation	Red, trough cross-bedded coarse-grained sandstones and conglomerates showing soft-sediment deformation	~ 3000	
	Diabaig Formation	Breccias, conglomerates, tabular sandstones and mudstones	< 100	
	Angular unconformity			
*STR GRP		Red sandstones and mudstones with a volcaniclastic member	< 2000	**MP***
	Unconformity: old land-surface			
LEWISIAN GNEISS COMPLEX		Rubha Ruadh (Laxfordian) granites Scourie Dyke Swarm		**PP***
		Mafic and felsic orthogneisses and paragneisses		**ARCHAEAN**

*STR GRP = STOER GROUP; *MP = MESOPROTEROZOIC; *PP = PALAEOPROTEROZOIC nated Stoer and Torridon groups, the Cambrian clastic sedimentary rocks of the Ardvreck Group, and the Cambro-Ordovician dolostones and limestones of the Durness Group. Each of these major lithological units gives rise to a distinctive type of scenery. A particularly spectacular feature of the area is the 'double unconformity', where the planar base-Cambrian unconformity cuts across the more irregular unconformity between the Torridon Group and the underlying Lewisian Gneiss Complex (Fig. 2). On many of the hills in the area, it is easy to pick out the distinct lithological changes across the unconformities at the base of the Torridon Group, and at the base of the Cambrian succession. The basal Cambrian unconformity, which must have been horizontal when it formed, is now tilted gently towards the south-east.

The Lewisian gneisses form a rocky plateau with a succession of ridges and low hills of bare rock, among which lie many lochs (cnoc-and-lochan scenery). Above this plateau rises a thick pile of nearly horizontal beds of Torridon Group sandstone, which forms many of the spectacular mountains of the North-west Highlands (Fig. 3). Characteristic features of these spectacular relic mountains are the terraced slopes and precipitous cliffs, with giant buttresses and pinnacles that have been sculpted by erosion.

The white Cambrian quartz arenites of the Ardvreck Group produce gleaming escarpments and long dip slopes, such as on the eastern faces of Quinag, Canisp and Foinaven. In contrast, the dolostones and limestones of the Durness Group form lower-lying valleys, typically with swards of green grass punctuated by outcrops of grey carbonate rocks, representing the largest area of karst landscape in Scotland.

Lewisian Gneiss Complex

The basement of the North-west Highlands is formed by the Lewisian Gneiss Complex. The early detailed surveys of this area (Peach *et al.*, 1907) recognised that the Lewisian Gneiss Complex could be separated into three districts (northern, southern and central), with the central district containing pyroxene-bearing gneisses (granulite facies) and the northern and southern districts being composed of hornblende-bearing gneisses (amphibolite facies). A simple chronology (Peach *et al.*, 1907; Sutton and Watson, 1951) was established, with a 'fundamental' complex that was metamorphosed prior to intrusion of a swarm of dykes, known as the Scourie Dyke Swarm. Following dyke intrusion, the northern and southern districts of the

Fig. 2 The 'double unconformity' of Loch Assynt, looking south towards Beinn Gharbh (539 m). Arkosic rocks of the Torridon Group (To) unconformably overlie the Lewisian Gneiss Complex (Le); the unconformity is of buried landscape type, with relief of several hundred metres on top of the Lewisian gneisses. The Torridon Group is in turn overlain by quartz arenites of the Lower Cambrian Ardvreck Group (Ar) at a planar, marine unconformity. The two unconformities intersect to the east (left), such that the Ardvreck Group directly overlies the Lewisian Gneiss Complex. (Photograph: © M. P. Smith)

Fig. 3 The peaks of Quinag, with Torridon Group sandstones overlain by pale grey Ardvreck Group quartz arenites which form the highest summits. (BGS Photograph: P670756, © NERC)

13

complex were reworked at high temperatures (the Laxfordian orogeny).

More recent research, notably aided by advances in radiometric dating, has recognised that the evolution of the Lewisian gneisses was rather more complex. A large body of work (summarised by Kinny *et al.*, 2005) has shown that the different districts have different protolith ages, as well as different metamorphic histories, and it has been suggested that they represent different crustal blocks or terranes. Two of these terranes lie within the area covered by this guide: the northern, 'Rhiconich' Terrane; and the central, 'Assynt' Terrane.

Most of the Archaean gneisses of the Assynt Terrane had a tonalitic or leucotonalitic protolith, formed at 3030–2960 Ma (Kinny and Friend, 1997). These rocks were metamorphosed in an early granulite-facies metamorphic event (the 'Badcallian'). The age of this event is currently unresolved; whilst many authors have obtained ages around 2700 Ma for the granulite-facies metamorphism (Pidgeon and Bowes, 1972; Corfu *et al.*, 1994; Zhu *et al.*, 1997), others have suggested that the main high-grade metamorphism occurred at *c.*2490 Ma (Friend and Kinny, 1995). The gneisses were later locally reworked by an amphibolite-facies event known as the Inverian, which formed a series of major shear zones (Evans, 1965; Attfield, 1987). This was followed by the intrusion of the Scourie Dyke Swarm, in the period 2400 to 2000 Ma (Heaman and Tarney, 1989). Further local reworking occurred during the Palaeoproterozoic, in the Laxfordian event, which has been dated at *c.*1740–1670 Ma (Corfu *et al.*, 1994; Kinny and Friend, 1997).

The Assynt Terrane is typified by grey pyroxene-bearing felsic gneisses, commonly having a marked gneissic banding, and consisting largely of quartz, locally bluish or opalescent, and plagioclase feldspar. These have been named the 'Eddrachillis gneisses' by Kinny *et al.* (2005). Away from zones of Inverian reworking, hypersthene is the principal ferromagnesian mineral; where the gneisses have been retrogressed, hornblende is common and biotite may be present. The felsic gneisses enclose bands and lenses of more mafic meta-igneous rock, of widely varying scales from a few centimetres to a few kilometres across. Unretrogressed mafic bodies contain clino- and ortho-pyroxene, locally with garnet; where retrogressed, they are dominated by hornblende. Examples of typical felsic and mafic gneisses of the Assynt Terrane can be seen in Excursion 12.

In a few areas, particularly just south of Loch Laxford (Davies, 1974; Excursion 13) and near Stoer (Cartwright and Barnicoat, 1987), the mafic bodies are associated with garnet-biotite-quartz schists and rare calc-silicate rocks (the Claisfearn supracrustals), which are considered to have had a sedimentary protolith. It has been suggested that this association of mafic and ultramafic rocks with metasedimentary rocks could represent an ocean-floor assemblage, tectonically accreted to the continental margin (Park and Tarney, 1987).

In contrast, the protoliths of the Rhiconich Terrane gneisses were mostly granodioritic, and have been dated at 2800–2840 Ma (Kinny and Friend, 1997). They show no evidence of early, granulite-facies metamorphism, but were affected by an undated metamorphic event prior to the intrusion of the Scourie Dyke Swarm (Chowdhary and Bowes, 1972). They were pervasively reworked during the Laxfordian event (1740–1670 Ma; Corfu *et al.*, 1994, Kinny and Friend, 1997). The amphibolite-facies gneisses of the Rhiconich Terrane are pink to grey in colour, with a strong gneissic banding, and commonly also show evidence of migmatisation. They contain both plagioclase and alkali feldspar, plus quartz, hornblende and biotite. Older mafic bodies are much less common in the Rhiconich than in the Assynt Terrane.

Both terranes are cut by a major swarm of NW-SE- to WNW-ESE-trending dykes, known as the Scourie Dykes (Excursion 12). The Scourie Dykes vary in width from a few centimetres up to tens of metres and are remarkably laterally persistent. In Assynt, the dykes fall into two main classes: an earlier and widely distributed NW-SE-trending set that includes olivine-gabbros, norites and, most commonly, quartz-dolerite; and a later, less abundant, set of east-west-trending picrites and NW-SE-trending dolerites (Tarney, 1973). Both sets clearly cross-cut the gneissic banding. Although some dykes in the Assynt Terrane still retain their primary igneous mineralogy and textures, most have undergone metamorphism at amphibolite facies. In the Rhiconich Terrane, all the Scourie Dykes have been metamorphosed to coarse-grained amphibolites, and they are typically pervasively deformed, with their margins broadly parallel to the foliation in the host gneisses. Their period of intrusion may have spanned a long time, but the main dyke swarm was probably intruded at about 2400 Ma during a period of crustal extension (Heaman and Tarney, 1989).

The Assynt Terrane is cut by a number of broadly NW–SE-trending shear zones, marked by intensely deformed and retrogressed gneisses with a steeply-dipping foliation. Some of the major shear zones (such as the Canisp Shear Zone; Excursion 2) were initiated during the Inverian event, prior to the intrusion of the Scourie Dykes, and reactivated during the Laxfordian at about 1740 Ma (Attfield, 1987; Kinny and Friend, 1997). From Kylesku, narrow shear zones increase in abundance northwards, culminating in the major Laxford Shear Zone (Beach *et al.*, 1974; Goodenough *et al.*, 2010) at the margin of the Assynt and Rhiconich terranes (Excursion 13). This shear zone is considered to represent the boundary along which the two terranes were accreted, and it has been suggested that this occurred prior to Scourie Dyke emplacement, during the Inverian event (Goodenough *et al.*, 2010). Further north, in the Rhiconich Terrane, Laxfordian deformation is pervasive. Laxfordian deformation in this terrane was associated with the intrusion of a large number of sheets of granite and pegmatitic granite, some of which are strongly foliated, whilst others are relatively undeformed.

The Lewisian gneisses within the Moine Thrust Zone typically show the same features as those in the foreland. The transition from granulite-facies gneisses of the Assynt Terrane to amphibolite-facies gneisses of the Rhiconich Terrane occurs in the thrust belt in the vicinity of Loch Glencoul, several kilometres to the south of the same boundary in the foreland.

Stoer Group

The Stoer Group includes some of the oldest undeformed sedimentary rocks and the oldest life forms in Europe, with Pb-Pb ages on samples of limestone indicating deposition at around 1200 Ma (Turnbull *et al.*, 1996). The rocks of the Stoer Group are well-exposed on the Stoer peninsula (Excursion 3) and south of Enard Bay (Excursion 4), and at both localities the base of the group lies unconformably on rocks of the Lewisian Gneiss Complex.

The Stoer Group is divided into three formations (Stewart, 2002). The lowest Clachtoll Formation comprises basal conglomerate overlain by massive muddy sandstone with further conglomerates, suggesting deposition in lakes fringed by debris fans (Stewart, 2002). The overlying Bay of Stoer Formation contains fluviatile sandstone. Within this formation is the Stac Fada Member, which can be traced for over 100km; it is generally considered to represent a volcaniclastic deposit (Sanders and Johnston, 1989), but has also been explained as a meteorite impact layer (Amor *et al.*, 2008). Above the Stac Fada Member is the Poll a'Mhuilt Member, comprising layered and massive mudstone, probably of lacustrine origin, with some indications of evaporitic activity (Stewart, 2002). This is followed by the sandstones of the Meall Dearg Formation, deposited in a fluviatile (or possibly aeolian) environment.

A glacial origin for the basal part of the Stoer Group was proposed by Davison and Hambrey (1996, 1997), but Young (1999) and Stewart (1997, 2002) showed that the conglomerates and breccias could be interpreted as locally derived fan head material or debris fans, formed in a tectonically active environment with no need for glacial activity. The critical exposures are described in Excursions 3 and 4.

Detrital zircons from the Stoer Group show a cluster of late Archaean ages, although the youngest zircon is dated at c.1740 Ma (Rainbird et al. 2001; Kinnaird et al., 2007). The adjacent Lewisian gneiss is therefore considered as the most likely source for the sediments. It is generally agreed that the Stoer Group was deposited in a rift basin (Stewart, 1982, 2002; Beacom et al., 1999; Rainbird et al., 2001), on the basis of a number of features. These include: abundant vertical and lateral facies changes, with a mixture of fluviatile, debris-fan, lacustrine, volcanic and evaporitic deposits; the local source for the sediments; the presence of syn-depositional extensional (transtensional) faulting within the sequence; and the existence of opposing palaeocurrents in different units, suggesting alternating fault displacement along bounding faults.

The Stoer Group is separated from the overlying Torridon Group by a distinct angular unconformity, which can be seen at Bay of Culkein near Stoer (Excursion 3), Enard Bay (Excursion 4) and Achiltibuie. Palaeomagnetic studies indicate that Scotland had drifted southwards by some 40 degrees between the deposition of the Stoer and Torridon groups, and thus that this angular unconformity represents a considerable time gap (Stewart and Irving, 1974; Smith et al., 1983; Torsvik and Sturt, 1987).

Torridon Group

The Torridon Group is divided into four formations, of which three are seen in the area described in this guide: the basal Diabaig Formation and the overlying Applecross and Aultbea formations. The lower two formations can be easily studied on the shores of Loch Assynt (Excursion 1). A comprehensive overview of the Torridon Group is provided by Stewart (2002).

The unconformity at the base of the Diabaig Formation preserves a

17

'fossil' Proterozoic landscape, which shows spectacular relief; for example, a Lewisian 'hill' about 200m high forms the lower slopes on the north side of Quinag. The Diabaig Formation, which typically infills this topography, varies in thickness from a few metres to about a hundred metres. The formation includes breccias, conglomerates, and tabular-bedded sandstones and mudstones. Clasts in the breccias and conglomerates include locally-derived Lewisian gneiss and Stoer Group sandstone (Excursion 4).

The Applecross Formation is up to about 1km thick in the area of this guide, and forms many of the distinctive mountains, such as Suilven and Quinag. The formation chiefly consists of dark red or purplish-red, cross-bedded, arkosic sandstones with conglomerate beds. Trough and planar cross-bedding is common (Fig. 4); over most of the Assynt area, palaeo-currents are towards the south-east, but around Cape Wrath they are more easterly-directed. Soft sediment contortions such as oversteepened cross-bedding, slump folds and water escape structures are common. Pebbles in the Applecross Formation conglomerates include vein quartz and quartzite (some with tourmaline), jasper, chert, and porphyritic rhyolite (Williams, 1969).

Deposition of the Torridon Group, in rivers flowing across the Rodinian supercontinent, occurred at around 1000 Ma (Turnbull et al., 1996; Rainbird et al., 2001). The depositional setting of this group is the source of continuing debate; some authors suggest that it was formed from large-scale alluvial fans and braided river systems in a rift valley of the order of 100km wide (Stewart, 1982; Williams, 2001), but evidence from sedimentary structures suggests a much larger river system (Nicholson, 1993) and detrital zircon ages suggest a more distal source area, possibly the contemporaneous Grenville orogenic belt (Rainbird et al., 2001; Kinnaird et al., 2007; Krabbendam et al., 2008). This would imply that the Torridon Group was deposited in a large-scale, orogen-parallel foreland basin to the Grenville orogen.

The Cambro-Ordovician succession

Following late Neoproterozoic rifting and the opening of the Iapetus Ocean, northern Scotland formed part of the eastern margin of Laurentia. The oldest undeformed sediments deposited on the continental margin are of early Cambrian age and record only the later phases of margin development, not the initial rifting. Evidence of rifting is preserved elsewhere in

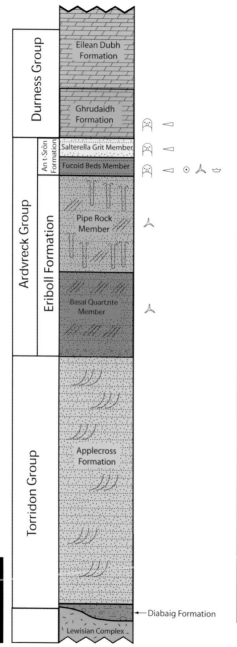

Fig. 4 Summary stratigraphic log for the Torridon, Ardvreck and basal Durness groups as seen in Assynt.

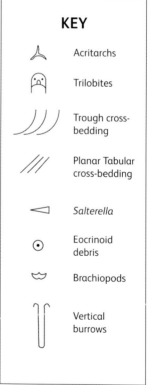

KEY

Symbol	Description
Acritarchs
Trilobites
Trough cross-bedding
Planar Tabular cross-bedding
Salterella
Eocrinoid debris
Brachiopods
Vertical burrows

19

Scotland, in the Dalradian Supergroup of the Grampian Highlands. Subsidence and deposition on the Laurentian margin was continuous from south-eastern USA, through maritime Canada and Newfoundland to North Greenland, a distance of several thousand kilometres. The subsidence history and stratigraphical record in the Newfoundland-Scotland-East Greenland sector of the margin show remarkable similarities that have been recognised since the early days of plate tectonic research (Swett and Smit 1972; Wright and Knight 1995; Higgins *et al.* 2001).

Within the North-west Highlands, rocks of Cambro-Ordovician age crop out in a narrow, almost continuous belt, rarely more than 10km wide, which stretches 170km from Loch Eriboll south-westwards to the Isle of Skye. The initial phase of Early Cambrian deposition comprised quartz-rich siliciclastic sediments, assigned to the Eriboll Formation (Ardvreck Group). These unconformably overlie both the Torridon Group and, where the Torridon Group rocks were eroded prior to Cambrian deposition, the Lewisian Gneiss Complex (Table A). This 'double unconformity' is spectacularly displayed in the Assynt area, particularly on the slopes of Canisp and Beinn Garbh to the south of Loch Assynt (Fig. 2, Excursion 1). The foreland succession in the Assynt area is shown in Fig. 4.

The Eriboll Formation is divided into two members: the older, pervasively cross-bedded Basal Quartzite Member (75–125m thick); and the overlying Pipe Rock Member (75–100m), which is also cross-bedded but extensively bioturbated by pipe-like, vertical *Skolithos* burrows. Despite the term 'Basal Quartzite', the rocks of the formation are actually sandstones and range from sub-arkoses to quartz arenites in composition.

The top few metres of the Eriboll Formation become more clay-rich and there is an abrupt change to the distinctive yellow-brown dolomitic siltstones of the Fucoid Beds Member (An t-Sròn Formation; 12–27m). These iron- and phosphate-rich rocks contain a diverse trace fossil assemblage that includes the ichnogenera *Palaeophycus*, *Skolithos* and *Cruziana*, together with a number of other fossils, particularly the trilobite *Olenellus*. The siltstone layers are punctuated by cross-bedded dolomitic grainstones, which represent storm events.

The succession from the base of the Eriboll Formation to the top of the Fucoid Beds Member represents an overall trend of sea-level rise, from tidally dominated shelf sedimentation in the Eriboll Formation, to background sedimentation below fair weather wave-base in the Fucoid Beds Member (McKie, 1990). The Fucoid Beds Member is conformably overlain by the arenaceous Salterella Grit Member (An t-Sròn Formation), which is typified by round millet-seed quartz grains and conical *Salterella* (commonly weathered out). This member is considered to be the product of relative sea-level fall and a return to tidally dominated shelf sedimentation (McKie, 1990); the round grain shapes probably indicate aeolian transport prior to deposition.

At the top of the An t-Sròn Formation, there is an abrupt change to carbonates of the Durness Group, and this shift from siliciclastic-dominated to carbonate-dominated sedimentation is seen along most of the Iapetus margin of Laurentia. The Durness Group comprises at least 935m of peritidal and shallow subtidal limestones and dolostones, which record deposition within a tropical setting – stromatolites and thrombolites (the products of microbially mediated sedimentation) are common, ooids are locally abundant, and evidence of former evaporites and early dolomite formation is found in parts of the succession. The lowest two units of the Durness Group, the Ghrudaidh and Eilean Dubh formations, are widely exposed along the Moine Thrust Zone; but only at the northern and southern ends of the thrust zone, in the Durness area and on the Isle of Skye, is a more complete succession represented (Fig. 5). Even here, the stratigraphic succession is truncated by thrusting (Excursion 14).

The Ghrudaidh Formation (65m) comprises lead-grey burrow-mottled or massive dolostones, of predominantly subtidal origin. The base of the formation contains *Salterella* and the trilobite *Olenellus*, indicative of the late Lower to earliest Middle Cambrian. The Ghrudaidh Formation is conformably overlain by the Eilean Dubh Formation (minimum thickness 135m), a unit of pale-weathering, laminated, very shallow subtidal and peritidal dolostones. Metre-scale shallowing upward parasequences (sea-level related cycles) are frequently seen in the lower and middle part of the formation, but tend to be absent in the upper part. The Eilean Dubh Formation contains stromatolites, but is otherwise unfossiliferous except for the uppermost few metres, where conodonts are recorded (Huselbee and Thomas, 1998) and provide evidence that the Cambrian-Ordovician boundary occurs in the upper few metres of the formation.

The overlying Sailmhor Formation (115m) constitutes a marked change to dark carbonates with conspicuous parasequences, and represents an earliest Tremadocian sea-level rise that has been documented globally (Nielsen, 2004). Burrow mottling and conspicuous chert concretions are common. Palmer *et al.* (1980) described a substantial unconformity surface

21

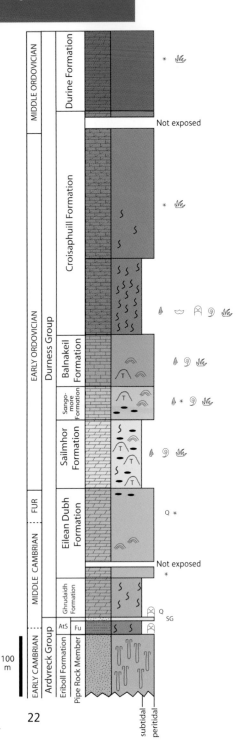

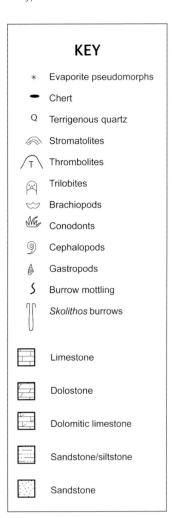

Fig. 5 Summary stratigraphic log for the Durness Group in its type area at Durness.

22

at the top of the Sailmhor Formation, with deep fissures and a significant time interval absent. However, these are now recognised to be Holocene erosion surfaces which expose Cenozoic fault breccias, and data from conodonts indicate that there is no significant temporal discontinuity in the succession.

Continuing up-sequence, the Sangomore Formation (55m) comprises generally light grey and buff finely laminated dolostones with some mid-grey thrombolitic limestones and stromatolites. The unit contains a reasonably diverse micro- and macrofauna that includes conodonts, gastropods and cephalopods. A significant sequence boundary, marked by a distinctive pebble bed, occurs at the top of the formation and may correlate with a similar 'megasequence' boundary in western Newfoundland (Knight and James, 1987). The overlying Balnakeil Formation (minimum thickness 85m) remains rich in microbialitic sediments, but with a conspicuous change to darker grey carbonates and a more subtidally dominated succession. The succeeding Croisaphuill Formation (minimum 350m) marks a shift from microbial-dominated carbonates to burrow-mottled limestones with dolomitised burrow systems. This shift represents the maximum flooding surface of the megasequence – a surface that can be correlated across most of Laurentia and is close to coincident with the Tremadoc–Arenig boundary (Haq and Schutter, 2009). The lower part of the Croisaphuill Formation is richly fossiliferous, yielding diverse and abundant cephalopod, gastropod and conodont faunas.

The youngest unit of the Durness Group, the Durine Formation (minimum 130m), records the abrupt, eustatic fall in sea-level at the Lower-Middle Ordovician boundary, which begins in the upper Croisaphuill Formation but is most pronounced at the boundary with the Durine Formation. This formation consists chiefly of lighter grey, fine-grained peritidal dolostones. The macrofauna is sparse, but conodonts are present and indicate that the youngest part of the formation is of early Middle Ordovician age (c.470 Ma). The top of the formation is everywhere truncated by faulting, and in Sango Bay the Moine Thrust juxtaposes mylonitised Eriboll Formation and Lewisian gneiss (Excursion 14).

(2) The Moine Supergroup

To the east of the Moine Thrust, the outcrop of the Moine Supergroup extends almost to the east coast of Scotland. The Moine Supergroup is divided into three groups (Morar, Glenfinnan and Loch Eil), of which only the Morar Group is present in the area covered by this guide. The whole of the Moine Supergroup is described in detail in *A Geological Excursion Guide to the Moine Geology of the Northern Highlands of Scotland* (Strachan *et al.*, 2010). Local inliers of 'Lewisianoid' Archaean basement occur within the Moine Supergroup, but none are present within the area described in this guide.

The rocks of the Morar Group are mainly psammitic, with subordinate beds of pelitic schist and, rarely, calc-silicates. Directly to the east of the Moine Thrust, these rocks show greenschist-facies metamorphism, with metamorphic grade increasing eastwards. The general dip of the Morar Group psammites is at low or moderate angles to the ESE, although to the east of the Assynt Culmination the strike trend varies so as to mimic the embayment of the Moine Thrust. The dominant linear structures plunge to the ESE or SE.

In the type area of Morar, Glendinning (1988) interpreted the Morar Group sediments as having been deposited in a fluvial or shallow marine environment. However, in the area to the east of Assynt, sedimentary features indicate that the Morar Group was deposited in a braided river system and can be correlated with the Torridon Group in the foreland, with both forming part of the foreland basin to the Grenville orogen (Krabbendam *et al.* 2008). The depositional environment of large parts of the Moine Supergroup, and linkages to rocks in the foreland farther south, remain unclear and would merit further study.

The age of the Moine Supergroup has long been controversial, but has largely been resolved by recent U-Pb geochronological studies. The rocks of the Morar Group were deposited after *c.*1000 Ma (the age of the youngest detrital zircon; Friend *et al.*, 2003). A general constraint for the minimum age of the Moine Supergroup comes from the intrusion of granitic and gabbroic rocks (the West Highland Granite Gneiss) into the southern part of the Moine Supergroup. These intrusions have been dated, using U-Pb on zircons, at *c.*870 Ma (Friend *et al.*, 1997; Millar, 1999; Rogers *et al.*, 2001), and it has been suggested that intrusion occurred in an extensional setting (Millar, 1999).

The age of metamorphism of the Moine rocks is also the subject of ongoing research. Parts of the Moine succession, particularly in Knoydart and Morar, show evidence for regional metamorphism between *c.*820 and 740 Ma (the Knoydartian event). In the type area of the Morar Group, this evidence includes pegmatites that have been dated at *c*.827 and *c*.784 Ma (Rogers *et al.*, 1998), and metamorphic ages of *c*.820–790 Ma obtained by dating of garnets (Vance *et al.*, 1998), as well as U-Pb ages for titanite that suggest that the Morar Group was affected by metamorphism at *c*.737 Ma (Tanner and Evans, 2003).

In east Sutherland there is evidence for metamorphism at *c*.470 Ma (Kinny *et al.*, 1999), but Caledonian regional metamorphism in the Morar Group in the area of this guide has been shown to have occurred at 435–420 Ma (Kinny *et al.*, 2003) and to be approximately coeval with movement on the Moine Thrust.

(3) The Moine Thrust Zone

The Moine Thrust Zone is a structurally complicated belt that stretches from Loch Eriboll in the north to the Isle of Skye in the south (Excursions 5 to 10 and 14 to 15). It is defined as the zone lying below the Moine Thrust (which carries the rocks of the Moine Supergroup, with local basement inliers), but above the Sole Thrust which separates the thrust zone from the undisturbed foreland. The Moine Thrust is everywhere a distinctive structure, but the Sole Thrust is rather variable, and locally includes structures with very little displacement. The rocks within the thrust zone are derived from the foreland, but show varying states of deformation. In some cases, the strain and accompanying recrystallization has been so intense as to make direct correlation with specific foreland units difficult.

The thrust zone varies widely in outcrop width, from just a few metres at Knockan Crag (Excursion 6), up to about ten kilometres in the Assynt Culmination. It comprises a number of major thrust sheets, which are themselves internally deformed by thrusting and folding. It has been considered as a classic example ever since the publication of the North-west Highlands memoir (Peach *et al.*, 1907) and the recognition that low-angle reverse faults (thrusts) could place older rocks on top of younger rocks. The term 'thrust' was coined by Geikie (1884), inspired by Charles Lapworth's work in the area around Loch Eriboll (Excursion 15).

The thrusting, and associated deformation, are the result of shortening of the Laurentian continental margin during the closure of the Iapetus ocean and the collision between the continents of Laurentia and Baltica, together with the docking of Avalonia. The thrust zone, which forms the front of the Caledonian orogen in northern Scotland, developed during the Silurian, in the Scandian event which is also recognised in eastern Greenland and Scandinavia.

Elliott and Johnson (1980) presented a 'piggy-back', foreland-propagating model for the Moine Thrust Zone; that is, the upper thrusts moved first, and these thrust sheets were carried further by subsequent movement along lower thrusts. In this model, the earliest movement in the Moine Thrust Zone was along the Moine Thrust itself – although it should be noted that a number of important earlier thrusts (including the Naver and Sgurr Beag thrusts) occur within the rocks of the Moine Supergroup further to the east. Displacement on the thrusts was broadly towards the WNW. The thrust sheet carried by the Moine Thrust was large; on the basis of current exposure on the mainland, it was over *c.*200km in strike length and *c.*10–20km in thickness. Furthermore, the presence of a klippe (outlier) of Moine rocks at Faraid Head (Excursion 14) shows that the Moine sheet extended westwards over the foreland for a distance of at least 10km beyond its present outcrop.

Although elegant, the simple 'piggy-back' model does not account for (a) the dual nature of the Moine Thrust, which is an early ductile shear zone in some places and a late brittle fault in others; and (b) the apparent truncation of lower faults by higher ones at some localities (e.g. in the klippen to the east of Knockan, south Assynt, Excursion 6). It is clear that the Moine Thrust Zone represents a rather more complex system. A variety of models have been proposed to explain some of these features, including late-stage extensional faulting (particularly in southern Assynt; Coward, 1982, 1983); synchronous movement along imbricate thrusts and roof thrusts (Butler, 2004); and extensional collapse episodes during the largely compressional evolution of the thrust wedge (Holdsworth *et al.*, 2006). Recent work has shown that detailed mapping of specific localities is essential to understand the different processes that have operated in the Moine Thrust Zone (Butler, 2004; Krabbendam and Leslie, 2004; Holdsworth *et al.*, 2006).

The Moine Thrust has traditionally been defined as the thrust that forms the base of the Moine Supergroup (and its Lewisianoid basement, where exposed), but this structure varies in character along its length. In places it is a ductile shear zone, represented by a thick pile of mylonites, as seen at the Stack of Glencoul and at Loch Eriboll (Excursions 11 and 15);

elsewhere (e.g. at Knockan Crag, Excursion 6), it is a polyphase brittle-ductile structure, the mylonites being brecciated by late, lower-temperature deformation (Coward, 1983). Mylonites are fine-grained, strongly layered rocks, formed by dynamic recrystallisation during ductile deformation (e.g. White, 1980), and they were first defined on the basis of examples from the Moine Thrust Zone (Lapworth, 1885).

Peach *et al.* (1907) noted that 'owing to the development of mylonites in association with the Moine Thrust, it is extremely difficult to determine everywhere its exact position', and this debate has continued to cause controversy for a century. Some workers prefer to place the Moine Thrust at the base of the Moine Supergroup (e.g. Christie, 1963; Law, 1987; Holdsworth *et al.*, 2006), so that the mylonites above the Moine Thrust have a Moine protolith, whereas mylonites derived from Torridonian, Lewisian or Cambro-Ordovician protoliths lie below the Moine Thrust. Others have placed the Moine Thrust at the base of the mylonite pile (e.g. Soper and Wilkinson, 1975; Elliott and Johnson, 1980). On the east side of Loch Eriboll, the main belt of foreland-derived mylonites lies above a brittle structure that has recently been named the Lochan Riabhach Thrust by Holdsworth *et al.* (2006), but the interpretation of this structure is also controversial (Butler *et al.*, 2006).

The mylonites associated with the Moine Thrust were developed largely under conditions of greenschist-facies metamorphism. Mylonites of different protoliths may be quite similar in appearance, and thus, as noted by Peach *et al.* (1907), in places it is difficult to accurately place the contact between different rock-types within the mylonite pile. An excellent place to study the mylonites is the Stack of Glencoul (Excursion 11) where a complex mylonite zone, reaching some 70m in thickness, has been derived from Lewisian gneiss, Cambrian quartz arenite and Moine psammites.

As ductile movement on the Moine Thrust ceased, displacement was transferred to the lower thrusts of the Moine Thrust Zone. Within the Moine Thrust Zone, numerous thrusts developed in the rocks of the foreland succession; the major thrusts are most easily studied in the Assynt Culmination (Fig. 6). Thrusts tend to follow weak layers, as they show a preference for 'easy gliding' surfaces. In the Moine Thrust Zone, this role has typically been filled by fine-grained clastic horizons, such as the Fucoid Beds Member or the mudstones of the Diabaig Formation, and thrusts are most commonly focused along these layers. Zones where a thrust runs along one horizon are known as *flats*, with *ramps* occurring in thrust

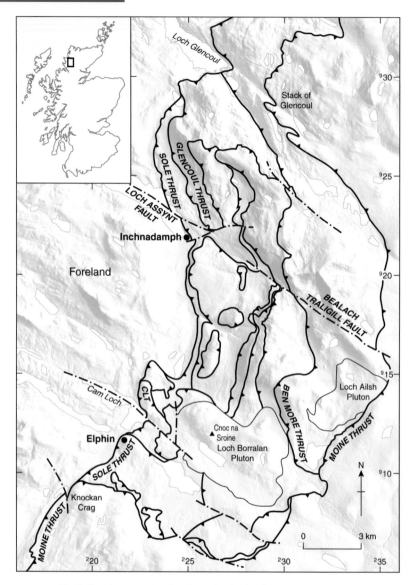

Fig. 6 Overview map showing the main structural features, thrusts, and intrusions within the Assynt Culmination. CLT = Cam Loch Thrust

Opposite page:
Fig. 7 Illustration of the formation of a duplex, with thrusts propagating from left to right.

planes where they cut up or down from one 'easy gliding' horizon to another. Thrusting typically placed older rocks over younger rocks, though variations to this pattern occurred. Breaching thrusts have 'reshuffled' sequences that have already been thrusted, emplacing younger rocks over older rocks; stratigraphic inversion was also caused by the development of thrust-related folds, such as the Sgonnan Mòr Syncline (Excursion 9) and the spectacular anticline/syncline pair on Na Tuadhan in Assynt (Excursion 8).

Even a superficial examination of the geological map of Assynt (British Geological Survey, 2007) or of Loch Eriboll (British Geological Survey, 2002a) reveals the arrays of many anastomosing minor thrusts within the major thrust sheets. These were described by Peach *et al.* (1907) as imbricate structures. Elliott and Johnson (1980) and Boyer and Elliott (1982) regarded these arrays as examples of *duplex structure*, a series of curved faults asymptotically related to a higher ('roof') thrust and a lower ('floor') thrust (Fig. 7). Each thrust-bounded body of rock within the duplex is termed a 'horse'. Unlike an imbricate fault, a duplex must have a roof thrust that does not truncate the thrusts in its footwall. Ideally the array of faults in a duplex is a system in which slip is partitioned both along the roof thrust and along the imbricates below. A small duplex or imbricate structure can be observed in the Stronchrubie cliffs (Excursion 16).

In many areas 'smooth' gliding occurred, but locally 'rough' gliding led to the piling up of lenticular thrust sheets and resulted in local thickening of the hangingwall. These piled-up thrust sheets pushed up the base of the overlying Moine Thrust Sheet, folding it to create a bulge or culmination (Fig. 8). The most spectacular example is the Assynt Culmination (Fig. 9), where the cause of the local 'rough' gliding may have been the presence of large amounts of igneous rocks. However, this explanation does not apply to other culminations in the Moine Thrust, and other factors must be involved elsewhere.

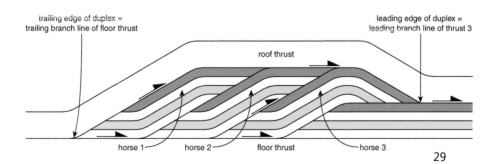

29

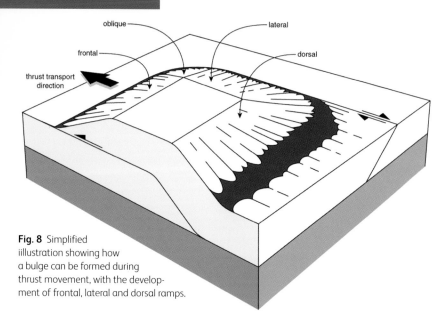

Fig. 8 Simplified
iillustration showing how
a bulge can be formed during
thrust movement, with the development of frontal, lateral and dorsal ramps.

Many estimates have been made for the displacement on the thrusts of
the Moine Thrust Zone, but some of them are based on disputable field
relationships. However, the offset of distinctive features in the Lewisian
gneisses in the thrust zone relative to the foreland (Clough in Peach *et al.*,
1907; Elliott and Johnson, 1980) indicates 20–25 km of displacement along
the Glencoul Thrust (now recognised as the northern part of the Ben More
Thrust; Krabbendam and Leslie, 2004). On the basis of balanced cross-
sections, Elliott and Johnson (1980) suggested a displacement of at least
77 km on the Moine Thrust. Slip on the Sole Thrust is probably only a few
kilometres, but in total the displacement across the Moine Thrust Zone is
likely to be at least 100 km. The direction of thrusting was towards what
is now the WNW (290°), as indicated by the stretching lineation in the
mylonites (Christie, 1963), the orientation of duplex and imbricate faults,
and the spectacular deformation of the *Skolithos* burrows in the Pipe Rock
(McLeish, 1971; Wilkinson *et al.*, 1975).

Two methods have been used to date the Moine Thrust Zone: indirect
dating of igneous rocks with clear relationships to the thrusting, and direct
dating of micas in mylonites formed during thrusting. Constraints on the
onset of thrusting are provided by U-Pb zircon dates for the Loch Ailsh
Pluton and the Canisp Porphyry Sills in Assynt, both of which pre-date
movement on thrusts within the Moine Thrust Zone (Excursion 9). For
some years, a date of 439 ± 4 Ma has been accepted for the Loch Ailsh

30

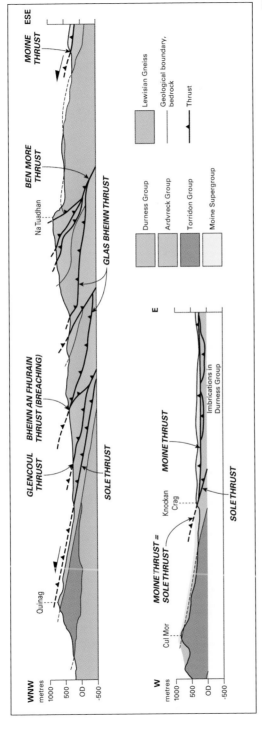

Fig. 9 Schematic cross-sections through the Moine Thrust Zone.

(a) Section through the Assynt Culmination, illustrating some of the complexity of this area, with numerous thrusts between the Moine and Sole thrusts.

(b) Section through the Moine Thrust at Knockan Crag to the south of the Assynt Culmination, illustrating the late nature of the brittle Moine Thrust in this area.

31

Pluton (Halliday *et al.*, 1987), but recent high-precision dating has dated this pluton at 430.6 ± 0.3 Ma, within error of the Canisp Porphyry Sills at 430.4 ± 0.4 (Goodenough *et al.*, 2011). In contrast, the later magmatic suite of the nearby Loch Borralan Pluton post-dates movement on the Ben More Thrust (Parsons and McKirdy, 1983; Excursion 10) and has now been dated at 429.2 ± 0.5 Ma (Goodenough *et al.*, 2011). Movement within the Moine Thrust Zone therefore took place over a relatively short period of one to two million years. Both earlier and later periods of movement took place on the Moine Thrust itself, as shown by the second method of dating used in this area.

Direct dating of micas from mylonites along the Moine Thrust, using Rb-Sr, K-Ar, and Ar-Ar techniques, has obtained a broader spread of results. Mylonitisation of the Moine rocks was accompanied by green-schist-facies metamorphism, at a temperature of approximately 400°C (Freeman *et al.*, 1998). This ductile deformation continued until at least 430 Ma, but locally appears to extend until 408 Ma (Kelley, 1988; Freeman *et al.*, 1998; Friend *et al.*, 2000; Dallmeyer *et al.*, 2001).

In general terms, the majority of displacement within the Moine Thrust System appears to have been confined to the interval from the middle to late Llandovery (*c.*435–428 Ma), with some displacement persisting into the early Devonian, and this timing is remarkably synchronous from Scotland to eastern North Greenland. Although the general pattern is clear, there continues to be considerable discussion about detailed relationships within this well-preserved ancient mountain belt.

B: Igneous rocks

The Assynt district contains a considerable range of igneous rocks, some of extreme composition and many unique in the British Isles, which were emplaced during the Caledonian orogeny and provide both relative and absolute chronology of displacements in the Moine Thrust Zone. The literature is complicated by archaic terminology as well as great minera-logical variety, summarised in Table B. A comprehensive overview has been provided by Parsons (1999).

The Loch Borralan Pluton (Excursion 10) is the only alkaline pluton in the British Isles that includes nepheline syenites. It also contains exotic, strongly ultrapotassic units and is associated with a small body of carbon-atite. The smaller Loch Ailsh Pluton (Excursion 9) is composed mainly of silica-saturated syenite. Abundant dykes and sills, ranging from calc-alkaline lamprophyres to peralkaline rhyolites, are found throughout the thrust sheets. In the foreland to the west, the Canisp Porphyry forms a large sill complex of quartz-microsyenite; and two mafic phonolite dykes, focussed on the Loch Borralan intrusion, reach the coast NW of Achiltibuie and near Achmelvich. Deformed sills of quartz-microsyenite ('nord-markite') occur close to the Moine Thrust, and extend eastwards into the Moine psammites. It must be borne in mind that crustal shortening of several tens of kilometres may have occurred between the intrusions near the Moine Thrust and the compositionally similar Canisp Porphyry Sills in the foreland.

The alkaline plutons are part of a strip of late Caledonian intrusions that occur along, and slightly to the east of, the Moine Thrust Zone, extending from Loch Loyal in the north to Glen Dessary in the south. The alkaline igneous activity represents the north-west edge of the slightly younger, calc-alkaline granitic magmatism that dominates the remainder of the Highlands and Southern Uplands. Like alkaline magmatism else-where it extended over a long period of time, from 448 ± 2 Ma at Glen Dessary (van Breemen et al., 1979b; Goodenough et al., 2011) to 425 ± 3 Ma at Ratagain (Rogers and Dunning, 1991). Alkaline magmatism is most commonly associated with extension of the crust, as in the rift-valleys of present-day East Africa, but the North-west Highlands are a region of marked crustal shortening. A westward-dipping subduction zone has been postulated to exist beneath the Scottish Caledonides and many of the alkaline igneous rocks in the North-west Highlands have affinities with shoshonites, subduction-related basaltic rocks unusually rich in potassium (Thompson and Fowler, 1986; Thirlwall and Burnard, 1990). The source of ultrapotassic magmas and carbonatites is usually placed in the mantle. It is possible that the alkaline magmas arose by partial melting, during subduction, of mantle enriched in alkalis during an earlier phase of carbon-atitic metasomatism, as has been postulated for subduction-related ultra-potassic rocks in Italy. However, this does not explain the localisation of alkaline magmatism to a narrow band near the Moine Thrust Zone.

The Loch Borralan Pluton, in southern Assynt, is divided into early and late suites (Woolley, 1970), the former being dominated by silica-undersaturated rocks that include pyroxenites and nepheline syenites (see Table B). Ultrapotassic rocks ('pseudoleucite syenites'), containing white spots made of nepheline and potassium-rich feldspar replacing the potas-sium-rich feldspathoid leucite, are mainly confined to the eastern end of the outcrop of the early suite. A carbonatite, which contains xenoliths of

Table B

Current rock names	Early names	Mineralogy
UNITS IN THE LOCH BORRALAN PLUTON		
Late suite		
Cnoc na Sroine quartz-syenite	Nordmarkite	Alkali feldspar, quartz, aegirine-augite and/or alkali amphibole, ± melanite garnet
Altnacealgach alkali-feldspar-syenite	Perthosite	Nearly monomineralic alkali-feldspar rock. Minor melanite.
Early suite		
Ledmore nepheline-syenite	Ledmorite	Alkali feldspar, nepheline, melanite garnet, diopsidic augite, biotite
Allt a'Mhuilinn pseudoleucite-syenite and associated rocks	Borolanite	Alkali feldspar, nepheline, melanite garnet, biotite in matrix. Alkali feldspar and nepheline intergrowths as pseudomorphs after leucite
Bad na h-Achlaise ultramafic rocks	Shonkinite	Diopsidic pyroxene in a matrix of alkali feldspar and zeolite replacing nepheline
Sòvite (calcite carbonatite)	Cromaltite	Diopsidic pyroxene and/or hornblende, ilmenomagnetite, biotite, apatite and melanite garnet
		Calcite ± phlogopite and apatite
DYKES AND SILLS		
Porphyritic trachyte swarm		Plagioclase phenocrysts in matrix of aligned alkali feldspar laths
Ledmorite swarm (nepheline-syenite)	Ledmorite	Phenocrysts of euhedral melanite garnet, aegirine and biotite in orthoclase and nepheline matrix
Nordmarkite swarm (quartz-microsyenite)	Nordmarkite	Alkali feldspar phenocrysts in matrix of alkali feldspar, quartz, biotite ± aegirine-augite, alkali amphibole
Peralkaline rhyolite swarm	Grorudite	Alkali feldspar and aegirine phenocrysts in quartz, feldspar, aegirine matrix
Canisp Porphyry (quartz-microsyenite)	Canisp Porphyry	Alkali and plagioclase feldspar phenocrysts in feldspar, quartz matrix
Hornblende-microdiorite swarm	Hornblende porphyrite	Phenocrysts of hornblende and plagioclase, ± biotite, in feldspathic matrix
Vogesite swarm	Vogesite	Hornblende phenocrysts, ± diopside, in plagioclase, hornblende, quartz matrix
UNITS IN THE LOCH AILSH PLUTON		
Loch Ailsh syenite S3	Aegirine-melanite-syenite	Nearly monomineralic alkali feldspar-syenite with small amounts of alkali pyroxene and melanite garnet
	Perthosite	Nearly monomineralic alkali feldspar rock with small amounts of aegirine-augite
Loch Ailsh syenite S2	Pulaskite and nordmarkite	Alkali feldspar syenite with aegirine-augite, ± riebeckite ± minor quartz
Loch Ailsh syenite S1	Pulaskite and nordmarkite	Alkali feldspar syenite with augitic pyroxene
Melanocratic pyroxene-syenite	Shonkinite	Diopside and biotite, ± hornblende, in clusters set in alkali feldspar.
Loch Ailsh ultramafic rocks	Pyroxenite and hornblendite	Diopsidic pyroxene, ilmenomagnetite, apatite, biotite. Hornblende sometimes replaces diopside

nepheline syenite, is emplaced in Durness Group dolostones 400m outside the main Loch Borralan Pluton, but is most probably related to the early suite (Young *et al.*, 1994). The late suite cuts through the undersaturated units and is composed of silica-saturated or quartz-bearing alkali feldspar syenites. The relationships between the multiplicity of rock types in the early suite are difficult to establish because of poor exposure, but strong crystal fractionation, much of it in magma chambers below the present level, is likely to have been involved. The quartz-bearing late suite cannot, however, have been derived directly from the early suite by crystal fractionation; no amount of fractionation can change a magma from being silica undersaturated to silica saturated.

The Loch Ailsh Pluton is less diverse and composed largely of very leucocratic alkali feldspar syenites, some with small amounts of quartz, formed in three magmatic pulses termed S1, S2 and S3 (Parsons, 1965a). As at Loch Borralan, ultramafic pyroxenites occur only where the magmas were in contact with Durness Group dolostone. In places there is clear evidence that some pyroxenites have been produced by reactions between silicate magma and dolomite, but at Loch Borralan there is good evidence that the main mass of biotite pyroxenite is intrusive. The reason for the association with dolostone is not understood. It would require extremely high temperatures to produce magmas of the composition of the diopside-biotite pyroxenites and emplacement as a cumulate mush is probable.

Dykes and sills of the North-west Highlands Minor Intrusion Suite are abundant throughout the Assynt Culmination, but are rare elsewhere (Sabine, 1953; Goodenough *et al.*, 2004). The main suite of minor intrusions varies in composition from lamprophyres, through hornblende diorites to peralkaline rhyolites, all of which have been deformed and were clearly intruded prior to thrusting. These intrusions are unevenly distributed through the thrust sheets. The most basic type comprises dark grey-weathering vogesites (hornblende-bearing lamprophyres) that occur predominantly in the Durness Group dolostones in the Sole Thrust Sheet. In contrast the most evolved type, the brick-red peralkaline rhyolites, mainly occur above the Ben More Thrust, and cut the slightly earlier Loch Ailsh Pluton. There is therefore a hint of regional variation in magmatism prior to crustal shortening. The various types of minor intrusive include both calc-alkaline and alkaline compositions, and are thought to have formed by fractionation from a common parental magma, formed in a mantle source modified by subduction-related components (Goodenough *et al.*, 2004).

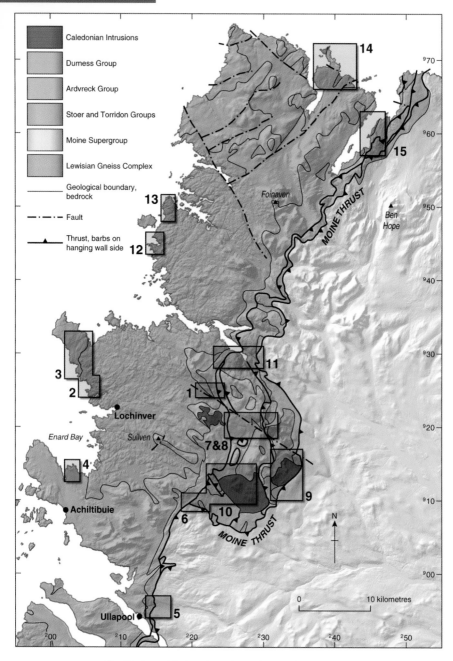

Fig. 10 A simplified geological map showing the areas covered by the excursions detailed in this guide.

Excursion 1

Loch Assynt and the Achmore Duplex

Paul Smith and Robert Raine

Purpose: To examine the stratigraphy and sedimentology of the foreland succession and the lower part of the Achmore Duplex, and to study the structural architecture of the duplex. A good general introduction for any party visiting the North-west Highlands.

Aspects covered: Clastic and carbonate sedimentology, Precambrian-Lower Cambrian stratigraphy, structural geology of duplexes.

Maps: OS: 1:50,000 Landranger sheet 15 Loch Assynt; 1:25,000 Explorer sheet 442 Assynt and Lochinver. BGS: 1:50,000 special sheet, Assynt district.

Terrain: Roadside outcrops on the first part of the itinerary; rough but low moorland and stream sections for the second half of the excursion. No part of the excursion is more than 500m from the road. There are a number of lay-bys at which it is possible to park, but the roadside part of the excursion is most easily accomplished by walking along the road, paying due attention to the traffic.

Time: The two halves of the trip divide conveniently into separate half-day excursions or a single full day.

Access: There are no access constraints for this excursion, although care should be taken at roadside stops. Please note that this is a very popular excursion, and that the outcrops should not be hammered.

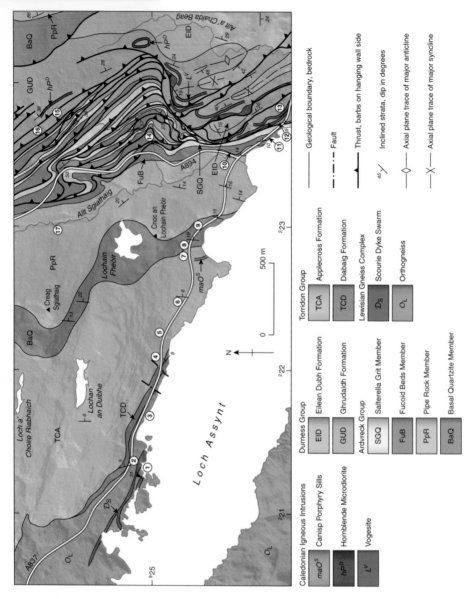

Fig. 11 Geological map of the Loch Assynt area, after British Geological Survey (2007), showing the localities described in Excursion 1.

Opposite page:

Fig. 12 Outcrops of Lewisian gneiss on the shore of Loch Assynt at Locality 1.1. (BGS photograph P531871, © NERC)

Torridon Group
TCA — Applecross Formation
TCD — Diabaig Formation

Lewisian Gneiss Complex
D_S — Scourie Dyke Swarm
O_L — Orthogneiss

Durness Group
EID — Eilean Dubh Formation
GUD — Ghrudaidh Formation

Ardvreck Group
SGQ — Salterella Grit Member
FuB — Fucoid Beds Member
PpR — Pipe Rock Member
BaQ — Basal Quartzite Member

Caledonian Igneous Intrusions
maO^S — Canisp Porphyry Sills
hP^D — Hornblende Microdiorite
L^V — Vogesite

—— Geological boundary, bedrock
—··—··— Fault
▲▲▲ Thrust, barbs on hanging wall side
^{45} ⟋ Inclined strata, dip in degrees
◇ Axial plane trace of major anticline
—X— Axial plane trace of major syncline

Excursion 1A:
The foreland succession of the Loch Assynt roadside

Locality 1.1 [NC 2125 2507]

Lewisian outcrops, Loch Assynt.

Park in the lay-by [NC 212 251] alongside the A837 to Lochinver from Skiag Bridge (second lay-by on the left). From the lay-by, walk down to a small east-facing bay on the shore of Loch Assynt (Fig. 11), adjacent to an island with two large Scots Pines and many dead trees. The bay [NC 2125 2507] contains a 9m-wide, ESE-trending ultramafic Scourie Dyke, intruded into Lewisian orthogneisses with a westward dipping foliation (Fig. 12). The core of the dyke is a fairly fresh, olivine-rich metaclinopyroxene-norite (Tarney, 1973). The host rocks are chiefly pyroxene-bearing felsic gneisses, consisting of quartz, feldspar and hypersthene, with hornblende and biotite also present. Lenses, pods and bands of both mafic and ultramafic rock are common and are generally unfoliated.

12

Locality 1.2 [NC 2134 2516]

Basal unconformity of the Torridon Group.

Return to the lay-by and examine the roadside cutting opposite the eastern entrance to the lay-by. Conglomerates and pebbly sandstones of the Diabaig Formation (Torridon Group) unconformably overlie highly weathered, pale green to cream Lewisian gneisses with some red staining. Two lithofacies are present in the Diabaig Formation; the first is a poorly lithified and poorly sorted, tabular-bedded, very coarse sandstone with a muddy matrix and matrix-supported pebbles composed principally of gneisses and vein quartz. The pebbles are rounded to sub-rounded and frequently preserve a desert varnish; wind-etched dreikanter pebbles are not uncommon.

The second lithofacies is better sorted and comprises very coarse sand to granule grade sediment with matrix-supported pebbles. Some beds have erosive bases and there is poorly developed inverse grading with concentrations of pebbles at bed tops. Parallel lamination is also evident at the top of some beds.

In both lithofacies the matrix is arkosic. Further evidence of terrestrial erosion comes from the presence of highly rounded, almost millet seed, sand grains within the matrix. Both facies are the product of alluvial fans interacting with lacustrine environments, and palaeocurrent data suggests that the fans may have been confined within valleys (Stewart, 2002).

The unconformity at this locality represents an enormous amount of 'missing' time. The Lewisian gneisses here have protolith ages of about 3000 Ma (Kinny and Friend, 1997), and the Scourie Dykes were intruded around 2400–2000 Ma (Heaman and Tarney, 1989). In contrast, the sandstones of the Diabaig Formation were deposited at about 1000 Ma (Turnbull *et al.*, 1996). Thus, over 20% of Earth history is missing at the unconformity surface.

Locality 1.3 [NC 2175 2503]

Relief on the basal Torridon Group unconformity.

Walk eastwards to the 'falling rocks' road sign. Beds of Diabaig Formation are truncated against a topographic high on the Lewisian gneiss erosion

40

surface. There has been some minor faulting on the flanks of the high during compaction, but the relationship is to a large degree the original stratigraphical one. To the east, the Diabaig Formation is visible in the top of the road cut for around 100m until it is thrown down on a normal fault [NC 2183 2499]. The Lewisian gneiss is highly weathered to at least 10m beneath the unconformity. Beyond the small fault, the Diabaig Formation reaches its greatest thickness in this section and is at least 25m thick – the variable thickness reflects the local derivation of sediment and the infilling of topographic hollows on the unconformity surface. Looking southwards across Loch Assynt, considerable topography can be seen on top of the Lewisian Gneiss Complex. Around Quinag, to the north of Loch Assynt, there is up to 400m of relief on the unconformity (Stewart, 2002).

Locality 1.4 [NC 2194 2497]

Base of the Applecross Formation.

Thirty metres before the end of the roadside safety barrier, the character of the road-cut changes and thick, trough cross-bedded sandstones of the Applecross Formation (Torridon Group) can be seen to conformably overlie the thinly bedded, poorly sorted, laminated granulestones of the Diabaig Formation (Fig. 13). The lithology of the Applecross Formation will be examined at Locality 1.6.

Fig. 13 Massive, trough cross-bedded sandstones of the Applecross Formation overlying flaggy Diabaig Formation strata at Locality 1.4. (BGS photograph P506431, © NERC)

41

Locality 1.5 [NC 2225 2489]

Glacial striae.

A small cutting by the road preserves well-developed glacial striae on the surface of ice-sculpted Applecross Formation sandstone (best seen on the southern side of the east end of the cutting). Striae are rarely seen on Torridon Group sediments, but here they have been protected from erosion by peat cover.

Locality 1.6 [NC 2248 2479]

Typical outcrops of Applecross Formation.

Continuing eastwards, just beyond an old road sign and set back 20m from the road next to a small holly is an easily accessible outcrop of typical Applecross Formation. The grain size varies from very coarse sand to granule and the clasts are angular to sub-angular; there is very little silt or clay, in common with most of the Applecross Formation. Compositionally, the sediment contains a high proportion of terracotta-coloured feldspar and lithic clasts in addition to vein and polycrystalline quartz. Trough cross-bedding is common throughout, with sets varying from 10–20cm (Fig. 14). On the upper surface of the outcrop, sets can be seen clearly in 3D with current directions towards 100°. The sediments were deposited by deep, perennial braided rivers that formed a very large-scale braidplain, with a mean current direction of 123° (Stewart, 2002).

Fig. 14 Trough cross-bedded arkosic sandstones and granulestones of the Applecross Formation at [NC 2164 2539]. One metre rule for scale; note the convolute lamination in the lowest bed. (Photograph: © M. P. Smith)

Locality 1.7 [NC 2273 2470]

The basal Cambrian unconformity.

The last outcrops of Applecross Formation by the road provide a good viewpoint north-westwards towards the summit of Spidean Coinich (764m), one of the summits of Quinag. White, well-bedded quartz arenites of the Eriboll Formation dip east at 12–15° and overlie the sub-horizontal Applecross Formation with angular unconformity, the boundary descending to the road just beyond a small stream.

The slabs of Applecross Formation by the road again preserve friction cracks and good striae at 113°, indicating westward transport of ice along the valley axis.

Locality 1.8 [NC 2291 2472]

The base of the Eriboll Formation.

The Applecross–Eriboll formation boundary is not exposed (though there are excellent exposures of this unconformity about 1.5km from the road at [NC 220 257]). The first roadside outcrop of the lower member of the Eriboll Formation, the Basal Quartzite Member, is just past the stream culvert. These are very light grey-weathering, very coarse sandstones–granulestones, which have a high content of terracotta-coloured feldspars, enough to be classified as sub-arkoses despite the name of the member. Small-scale cross-bedding is evident.

Locality 1.9 [NC 2308 2453]

Typical outcrops of the Basal Quartzite Member.

A large cutting within the Eriboll Formation lies 200m farther eastwards. Much of the sedimentary detail is obscured by mineral-coated joint faces, including slickensides, but good exposures lie around 20m before the end of the safety barrier, within the upper part of the Basal Quartzite Member. The sediment is generally finer than at the base, but there is still granule-grade material on the bounding surfaces. The proportion of feldspar has also decreased and the sediments here are true quartz arenites. Well-developed planar tabular cross-bedding forms 5–20cm sets. Bipolar current directions are evident (towards 290° and 055–110°) and, in places, well-developed herringbone cross-bedding is present. A small-scale duplex structure that shows floor and roof thrusts and several imbricate slices can also be seen within this outcrop.

The youngest beds in the cutting [NC 2313 2451] contain very faint, but clearly distinguishable, *Skolithos* 'pipes', indicating that the Basal Quartzite–Pipe Rock Member boundary lies a few metres from the top of the exposed succession. In beds where *Skolithos* is ambiguously developed in vertical profile, this can often be verified by looking for the tell-tale dimples and corresponding warts on the bedding surfaces where the burrows pass through.

Locality 1.10 [NC 2349 2440]

Classic outcrops of the Pipe Rock Member.

Twenty metres up the Kylesku road from Skiag Bridge lie some of the most photographed trace fossils in the United Kingdom. The matrix of the Pipe Rock Member is here stained red by diagenetic iron oxide, but the *Skolithos* burrows remain white as a result of differential early diagenesis (Fig. 15). Somewhat masked by the red staining and the abundant *Skolithos* burrows, the Pipe Rock Member contains abundant large-scale planar tabular cross-bedding in sets of 0.5–1.5m; each set is divided by green mudstone seams from which sphaeromorph acritarch floras have been recovered. The *Skolithos* burrows are *c.* 1cm wide with lengths of many tens of centimetres: precise maximum lengths are difficult to estimate since outcrop faces are not coincident with the burrow axes.

Locality 1.11 [NC 2359 2423]

Outcrops of the Fucoid Beds Member.

Return to the junction and continue eastwards along the lochside road towards Inchnadamph. The Pipe Rock Member is conformably overlain by the orange-brown Fucoid Beds Member (An t-Sròn Formation) a short

Fig. 15 Distinctive surfaces
of Pipe Rock Member at
Skiag Bridge, Locality 1.10.
(BGS photograph P531881,
© NERC)

Fig. 16 Close-up of Fucoid
Beds Member at Skiag Bridge,
Locality 1.11. (BGS photo-
graph P531882, © NERC)

distance east along the roadcut, and
typical lithofacies are exposed 10m east
of the brown tourist sign (Fig. 16). Two
lithofacies are present, the dominant
one being dolomitic wavy bedded siltstones. *Skolithos* and *Palaeophycus* are
common, but a diverse assemblage of
other trace fossils is present, including
Planolites, *Cruziana* and *Rusophycus*.
Together these are characteristic of the

Cruziana ichnofacies, which is indicative of a position above storm wave
base but beneath fair weather wave base. It was the occurrence of abundant
black burrows on bedding surfaces that early geologists mistook for fossil
seaweeds, giving rise to the name of the member. The Fucoid Beds Member
is the earliest unit in the Cambrian succession to contain abundant body
fossils as well as trace fossils, and trilobites that have been found in this
member indicate a position within the *Bonnia–Olenellus* Biozone (late
Early Cambrian to earliest Middle Cambrian).

The less abundant lithofacies comprises distinctive 10–30cm beds of
dolomitic grainstones in which the dominant allochems are echinoderm
fragments. McKie and Donovan (1992) identified eocrinoid fragments
amongst the debris. The grainstones are cross-bedded with E- to NE-
directed palaeocurrents and are interpreted as storm event beds.

Locality 1.12 [NC 2372 2408]

Outcrops of the Salterella Grit Member and Ghrudaidh Formation.

The Fucoid Beds Member is conformably overlain by the Salterella Grit Member, which forms the upper part of the An t-Sròn Formation and marks a return to cross-bedded quartz arenite deposition. The roadside outcrop contains prominent *Skolithos* and less conspicuous examples of the body fossil *Salterella*. The latter is an organism of unknown affinity, but may be a primitive mollusc that produced an agglutinated rather than microcrystalline shell. In hand specimen, it appears as a cone a few milli-metres long that produces dark, circular or v-shaped profiles depending on the section; very occasional 3D specimens are white or black, but the shell is frequently dissolved out leaving distinctive mouldic cavities. *Salterella* occurs from the upper part of the Pipe Rock Member through to the base of the Ghrudaidh Formation, but is particularly abundant in the epony-mous member. The genus is stratigraphically restricted to the *Bonnia–Olenellus* Biozone. Other shell material is present as small fragments.

The Salterella Grit Member is conformably overlain by lead grey dolostones of the Ghrudaidh Formation (Durness Group), marking a major shift in depositional style on the Laurentian margin from clastic- to carbonate-dominated (Fig. 17). In the roadside section the boundary is gradational over a metre or so, marked by a rubbly sandy dolostone. This is significantly different to the boundary exposed a few hundred metres away in the lowest horses of the Achmore Duplex (see Locality 1.14) where a low

Fig. 17 White quartz arenites of the Salterella Grit Member overlain by grey dolostones of the Ghrudaidh Formation at Locality 1.12. This boundary is also the Ardvreck–Durness group boundary. (Photograph: © M. P. Smith)

energy, dolomitic siltstone marks the boundary. The dolostones in the road cut are faintly mottled as a result of differential dolomitisation in burrow systems, and there are occasional quartz sands with intraclasts. Towards the top of the outcrop, irregular white vugs become common and represent pseudomorphed evaporite nodules, probably of anhydrite.

Locality 1.13 [NC 2382 2403]

Vogesite sills and Sole Thrust.

Beyond the end of the lay-by, the top of a vogesite (hornblende lamprophyre) sill that intrudes the Ghrudaidh Formation is seen by a culvert. Ten metres farther east is a 5 m-thick vogesite sill with a rubbly base, which has been interpreted as the floor thrust of the Achmore Duplex, and the lowest thrust (Sole Thrust) of the Moine Thrust Zone in this area.

Excursion 1B:
The stratigraphy and structure of the Achmore Duplex and adjacent foreland

Park in the first car-park on the left [NC 234 248] on the road to Kylesku and Scourie from Skiag Bridge. From the lay-by, walk up the road to a gate on the right [NC 2349 2514] and then walk eastwards along a grassy track to a ford over a small stream [NC 2366 2509]. Proceed up the stream, which may be a dry bed or (very) wet. CAUTION: please do not hammer at any of the localities, this is a popular excursion and hammer scarring is becoming evident.

The Sole Thrust lies below the ford in the boggy ground, and most of the excursion is within a duplex developed beneath the Glencoul Thrust sheet. The stratigraphy of the horses within the duplex comprises the Fucoid Beds and Salterella Grit members of the An t-Sròn Formation (Ardvreck Group) and the lower part of the Ghrudaidh Formation (Durness Group). The duplex is of large scale, with a vertical distance of around 150m from floor thrust to roof thrust, but the local stratigraphy means that each individual horse is very thin, and the bounding thrusts are rarely separated by more than a few tens of metres.

Locality 1.14 [NC 2366 2509 to NC 2369 2528]

Imbricates in the stream section west of Achmore Farm.

At the ford, where a grassy track crosses the small stream [NC 2366 2509], the Salterella Grit Member forms the base of a waterfall and is conformably overlain by the Ghrudaidh Formation. In contrast to the foreland section along the lochside, the base of the Ghrudaidh Formation here comprises 2m of dark grey dolomitic siltstone that is superficially similar to some parts of the Fucoid Beds Member. This is overlain by typical buff grey weathering dolostones but, at the top of the second cascade, orange-weathering dolomitic siltstones of the Fucoid Beds Member are thrust over the Ghrudaidh Formation to the left of the waterfall (all directions given looking upstream). The thrust plane is exposed and dips at 28° towards the north-east.

Continuing up the stream, the Fucoid Beds – Salterella Grit – Ghrudaidh Formation succession is repeated by a number of small thrusts. Some horses do not contain all three units; for instance, the Fucoid Beds Member is thrust over the Salterella Grit at [NC 2368 2518]. At a sharp left hand bend where the Salterella Grit Member crosses the stream [NC 2369 2518], the topographic expression of the duplex across the hillside becomes clearly visible. The bedding is steeply dipping, and ridges of Salterella Grit Member trend NW–SE. Behind some of the ridges are trenches that contain the Ghrudaidh Formation, evidenced by the vegetation and the presence of shake holes, together with scattered outcrops of the shaley base of the formation and the more typical overlying dolostones. Within the shaley base at [NC 2367 2520] is the key fossil locality from which Huselbee and Thomas (1998) described *Olenellus lapworthi* and *Salterella maccullochi*, indicating a *Bonnia–Olenellus* biozone (late Early Cambrian to earliest Middle Cambrian) age for the base of the Durness Group. Above each trench, a steep bank of Fucoid Beds Member leads up to the next ridge of Salterella Grit Member. The stream flows along the trenches on the uphill side of the ridges, before cutting through the Salterella Grit and cascading down the steep banks.

Several more horses are crossed to a fence [NC 2369 2528], from where there is an excellent view across Loch Assynt to the 'double unconformity' (see Excursion 16). Above this point, the exposure becomes more sporadic.

Locality 1.15 [NC 2381 2558]

Follow the stream northwards to where it emerges from a small rising. Above this point the stream bed is dry, with occasional collapses into the underlying karst drainage. This is indicative of a change in the character of the duplex – above this point the horses are entirely composed of carbonates of the Durness Group, without the An t-Sròn Formation units seen at lower structural levels.

Locality 1.16 [NC 2363 2570]

From a short distance downstream of Locality 1.15, follow the last ridge of Salterella Grit Member north-westwards to another stream that offers a further section through the lower part of the duplex. On the way to this stream the highest point of the ridge offers an excellent viewpoint from which to survey the geology of Loch Assynt.

To the north-east, on Glas Bheinn (776m), the Eriboll Formation sequence is repeated by a number of thrusts. The Glencoul Thrust occurs at the break in slope below the quartzite screes. To the south-west, the famous 'double unconformity' can be seen on the hill of Beinn Gharbh (539m), with Lewisian gneisses overlain by Torridon Group units that are in turn overlain by quartz arenites of the Ardvreck Group (the latter intruded by sheets of Canisp Porphyry). To the west lies the foreland, with the dipslope of the Eriboll Formation unconformably overlying the arkoses of the Applecross Formation (Torridon Group) on Quinag.

At [NC 2363 2570], the ridge of Salterella Grit Member that has been followed across the moor crosses a second stream. The Fucoid Beds Member is thrust over this unit and a short distance upstream, the carbonate-dominated duplex begins. Proceed downstream (all directions now refer to looking downstream).

The stream descends back through the imbricated sedimentary sequence, with the same topographic features as at Location 14, but with rather fewer exposures of Ghrudaidh Formation dolostones. Farther downstream, thick units of Fucoid Beds Member with variable strike values and abrupt discontinuities in dip provide evidence for internal thrusts within this member. The reason for the contrast in stratigraphical composition of the horses in the first stream (Locality 1.14) with that seen here lies in the presence of a low angle lateral ramp, such that the older units are progressively cut out south-eastward between the two streams.

At the foot of a steep descent just above the road is a 5m waterfall with a birch tree. The dip of the Fucoid Beds Member in the waterfall is 52°, whereas a few metres lower down the valley, across a bounding thrust, the same unit has the gentle dips of the foreland. The Salterella Grit Member crops out by the culvert under the road, and between this and the last out-crop of Fucoid Beds Member lies the floor thrust of the Achmore Duplex – the Sole Thrust. This relationship is also seen slightly farther down the road [NC 2340 2546] and the Sole Thrust then lies a short distance above the road for several hundred metres down the hill. Good sedimentary structures are seen in the Salterella Grit Member in a small roadside quarry [NC 2340 2539]. Metre-scale planar tabular cross-bedding is well-exposed in the 3D outcrop, with laminae sharply defined by heavy minerals, though *Salterella* is scarce. Current directions are mainly directed towards the east and south-east. Topographically below and to the west of the quarry lies the foreland.

From the quarry, cross the road to rejoin the stream and follow it down-stream. The same, foreland, Salterella Grit Member is seen across the deeply incised stream valley beneath a rowan tree, and directly below this lies an outcrop of foreland Fucoid Beds Member. Farther downstream, close to the junction of the stream with Allt Sgiathaig, are outcrops of the Pipe Rock Member.

Locality 1.17 [NC 2310 2540]

From the stream junction, walk north-west up the Allt Sgiathaig across more or less continuously exposed Pipe Rock Member, passing one bedding surface [NC 2316 2533] with very well-developed *Monocraterion* – a burrow system similar to *Skolithos* but with a distinctive cone or 'trumpet' at the top of the burrow. Continue past a sharp bend and waterfall to where the stream flows over large bedding surfaces with a two-tiered cliff forming the east bank. On the west bank [NC 2305 2548] are bedding surfaces with fine calibre *Skolithos* and small *Monocraterion* (2–3cm tops with 0.5cm diameter burrows). The bedding has a maximum thickness of 20–40cm and is wedge-shaped at outcrop-scale. Wavy set boundaries indicate the presence of ripples on top of the dunes.

Recross to the east bank and climb to the top of the first tier of outcrop. The bedding surface contains densely packed *Skolithos* and occasional *Monocraterion*. Above this prominent surface are two further beds with *Skolithos*, but these are overlain by a 30cm bed and then a 5m-thick massive bed, first recognised by Peach *et al.* (1907), which forms the second tier (Figs 18, 19). This pale-weathering massive bed forms a distinctive marker horizon a short distance below the top of the Eriboll Formation, recognisable along much of the Cambro-Ordovician outcrop belt from Loch Eriboll in the north to the Isle of Skye, and represents a sequence boundary within the formation. Although most of the bed is structureless, the top surface contains planar lamination, ripple lamination and dewatering structures. The massive bed is overlain by a more heterolithic succession of interbedded sandstones and silty mudstones, representing the maximum flooding surface. The sandstones are planar-laminated and cross-bedded and contain red *Skolithos* in a red matrix. Several of the beds exhibit shearing of the *Skolithos* burrows (top to the NW). The 1.5m heterolithic succession is overlain by typical Pipe Rock Member before outcrop is lost.

Walk down the bedding plane on the top of the massive bed to rejoin the Allt Sgiathaig and return to the lay-by, which is visible ahead. If time permits, it is worth driving northwards over the pass towards Kylesku, where a viewpoint at Newton (Locality 16.10) provides an excellent view down Loch Glencoul and context for the structural position of the Achmore Duplex beneath the Glencoul Thrust.

Fig. 18 Large bedding surface within the Pipe Rock Member at Locality 1.17 [NC 2310 2540] with dense concentrations of *Skolithos* and *Monocraterion* overlain by a distinctive, pale-weathering 5m-thick massive bed which forms a distinctive marker horizon a short distance below the top of the Eriboll Formation. The yellow rule in the dotted circle is one metre. (Photograph: © M. P. Smith)

Fig. 19 A bedding plane with abundant *Monocraterion* burrows immediately below the massive bed in Allt Sgiathaig, at Locality 1.17. The conical tops of the burrows are seen from above. (Photograph: © M. P. Smith)

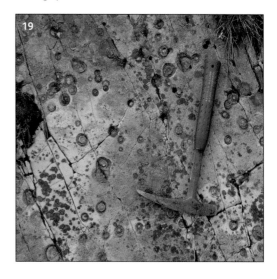

Excursion 2

A Transect through the
Canisp Shear Zone, Achmelvich

Robert Wilson, Bob Holdsworth and Ruth Wightman

Purpose: To examine the Canisp Shear Zone, which preserves a complex history of deformation and reactivation, from Archaean to Cenozoic time. To study rocks of the Lewisian Gneiss Complex deformed at progressively shallower depths, starting in deep Badcallian basement structures, followed by exposures of Inverian, Laxfordian and later deformation events.

Aspects covered:

Badcallian, Inverian and Laxfordian deformation events of the North-west Highlands;

Granulite- to greenschist-facies metamorphism;

Transpressional shear zone structures and fabrics;

Reactivation and strain localisation processes;

Non-Andersonian fracturing and 3D strain.

Maps: OS: 1:50,000 Landranger sheet 15 Loch Assynt; 1:25,000 Explorer sheet 442 Assynt and Lochinver. BGS: 1:50,000 sheet S107E, Point of Stoer.

Terrain: 4 km walk along rough coastal footpaths and over moderate terrain; sturdy footwear and waterproofs are advised. Some scrambling may be required and extreme care should be taken on low cliff sections, especially during windy weather. It is not advised to access the coast during storms, especially if there is a substantial ocean swell, as there is a risk of being caught by large breaking waves.

Time: This is a full day excursion.

Access: There are no access constraints for this excursion, although care should be taken on coastal sections. Please note that as the area includes an SSSI, the use of hammers is prohibited.

53

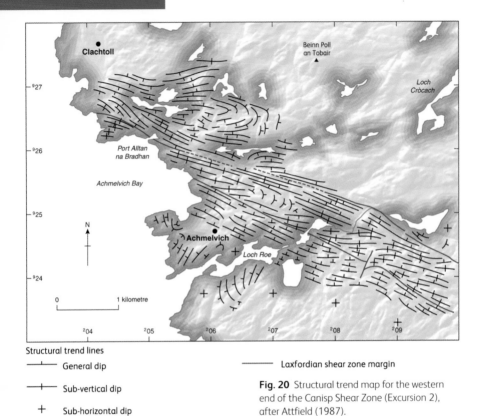

Structural trend lines

───┴─── General dip

───┼─── Sub-vertical dip

╋ Sub-horizontal dip

────── Laxfordian shear zone margin

Fig. 20 Structural trend map for the western end of the Canisp Shear Zone (Excursion 2), after Attfield (1987).

Locality 2.1 [NC 0753 2554]

Surface expression of Lewisian basement fabrics – viewpoint looking inland towards Canisp.

Travelling west from Loch Assynt (or east from Lochinver) on the A837, turn north on the B869 (following signs for Stoer and Drumbeg). After about 3 km a viewpoint is reached at the top of a hill. From here there is a wonderful panoramic view of Sutherland's hills and the Assynt Culmination. A number of distinct valleys may be seen running inland towards the hills of Canisp and Suilven, which can also be easily picked out on maps, aerial photos and satellite images. Some of these valleys are fault controlled, including a number that follow the surface expression of the major Canisp Shear Zone (CSZ). Looking around at the gneissic rocks in the area you should be able to pick out a steeply dipping foliation trending ESE–WNW. This is the characteristic fabric of the CSZ (Fig. 20). The CSZ was formed during the Inverian (pre-Scourie Dyke) and reactivated in the Laxfordian (post-Scourie Dyke). This excursion provides a transect across it.

Locality 2.2 [NC 0565 2503]

Badcallian gneiss on Achmelvich beach.

Drive for another 1.5km NW along the B869 until you reach a turning on your left side (near Alltan na Bradhan, [NC 0589 2600]). Park in the old quarry/lay-by. From here follow the track for about 100m and you should see a footpath on your left that will take you south to Achmelvich. After a short (20-minute) walk south along the inland footpath you come to a car-park and campsite (NOTE: you can drive here directly from a turning on the B869, but the road is very narrow and is not suitable for large vehicles such as buses). From the car-park, make your way over the dunes to the beach (Fig. 21). Here you can look at the water-washed exposures on the north (and south) side of the beach and examine the general lithology, metamorphic state and structure of the felsic gneiss (Fig. 22). There is good evidence for high temperature metamorphism with partial melting, with widespread preservation of schlieren textures that wrap lens-shaped inclusions of coarse-grained mafic to ultramafic material up to one metre across. Here we see dominantly shallowly dipping Badcallian deformation fabrics and cm-scale intrafolial folds, although small, steeply-dipping dextral Laxfordian shear zones and faults may be found trending ~NW–SE. This locality lies within the central part of the Lochinver Monocline (Fig. 23).

Locality 2.3 [NC 0570 2512]

Little-deformed Scourie Dyke and localised Laxfordian dextral shear.

Walk north round the coast to a 20m-wide WNW–ESE Scourie Dyke, which cuts the north limb of the Lochinver Monocline. Here the discordant, intrusive relationships between the gneisses and the medium to coarse-grained doleritic dyke can be studied. Xenoliths of felsic gneiss and little-deformed igneous textures are well preserved in the centre of the dyke, and the margins clearly cross-cut the gneissic banding (Fig. 24). Laxfordian features

55

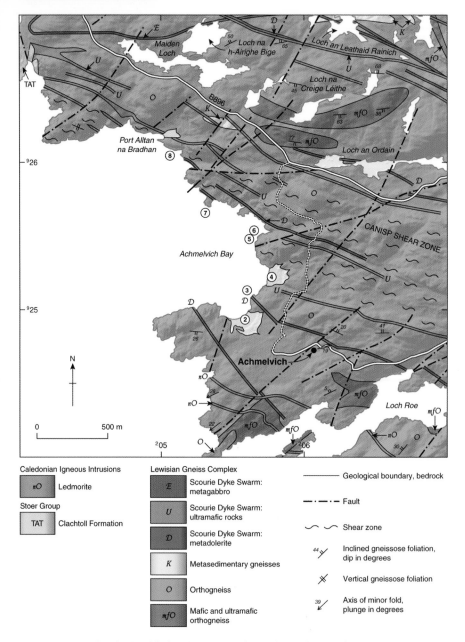

Fig. 21 Simplified geological map of the Achmelvich area, after British Geological Survey (1998), showing the localities described in Excursion 2.

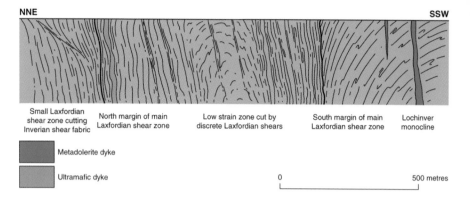

NNE   SSW

Small Laxfordian
shear zone cutting
Inverian shear fabric

North margin of main
Laxfordian shear zone

Low strain zone cut by
discrete Laxfordian shears

South margin of main
Laxfordian shear zone

Lochinver
monocline

Metadolerite dyke

Ultramafic dyke

0   500 metres

Above:

Fig. 23 Schematic cross-section across the extreme western end of the Canisp Shear Zone, after Attfield (1987).

Fig. 22 Photograph of typical Badcallian gneisses outwith the Canisp Shear Zone, Achmelvich beach, Locality 2.2. (Photograph: © R. E. Holdsworth)

Fig. 24 Cross-cutting Scourie Dyke with xenoliths of acid gneiss at Locality 2.3. (Photograph: © R. E. Holdsworth)

here are typical of much of the Assynt Terrane Lewisian outside the Canisp Shear Zone. The effects of later Laxfordian shearing are localised in mm- to cm-wide shear zones along dyke margins, with retrogression of both felsic gneisses and dyke to form greenschist-facies biotite-muscovite schists and hornblende-biotite schists respectively. Small foliation-parallel quartz veins are associated directly with this retrogression. Associated mineral stretching lineations are sub-horizontal with numerous examples of dextral shear criteria preserved.

57

Locality 2.4 [NC 0591 2525]

Inverian deformation on north beach.

Walk north to the middle of the next sandy beach. Note how the foliation steepens into the Inverian part of the Canisp Shear Zone, and marking the northern flank of the Lochinver Monocline. Features to be studied include the general lithology, metamorphic state and structure of felsic gneisses associated with Inverian deformation. Characteristic structures include a steeply dipping foliation, moderately to steeply SE-plunging lineation and isoclinal folds.

Locality 2.5 [NC 0575 2551]

Faulted margin of the Laxfordian Canisp Shear Zone.

Walk farther north up onto the low crags and round into a marked cleft in the coastline which marks the faulted south margin of the Laxfordian Canisp Shear Zone. The foliation in the gneisses steepens further to sub-vertical between Localities 2.4 and 2.5 and, across the faulted margin, becomes much more attenuated, with a shallowly SE-plunging mineral lineation developing. Later foliation-parallel and cross-cutting faults, together with numerous foliation-parallel quartz veins up to 30cm thick, are also much more common. Look WNW out along the coast for a good view of the NW–SE-trending CSZ fabrics and associated faults, many of which produce distinctive 'clefts' in the landscape, including one crossed on the headland at Locality 2.7.

Locality 2.6 [NC 0575 2556]

Ductile and brittle Laxfordian shear fabrics indicating multiple deformation events.

The intense ductile fabric (Fig. 25) largely obliterates the pre-existing gneissose texture, with the widespread development of biotite and musco-vite suggesting upper greenschist- to lower amphibolite-facies metamorphic conditions during Laxfordian reworking. Despite the very well-developed shallowly ESE-plunging mineral stretching lineation (Fig. 26), there are very few unambiguous asymmetric ductile shear sense criteria preserved at this locality, although a dextral sense of shear is inferred (see below). Schistose dark green lenses of amphibolite may represent highly attenuated and retrogressed Scourie Dykes sheared into parallelism with the CSZ foliation. At this locality, the foliation is ubiquitously reactivated by 'Late Laxfordian' foliation-parallel sinistral faults and associated Riedel shear systems indicating sinistral senses of shear. These are widely developed, often with spacings of a few cm or less, and they are commonly associated with mainly sinistral-verging brittle-ductile folds. All these structures are cross-cut at high angles by characteristically iron-stained, 'ladder-like' systems of faults, fractures and brecciation thought to be related to Stoer Group rifting (Fig. 27). The geometry of these fractures reflects a non-Andersonian fracture pattern which may be associated with 3D strain, possibly during oblique extension (transtension).

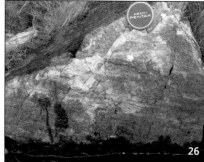

Fig. 25 Typical mylonitic gneisses within the Canisp Shear Zone (Locality 2.6).

Fig. 26 Shallowly plunging mineral lineations typical of Laxfordian CSZ.

Fig. 27 Late faults and fractures, thought to be associated with Stoer Group rifting, at Locality 2.6.

(All photographs: © R. E. Holdsworth)

59

Locality 2.7 [NC 0533 2574]

Unfaulted margin of the Laxfordian Canisp Shear Zone.

Follow footpaths along the coast round to a prominent peninsula cut by a distinct cleft (Fig. 21). If tide and sea conditions permit, you can climb across this cleft (extreme care should be taken here, and you should not attempt to cross if alone!) to look at exposures of the unfaulted margin of the Laxfordian Canisp Shear Zone. The outer part of the headland comprises relatively little-deformed felsic gneisses, while the inner part is mainly schistose mylonite with shallowly plunging mineral stretching lineations derived from felsic gneiss with numerous concordant quartz veins. The original ductile boundary of the Laxfordian CSZ is preserved here and shows clear evidence for a dextral sense of shear based on the asymmetric bending-in of the fabric in the few centimetres adjacent to the shear zone margin.

In the schistose section of mylonites, the foliation is very strongly reactivated by 'Late Laxfordian' foliation-parallel faults and associated Riedel shear systems indicating sinistral senses of shear. Once again, these are closely spaced and they are commonly associated with mainly sinistral-verging brittle-ductile folds.

Looking back along the coast to the south-east we can see a good cross-sectional view across the CSZ. It is possible to pick out the changes in dip indicating the presence of the Lochinver Monocline, changes in the basement fabric appearance and strain intensity due to the development of the CSZ (from south to north: Badcallian, Inverian and Laxfordian respectively) and the presence of a number of large foliation-parallel faults.

Locality 2.8 [NC 0508 2611]

Refolded folds, sheath folds and reworked Scourie Dykes.

Using rough footpaths, follow the coast round to the prominent peninsula at Port Alltan na Bradhan (Fig. 21). Care should be taken in this section as cliff sections are very exposed in windy conditions and relatively steep in places, and surfaces may be slippy. If weather conditions are windy, it is possible to cut inland to access the next set of exposures or return to the parking spot.

The best exposures lie on the south side and western end of the peninsula (Fig. 28). Spectacular 3D exposures of strongly reworked, locally folded yet commonly discordant, Scourie Dykes can be seen; these now occur as foliated amphibolites with little or no igneous mineralogy or textures preserved. Nests of complex Laxfordian folds occur on centimetre to metrescales and locally refold early intrafolial isoclines (possible Badcallian or Inverian structures?). Mineral lineations and minor Laxfordian folds plunge predominantly SE at low angles but are locally highly variable, with complex curvilinear geometries and eye-structures that suggest the presence of highly curvilinear fold structures. In detail, these structures that fold the local mineral lineations appear to show curvature arcs about different directions in different localities. There is little evidence to suggest that the folds are regional polyphase structures and a preferred explanation is that they are flow perturbation folds formed during CSZ shearing. The complexity seems atypical of the shear zone as a whole and may reflect flow partitioning localised here due to the presence of a very large basic pod which is visible in the cliff south-east of the main peninsula (Fig. 21). This probably represents a large Scourie Dyke as it is strongly wrapped by the shear zone foliation.

Cross the stream to the north of the peninsula and follow the footpath inland back to the parking spot (NOTE: the footpath crosses back over the stream after about 200m and cuts up the hillside leading to a gravel track.)

Fig. 28 Tight Laxfordian folding in gneisses in the Canisp Shear Zone at Locality 2.8. (BGS photograph P618162, © NERC)

61

Excursion 3

Stoer Group at Stoer Peninsula

Maarten Krabbendam

Purpose: To examine the stratigraphy and sedimentology of the late Mesoproterozoic Stoer Group, and its unconformable relationships with the underlying Lewisian gneiss and overlying Torridon Group.

Aspects covered: Basal unconformity with breccia and neptunic dykes; fluviatile and lacustrine deposits (Clachtoll Formation), fluviatile sandstone (Bay of Stoer Formation) and volcaniclastic Stac Fada Member. The upper part of the Stoer Group is best studied at Enard Bay (Excursion 4).

Maps: OS: 1:50,000 Landranger sheet 15 Loch Assynt; 1:25,000 Explorer sheet 442 Assynt and Lochinver. BGS: 1:50,000 107W Point of Stoer.

Terrain: Mainly coastal outcrops with relatively easy access. Most outcrops can be visited at any state of the tide, with some exceptions (e.g. Locality 3.1). Many boulders and bedding planes can be extremely slippery, especially below high tide mark. The excursion is not recommended during stormy conditions.

Time: A full day allows leisurely study; if pressed, a half day would suffice.

Access: There are no access constraints for this excursion, but it is largely on or near crofting land and care must be taken with livestock – dogs should be kept on a lead at all times. Please note that this is a very popular excursion, and that the outcrops should not be hammered.

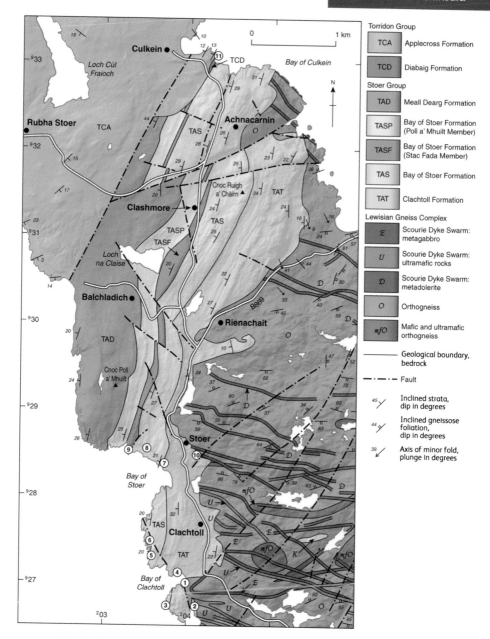

Fig. 29 Geological map of the Stoer area (after British Geological Survey, 2002b), showing the localities described in Excursion 3.

Locality 3.1 [NC 0404 2702]

Bay of Clachtoll: Stoer Group – Lewisian Gneiss Complex unconformity
(low tide only).

Park in the car-park near Clachtoll beach [NC 0395 2730)], which has
public toilets and a Ranger Hut with a small display on the local natural
history. A' Chlach Thuill (the 'Split Rock') is visible on the shore to the
south-west. From the car-park, walk across the dunes and then the beach
in a southerly direction (Fig. 29).

At the southern end of the beach, cobbly breccio-conglomerate – the
basal Clachtoll Formation – overlies Lewisian gneiss via a sharp unconformity. Note the strong subvertical east-west foliation of the Lewisian gneiss,
which lies within the Stoer Shear Zone (similar to the Canisp Shear Zone –
see Excursion 2). Towards the north-west, the conglomerate passes laterally
into brick-red muddy sandstone, indicating much quieter depositional
conditions. The depositional setting has been interpreted as an apron of
debris-fans (bajada) fringing a lake (Stewart, 2002).

If the tide is low, follow the beach south-east to a wide sandy gully, and
follow this south to a small bay at [NC 0405 2674]. If the tide is high, walk
to the south-east corner of the beach and ascend towards a fence. Turn right
and follow a faint path along the fence, which it crosses and re-crosses, and
walk south past a ruin to a small bay at [NC 0405 2674].

Lewisian gneiss occurs on the east of this little bay, while sandstone
occurs to the west; the bay marks a fault. From here, climb over the gneiss
knoll to the east, following an old fence, turn right through a gap and right
again to a small south-east-facing cliff.

Locality 3.2A [NC 0412 2672]

Stoer Group – Lewisian Gneiss Complex unconformity.

The small cliff of Lewisian gneiss shows numerous veins of red mudstone
and locally fine sandstone, injected into cracks and fractures. Locally, the
gneiss is brecciated, with angular blocks surrounded by a matrix of injected
mudstone. Some of the most photogenic examples occur in loose boulders
below the cliff. In the gully below the cliff, a small stream marks the

boundary between a mafic Scourie Dyke and brecciated, faulted Lewisian gneiss. On the far (western) side of the cliff, subhorizontal slickensides (suggesting a component of strike slip movement) occur in mudstone, plastered against gneiss. The cliff and gully mark a fault, which operated during Stoer Group deposition; Beacom *et al.* (1999) showed that deposition occurred during sinistral transtension.

Locality 3.2B [NC 0412 2666]

Basal Stoer Group breccio-conglomerate.

Cross the stream and follow a sheep path for *c.*50m to the south, then clamber over some gneiss until you see an outcrop of conglomerate. This conglomerate is the basal part of the Clachtoll Formation. It is confined to a small palaeovalley (notice the large knoll of gneiss to the east; Fig. 30). The unconformity is sharp and does not show signs of weathering. The breccio-conglomerate contains clasts of mafic and intermediate gneiss, metadolerite, ultramafic rock, and vein quartz that can be matched with the adjacent Lewisian gneiss, all within a gritty matrix. Together with locality 3.2A, this shows that the base of the Stoer Group was deposited during extension with locally high palaeorelief.

Fig. 30 Basal breccia of the Stoer Group in a palaeovalley (centre) resting unconformably against Lewisian gneiss on both sides. (BGS photograph P524833, © NERC)

65

Fig. 31 A' Clach Thuill, the Split Rock, formed of sandstone of the Bay of Stoer Formation. (BGS photograph P661223, © NERC)

Locality 3.3 [NC 0384 2673]

A' Chlach Thuill ('Split Rock').

Retrace your steps for about 100m, and then head west over grass towards a prominent rocky knoll on the peninsula. This is A' Chlach Thuill ('Split Rock'; Fig. 31). Most of the peninsula consists of the brick-red, massive muddy sandstone of the Clachtoll Formation, well exposed to the north and south of A' Chlach Thuill. The knoll marks the sudden incoming of pale, pink cross-bedded medium-coarse sandstone of the Bay of Stoer Formation (Fig. 32). Stewart (2002) reports horizons of dessicated limestone laminae within the mudstone of the upper part of the Clachtoll Formation, but the outcrops are difficult to find and in hazardous locations.

Retrace your steps to the beach of Bay of Clachtoll. Looking north, note the clear change of landscape that coincides with the unconformity between Lewisian gneiss and the Stoer Group: the characteristic, rough 'cnoc-an-lochan' landscape has developed on the gneiss, whilst to the east the Stoer Group underlies a gentler landscape with good pasture.

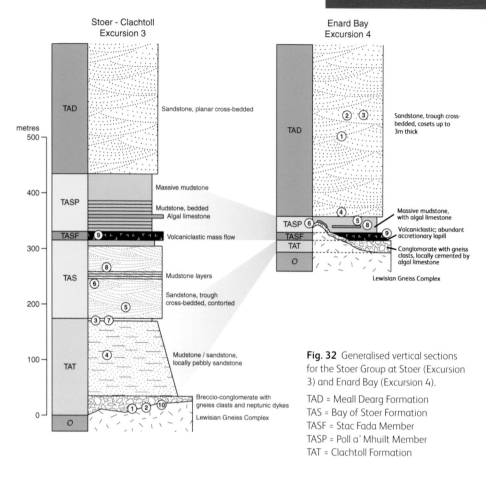

Fig. 32 Generalised vertical sections for the Stoer Group at Stoer (Excursion 3) and Enard Bay (Excursion 4).

TAD = Meall Dearg Formation
TAS = Bay of Stoer Formation
TASF = Stac Fada Member
TASP = Poll a' Mhuilt Member
TAT = Clachtoll Formation

Locality 3.4 [NC 0405 2715]

Bay of Clachtoll beach: Clachtoll Formation.

The large knoll in the middle of Bay of Clachtoll beach consists of thick bedded, red muddy sandstone, typical of the Clachtoll Formation. From here, make your way to the white building on the north-west side of the bay – this is the Salmon Bothy, and contains a small exhibition illustrating the history of salmon fishing in Clachtoll.

Outcrops at high-water mark just north of the Salmon Bothy show thinner bedded muddy sandstone, locally with desiccation cracks on bedding surfaces, indicating periods of subaerial exposure.

67

From here, follow the coast north to a monument to the Reverend Norman MacLeod, founder of the Normanite Presbyterian movement. The monument is made from Ledmore Marble (see Excursion 10). Follow the 'walkers' signs through the various gates and stiles past the croft of Clachtoll Cottage. Beyond the croft follow a path over grass, then turn west to a patch of boulders with low outcrops.

Locality 3.5 [NC 0361 2726]

Aird na Mòine: Bay of Stoer Formation.

The low outcrops here comprise medium-coarse pink sandstone (Bay of Stoer Formation) and show trough cross-bedding, indicating flow along a north-south axis. Dewatering structures and other soft-sediment deformation structures indicate rapid deposition. These sandstones were deposited in a fluviatile environment, possibly in braided rivers or alluvial fans.

Work your way northwards, following the top of the outcrops, past a perched erratic of Lewisian gneiss. Extensive, sloping bedding planes alternate with small cliffs; head towards the second of these.

Locality 3.6 [NC 0358 2751]

Sgèir na Tràghad: Bay of Stoer Formation.

A series of mudstone-sandstone alternations (*c.*10 cm scale beds), bounded at top and bottom by thicker bedded sandstone, are seen at this locality (Fig. 33). The mudstone (locally siltstone) contains both planar and ripple laminations. The sandstone sharply overlies the mudstone intervals and contains pebbles of vein quartz. Small-scale, syn-depositional extensional faulting disrupts the beds. This facies has considerable lateral extent (see also Locality 3.8) and this suggests a lacustrine interval within an overall fluviatile sequence. In total, five mudstone-sandstone cycles occur in the Bay of Stoer Formation (Stewart, 2002)

Continue northwards past An Dun, a ruined Iron Age broch, to the cobble beach of Bay of Stoer. Continue along the beach to reach outcrops at sea level on the north-west side of the bay.

Fig. 33 Outcrops of the Bay of Stoer Formation, containing alternating mudstone and sandstone beds, at Locality 3.6. (BGS photograph P518638, © NERC)

Fig. 34 Rippled sandstone surface in the Clachtoll Formation, Locality 3.7. (BGS photograph P518651, © NERC)

Locality 3.7 [NC 0379 2834]

Bay of Stoer: Clachtoll – Bay of Stoer formation boundary.

Take care at this locality as the bedding planes can be very slippery. The outcrops forming the wave-cut platform are in the Clachtoll Formation and show muddy sandstone with desiccation cracks and ripple marks (Fig. 34). Locally pebbly, gritty sandstone occurs, possibly indicating sheet floods. At the west end of the wave-cut platform is a small cliff of sandstone, marking the sharp, locally erosive, change into the Bay of Stoer Formation, characterised by thick-bedded and cross-bedded sandstone with local contortions.

Go a short distance to the east and ascend a grassy slope towards a wall; follow the path to the west along the wall. At the end of the wall, go through the gate; after about 50m, cross a small stream.

Locality 3.8 [NC 0355 2853]

The same thin mudstone-siltstone beds are exposed here as at Locality 3.6, showing considerable lateral extent. From here, continue west along the path to a rocky promontory.

Fig. 35 Outcrops of the Stac Fada Member on the Stac Fada peninsula. (BGS photograph P512723, © NERC)

Locality 3.9 [NC 0333 2854]

Stac Fada: Stac Fada Member.

The promontory marks the Stac Fada Member (Fig. 35). This consists of a *c.*12m thick massive deposit of greenish, poorly sorted muddy sandstone, full of angular dark green or black volcanic fragments (max. 5cm long), including pumice and (now devitrified) volcanic glass. At the top of the unit are round pea-sized spheres or accretionary lapilli (better preserved at Locality 4.9). The geochemistry of the volcanic fragments points to a mafic volcanic source (Young, 2002). Sanders and Johnston (1989) report folded vesicle trails up to 3m long within the member.

There appear to be two volcaniclastic units in the area (although Stewart [2002] suggests that these are the same unit repeated by faulting). The upper, thickest unit is seen in the north to be wedged in with sandstone; some metres above this lies a raft of sandstone some 20m long. Smaller rafts, some of which are contorted, occur to the south. The sandstone below the lowest unit is locally strongly warped, especially in the south.

A number of different interpretations have been proposed for the exact genesis of the Stac Fada Member. All interpretations have to take into account the fact that the underlying sediments were unlithified, and deformed and fragmented by the emplacement of the unit. This therefore suggests some sort of mass-flow, flowing at fairly high speed and covering a wide area. The presence of vesicle trails suggests that (at least at Stac Fada itself) emplacement was hot enough to produce gas or steam from underlying wet sediment, as the unit was emplaced. Lawson (1972) suggested an origin as an ash or pyroclastic flow. Sanders and Johnston (1989, 1990) suggested the unit had a peperitic origin (as a mixture of magma and wet sediment), with the lowest unit at Stoer representing the feeder. A difficulty with this interpretation is that peperite normally develops at the margins of large sills or at the base of lava flows, and that having the feeder exposed would be something of a coincidence. Young (2002) suggested that there are at least three units, representing three individual volcanic mudflows, some with opposing palaeocurrent indicators, suggesting different sources. However, Stewart (1990, 2002) favours the interpretation of a single volcanic mudflow. Most recently, Amor *et al.* (2008) have recognised grains of shocked quartz in the Stac Fada Member and have proposed that it is not volcanic in origin, but that it represents a proximal ejecta blanket formed by the impact of a meteorite into the underlying Stoer Group sandstones. This theory is difficult to reconcile with the evidence for mafic volcanic fragments (Young, 2002), which could not have been sourced from the local country rocks, and so the origin of the Stac Fada Member remains controversial.

In all cases, the presence of accretionary lapilli, which are formed as airborne ash particles coalesce into 'volcanic hailstones', suggests a component of direct ash fall, since lapilli are relatively fragile and are unlikely to survive redeposition. Such ash falls would, in all cases, follow the main depositional event, be it peperitic, mud flow, pyroclastic flow, or impact-related.

West of Stac Fada, the remainder of the Stoer Group stratigraphy can be seen: first stratified mudstone, followed by massive mudstone with rounded outcrops (Poll a' Mhuilt Member). At the western end of the bay steeper cliffs mark the start of the sandstone strata of the Meall Dearg Formation. These outcrops can only be studied at low tide and access is treacherous. The detailed stratigraphy of the section is described by Stewart (1978, 2002).

Take the path back, and keep following tracks past a white cottage left of the beach to meet the tarred road. Go left for 100m, then turn right on the tarred road towards Stoer Burial Ground (the upper, older cemetery; a newer cemetery lies to the south). Just past the cemetery is a gate, and behind this is Locality 3.10.

71

Locality 3.10 [NC 0411 2842]

Stoer cemetery: basal Stoer Group conglomerate.

Basal breccia and conglomerate, with gneiss cobbles up to 60cm across, directly overlie gneiss. The gneiss does not show signs of weathering. Notice the strong pre-Stoer Group topography.

Return to the road, go left and follow the road back to Clachtoll Beach car-park.

Locality 3.11 [NC 042 329]

Culkein – Port Feadaig: Stoer Group /Torridon Group unconformity.

From Clachtoll, drive north through Stoer, take the first left towards the lighthouse, then continue north towards Culkein. As you approach the sea, park in a lay-by approximately 50m before (east of) a white cottage. There is a parking place for one or two minibuses at [NC 0431 3275]. Walk west past the white cottage and descend north across a field (use the gate) to a small bay, Port Feadaig. In decent weather there is a good view to the north-east toward Scourie and the quartzite mountains of Arkle and Foinaven.

On the eastern side of the bay are strata of the Stoer Group, dipping c.25–30° to the west, whilst on the western side are gently dipping strata of the Torridon Group. Note the large hill of Lewisian gneiss (Cnoc na Buaille) to the south-east, again showing considerable relief in the pre-Stoer and pre-Torridon Group topography.

On the eastern side of the bay [NC 0426 3291] the Stoer Group sandstone is thickly bedded, medium- to coarse-grained, and locally cross-bedded, and probably fluviatile. These outcrops belong to the Bay of Stoer Formation (the thin cyclic muddy sandstone-mudstone cycles as seen at Localities 3.6 and 3.8 occur just east of Port Feadaig).

Also in this area are large metre-sized boulders (not *in situ*) of conglomerate, mainly with rounded clasts of Lewisian gneiss in them, suggesting moderate transport distance. The boulders are presumably derived from the basal Torridon Group conglomerate, and are remnants of the unconformity between the Stoer and Torridon groups, which would have occurred just above the present-day erosion surface.

Just west of the centre of the bay is a somewhat overgrown outcrop with gently north-east dipping strata of laminated siltstone, mudstone and sandstone, belonging to the Diabaig Formation of the Torridon Group. On the north-west side of the bay [NC 04205 3296] are coarse pebble beds, with round clasts of vein quartz and red chert, forming the lowest parts of the Applecross Formation of the Torridon Group. Massive, thick-bedded (up to 5 m thick) pebbly sandstones with conglomerate occur higher up.

Further north, the Applecross Formation rests directly on west-dipping sandstone of the Bay of Stoer Formation and the Diabaig Formation is not present, suggesting the existence of a small palaeovalley in the centre of the bay. The unconformity itself can only be seen at low tide.

To the east of Port Feadaig is a good section through the Stoer Group, which shows considerable lateral facies changes compared with the sequence at Clachtoll and Stoer. Details can be found in Stewart (1978, 2002).

Excursion 4

Stoer Group at Enard Bay

Maarten Krabbendam

Purpose: To examine the stratigraphy and sedimentology of the late Mesoproterozoic Stoer Group, and its unconformable relationships with the underlying Lewisian gneiss and overlying Torridon Group. The upper part of the Stoer Group is best examined here, whilst the lower part is best seen on the Stoer Peninsula (Excursion 3).

Aspects covered: Clastic sedimentology in a Mesoproterozoic rift environment, including algal limestone (the oldest life forms in Britain), putative drop stones, accretionary lapilli in the Stac Fada Member, and two well-exposed unconformities with distinct palaeo-relief.

Maps: OS: 1:50,000 Landranger sheet 15 Loch Assynt; 1:25,000 Explorer sheet 439 Coigach and Summer Isles. BGS: 1:50,000 101W Summer Isles.

Terrain: Mainly coastal outcrops with relatively easy access; a moderately good path links most of the localities. Most outcrops can be visited at any state of the tide, but some critical localities (e.g. Locality 4.6) are best seen at medium to low tide. Many boulders and bedding planes can be extremely slippery, especially below high tide mark. The excursion is not recommended during stormy conditions. Inland, recently planted forestry has created rough hummocky ground.

Time: Between a half and a full day.

Access: There are no access constraints for this excursion, but much of it is on or near crofting land and care must be taken with livestock – keep dogs on a lead at all times. Please note that the outcrops should not be hammered.

Park at the large lay-by [NC 0211 1241] at the road junction at Achnahaird Bay. Parties with several cars could leave one car near the bridge south of Loch Garvie [NC 0392 1300], as this saves a walk back along the road.

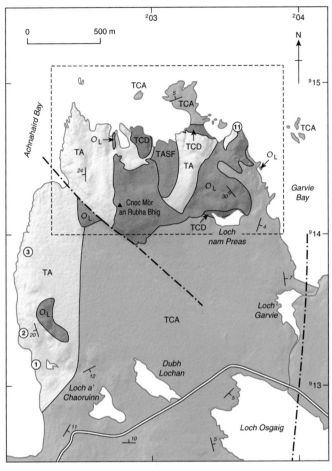

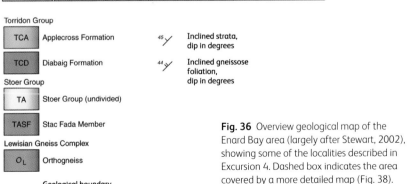

Torridon Group

| TCA | Applecross Formation |
| TCD | Diabaig Formation |

Stoer Group

| TA | Stoer Group (undivided) |
| TASF | Stac Fada Member |

Lewisian Gneiss Complex

| O_L | Orthogneiss |

——————— Geological boundary, bedrock

—·—·— Fault

$45 \diagup$ Inclined strata, dip in degrees

$44 \diagup$ Inclined gneissose foliation, dip in degrees

Fig. 36 Overview geological map of the Enard Bay area (largely after Stewart, 2002), showing some of the localities described in Excursion 4. Dashed box indicates the area covered by a more detailed map (Fig. 38).

75

Locality 4.1 [NC 0221 1312]

Achnahaird Bay: Meall Dearg Formation.

Walk along the road to the north-east for about 500m. At a sharp bend to the right, turn left off the road and walk through heather and bog in a NNW direction to a small knoll between a lochan and the bay [NC 0221 1312]; Fig. 36.

The rocks here are part of the Meall Dearg Formation, the uppermost formation in the Stoer Group. The outcrops show west-dipping strata with well-bedded, locally cross-bedded coarse sandstone. Close to the high-water mark is a pebble bed, with rounded pebbles of quartzite and vein quartz; this is one of the few pebble beds within the Meall Dearg Formation.

Continue north along the shore, walking underneath dip slopes of sandstone. Some 50m before the grass ends at a pebble beach, there is a small hollow on the right.

Locality 4.2 [NC 0215 1335] to [NC 0217 1400]

Achnahaird Bay: Meall Dearg Formation.

From this point northwards along the eastern shore of Achnahaird Bay there are good outcrops of trough cross-bedded sandstone. Walk north along the pebble beach and then along a path. Good three-dimensional outcrops of planar cross-bedded sandstone, with co-sets up to 2m thick, can be seen along the high-water mark. Cross-beds dip west (steeper than normal bedding) indicating palaeocurrents to the west. Wave-rippled sandstone can be seen between the larger cross-bedded sets.

Fig. 37 Sandstone with large-scale cross-beds, Meall Dearg Formation, Camas a' Bhuailte, just north of Locality 4.3. (BGS photograph P668334, © NERC)

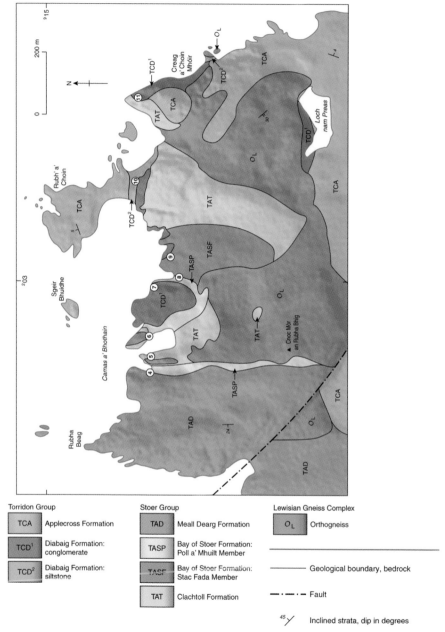

Torridon Group

TCA	Applecross Formation
TCD¹	Diabaig Formation: conglomerate
TCD²	Diabaig Formation: siltstone

Stoer Group

TAD	Meall Dearg Formation
TASP	Bay of Stoer Formation: Poll a' Mhuilt Member
TASF	Bay of Stoer Formation: Stac Fada Member
TAT	Clachtoll Formation

Lewisian Gneiss Complex

O_L	Orthogneiss

——————— Geological boundary, bedrock

—·—·—·— Fault

^{45}⟋ Inclined strata, dip in degrees

^{44}⟋ Inclined gneissose foliation, dip in degrees

Fig. 38 Geological map of the area around Camas a' Bhothain (largely after Stewart, 2002), showing some of the localities described in Excursion 4.

Locality 4.3 [NC 0222 1419]

A thick set (*c*.3m) of cross-bedded sandstone is excellently exposed here (Fig. 37) and appears to form a huge, 50m-wide channel or possibly barchan dune. Features such as pebble beds (Locality 4.1) and wave ripples suggest an overall fluvial origin for the Meall Dearg Formation (Gracie and Stewart, 1967; Stewart, 2002), possibly in braided rivers or alluvial fans.

Cross a stile, turn right (east) and skirt a small bay (Camas a' Bhuailte), all the time following a rough path around the headland of Rubha Beag, where the path turns east again. Pass a small bay with a pebble beach. Continue across the broad rocky promontory until you encounter a narrow, rectangular inlet on your left, and then descend steeply to the shore.

Locality 4.4 [NC 0271 1464]

Camas a' Bhothain: Meall Dearg Formation – Poll a' Mhuilt Member boundary.

The rectangular inlet is eroded into the softer mudstone of the Poll a' Mhuilt Member, the highest member of the Bay of Stoer Formation (Fig. 32). On the left (west) side of the inlet is the contact between red mudstone of the Poll a' Mhuilt Member and the overlying sandstone of the Meall Dearg Formation (Fig. 38). The red mudstones are locally laminated but also massive in places. The contact is sharp and locally erosive, and shows the sudden change from a calm, possibly lacustrine to a higher-energy fluviatile environment (Stewart, 2002).

The mudstone is only a few metres thick, as exposures on the east side of the inlet are of breccia and conglomerate, with large clasts of gneiss up to 1m across, in a sandy, gritty matrix. The breccia is a couple of metres thick and directly overlies Lewisian gneiss basement, which forms a prominent ridge just east of the inlet (Fig. 39). Note that the Stac Fada Member is not present here, suggesting that the basement ridge was exposed during deposition of this member.

Return to the path, and continue east, crossing the gneiss ridge into another, more rounded bay with the ruins of a salmon bothy. Walk to the west side of the bay.

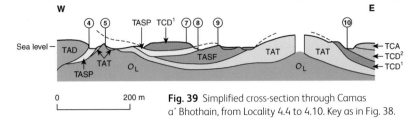

Fig. 39 Simplified cross-section through Camas a' Bhothain, from Locality 4.4 to 4.10. Key as in Fig. 38.

Locality 4.5 [NC 0278 1463]

'Salmon Bothy' Bay, west side: 'drop stones' in the Clachtoll Formation.

Just above high-water mark, metre-sized gneiss blocks are embedded in laminated red mudstone and sandstone. These outcrops have been the source of significant controversy, with the blocks being variously interpreted as ice-rafted drop stones (Davison and Hambrey, 1996) and as mass-flow deposits (Young 1999). Bedding in the surrounding mudstone and sandstone has been deformed; generally there is more deformation on the south side, suggesting southward, lateral rather than vertical emplacement. Towards the south, at the level of the gneiss boulders, oscillation ripples and desiccation cracks occur on bedding planes; Young (1999) noted that these indicate shallow to subaerial conditions of deposition, whereas ice-rafting of dropstones >1m across would have necessitated significant water depths. To the north and on the wave-cut platform, the mudstone passes laterally into a boulder conglomerate. Young (1999) suggested that these conglomerates were formed in debris fans along the margins of lakes, with blocks of gneiss from adjacent basement highs or scarps periodically sliding into the lakes, and a similar model was favoured by Stewart (2002).

Walk past the ruined salmon bothy to the east side of the bay, and cross a prominent C-shaped tidal inlet onto a small peninsula – this is possible at all but the highest tide.

Locality 4.6 [NC 0286 1462]

'Salmon Bothy' Bay, east side: basal conglomerate and algal limestone, Poll a' Mhuilt Member.

Most of the peninsula is developed on Lewisian gneiss basement, and the gneiss forms palaeohills which are smoothed and have asymmetrical shapes. Davison and Hambrey (1996) interpreted these palaeohills as roches

79

moutonnées, and this was used to support their suggestion of glacial conditions during basal Stoer Group deposition.

Along the C-shaped inlet are outcrops of conglomerate with gneiss cobbles, sharply and directly overlying the gneiss. Much of the conglomerate is 'glued' together by a matrix of laminated microbial, algal limestone (note that the limestone is brick-red, presumably due to staining from the overlying red mudstones). At the east end of the peninsula, laminated algal limestone is seen to overlie the breccia, but also contains large clasts of gneiss. This limestone represents the oldest life form on the British Isles; please do not hammer it.

The algal limestone is overlain by red mudstone, belonging to the same unit (Poll a' Mhuilt Member) as at Localities 4.4 and 4.5. The C-shaped inlet has eroded most of the mudstone.

South of the inlet, the mudstone is overlain by a thick unit of boulder conglomerate, with large clasts of sandstone in a sandy matrix (Fig. 40); this is interpreted as the basal conglomerate of the Diabaig Formation, forming the base of the Torridon Group.

Follow the path farther east.

Locality 4.7 [NC 030 146]

Camas a' Bhothain: Diabaig Formation.

Along the path are massive, thick-bedded red sandstone outcrops, mapped as belonging to the Diabaig Formation. Curiously, many bedding planes are steep, possibly due to large-scale slump folding.

Fig. 40 Red stained algal lime-stone draped over Lewisian gneiss (in the foreground), overlain by red mudstone (Poll a' Mhuilt Member) largely eroded by wave action, overlain by boulder conglomerate (Diabaig Formation). Locality 4.6, east side of Salmon Bothy Bay. (BGS photograph P661241, © NERC)

Follow the path around until you are above a small cliff. Follow the cliff top until you can safely descend, then turn north towards the left-hand (west) side of the bay.

Locality 4.8 [NC 0301 1456]

Camas a' Bhothain: Poll a' Mhuilt Member.

At the high-water mark are outcrops of red planar laminated algal limestone, which locally enclose clasts of gneiss up to 10cm across; please do not hammer these. The limestone is followed upwards by laminated mudstones (Poll a' Mhuilt Member), which are in turn overlain by boulder conglomerate with sandstone clasts up to 2m across, forming the cliff above (Diabaig Formation, Torridon Group).

To the north, on the island of Sgeir Bhuidhe and on Rubh' a' Choin, note the sub-horizontal, thick-bedded sandstones of the Applecross Formation. Continue along the bay as far as a large wave-cut platform.

Locality 4.9 [NC 0308 1456]

Camas a' Bhothain: Stac Fada Member.

The Stac Fada Member here (stratigraphically below the Poll a' Mhuilt Member of Localities 4.6 and 4.8) consists of sandstone beds, with pea-sized accretionary lapilli in the top part, best seen on bedding surfaces. In some cases, the insides of the lapilli are seen to be concentric. Accretionary lapilli are formed when ash particles are amalgamated in moist ash clouds (similar to hailstones); they are relatively fragile and generally have a poor preservation potential. The unit with accretionary lapilli is thicker here than at Stoer, but the volcanic fragments seen at Stoer are absent here. Thus the Stac Fada Member changes character, over a distance of $c.15$km, from a mass-flow deposit to an ash fall dominated unit.

The lower part of the member here consists of massive sandstone, locally with gneiss clasts. Continue along the bedding planes as far as a horizontal platform of breccia, just before a small inlet with loose cobbles. Some unsightly paleomagnetic drill holes are nearby. The platform [NC 0311 1457] consists of red breccia, with cobble-sized clasts which contain accretionary lapilli and are thus derived from the surrounding Stac Fada Member. The breccia, the lowest part of the Diabaig Formation, is lower than the surrounding outcrops of the Stac Fada Member and clearly occupied a palaeohollow.

Continue west along the path, past the little inlet, passing sandstones that form part of the lower Stoer Group. Continue to the north-west on the rough path, to a spit formed by large cobbles.

Locality 4.10 [NC 0331 1469] to [NC 0339 1462]

Rubh' a' Choin: Torridon Group.

The cliff to the south of the cobble beach consists of conglomerate with both gneiss and sandstone cobbles and mudstone intercalations. This is Diabaig Formation, which is plastered against a paleocliff of Stoer Group conglomerates. Walk over the cobbles to a low rock wall or plateau some 50m to the north-west.

The base of this outcrop [NC 0335 1471] consists of laminated fine sandstone and red and grey siltstone and mudstone of the Diabaig Formation. This is overlain by the Applecross Formation with a sharp, locally erosive contact. The Applecross Formation here consists of thick-bedded, coarse, gritty to pebbly red sandstone, with clear east-dipping cross-bedding, suggesting palaeocurrents to the east.

The cobble-covered spit and the bay to the east have clearly been eroded out at the level of the mudstone/siltstone part of the Diabaig Formation.

Return to the cliff and follow it to the left (east) until a large corner, where the cliff is at its highest [NC 0339 1462]. Cobble conglomerate, with clasts of gneiss and sandstone, is overlain first by pebbly sandstone and higher up by fine sandstone and mudstone (Diabaig Formation). Higher up is more conglomerate.

Follow the path farther east and skirt the bay (with outcrops of Lewisian gneiss), then follow the path towards the headland north of Creag a' Choin Mhóir.

Locality 4.11 [NC 0360 1467]

Headland of Creag a' Choin Mhóir: conglomerate of the
Stoer and Torridon groups.

Approaching the headland, you walk over dip slopes of conglomerate with
gneiss boulders (base of the Stoer Group), which dip *c*. 10° to the west. At
the farthest point north along the path, there is a sloping wall some 20 m
north of the path. Here there are two conglomerates apparently overlying each other, separated by a sharp unconformity (Stoer Group below;
Diabaig Formation on top; Fig. 41). Both contain gneiss clasts, up to 0.5 m
across. The upper part of the Diabaig Formation conglomerate grades into
stratified gritty sandstone.

From the headland follow the track south over Creag a' Choin Mhóir
(keeping high where possible), passing outcrops of thick-bedded sandstone
of the Applecross Formation on the way. At [NC 0365 1447] the Diabaig–
Applecross formation boundary occurs down at the high-water mark. After
about 1 km, the path drops down towards Garvie Bay, crossing gently
dipping Applecross Formation strata. At the beach of Garvie Bay follow the
path inland and skirt Loch Garvie on its west side (boggy in places). Keep
following the path until you meet the road; turn right (west) and back to the
car-park.

Fig. 41 Two basal breccias:
the basal breccia of the
Stoer Group below, overlain
via a sharp unconformity
by breccia of the Diabaig
Formation, Torridon Group.
Locality 4.11, Creag a'
Choin Mhóir. (BGS photo-
graph P661251, © NERC)

83

Locality 4.12 [NC 0242 0678]

Rubha Dunain, Achiltibuie: unconformity between the Torridon and Stoer groups.

To see further outcrops of the unconformity between the Torridon and Stoer groups, park at the village hall in Achiltibuie and pick up a path in a westerly direction. The path turns SSE, past Achlochan cottage, and continues to the coast.

South of Achiltibuie, on the east side of the headland of Rubha Dunain at [NC 0242 0678], the Torridon Group-Stoer Group unconformity is well exposed. Below the unconformity, Stoer Group sandstones dip $c.30°$ to the west. Above the unconformity, gently dipping basal Diabaig Formation conglomerates contain sandstone boulders up to 4m across, derived from the underlying Stoer Group. The conglomerate is followed upwards by red sandstone and grey shale (Stewart, 2002).

Locality 4.13 [NB 962 147]

Reiff: Applecross Formation.

From Achiltibuie take the road to Reiff and park near the end of the road. Cross a stream and walk north-west towards Roinn a' Mhill. Excellent three-dimensional exposures of Applecross Formation sandstones can be found north-west of Reiff between [NB 962 147] and [NB 962 150]. Features include thick bedding, with cross-beds up to 2m thick, commonly oversteepened and contorted. The outcrops are extensively used by rock-climbers, so please do not hammer.

Excursion 5

Ullapool River, Creag nam Broc and Glen Achall

Graham Leslie and Kathryn Goodenough

Purpose: To examine the Ullapool River section and the geology of Creag nam Broc; exposures within a structural window through the antiformally folded Moine Thrust into the underlying Ullapool Thrust Sheet (and Ullapool Thrust).

Aspects covered: Lithologies in the Ullapool Thrust Sheet; thrust geology of Creag nam Broc.

Maps: OS: 1:50,000 Landranger sheet 20 Beinn Dearg and Loch Broom; 1:25,000 Explorer sheet 439 Coigach and Summer Isles. BGS: 1:50,000 sheet 101E, Ullapool.

Terrain: The excursion comprises a number of localities close to the town of Ullapool, including some rough and pathless ground on the rocky northern slopes of the Ullapool River and around Creag nam Broc [NH 147 958].

Time: This is a full day excursion.

Access: Localities should have no problems with access at most times of the year. Good footwear is required as much of the excursion is in rough ground. Note that working quarries at Torr an Eas [NH 144 950] may provide additional material; permission for access should be obtained from the quarry manager (Tel: 01854 612336) and hard hats and high visibility jackets would be required.

The Moine Thrust is deformed across the Ullapool River by an open upright east-west trending culmination axis, such that a number of minor thrust sheets can be recognised in the footwall of the Moine Thrust, over-riding the 'normal' foreland sequence. The most significant of these thrust sheets is the Ullapool Thrust Sheet, composed mainly of metagranitoid rocks (the Ullapool Gneiss; part of the Lewisian Gneiss Complex) unconformably

85

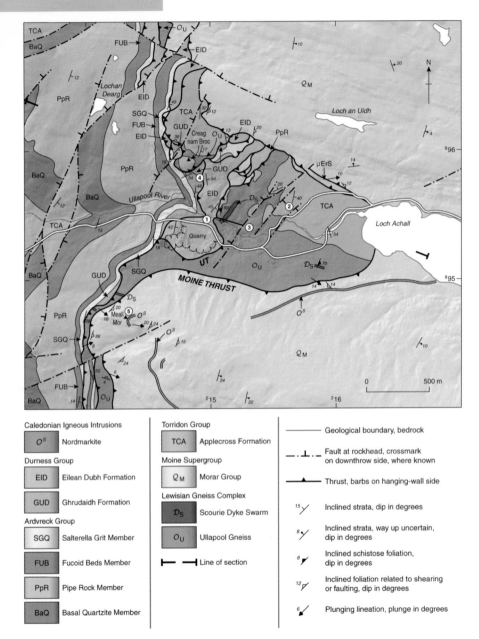

Fig. 42 Simplified geological map of the Glen Achall area, after British Geological Survey (2008), showing the localities described in Excursion 5. UT = Ullapool Thrust.

Caledonian Igneous Intrusions

O^S Nordmarkite

Durness Group

EID   Eilean Dubh Formation

GUD   Ghrudaidh Formation

Ardvreck Group

SGQ   Salterella Grit Member

FUB   Fucoid Beds Member

PpR   Pipe Rock Member

BaQ   Basal Quartzite Member

Torridon Group

TCA   Applecross Formation

Moine Supergroup

Q_M Morar Group

Lewisian Gneiss Complex

D_S Scourie Dyke Swarm

O_U Ullapool Gneiss

├──────┤ Line of section

───────── Geological boundary, bedrock

_.._⊥_.._ Fault at rockhead, crossmark on downthrow side, where known

──────▲ Thrust, barbs on hanging-wall side

$^{15}\!\diagup$ Inclined strata, dip in degrees

$^{8}\!\diagup$ Inclined strata, way up uncertain, dip in degrees

$^{6}\!\diagup$ Inclined schistose foliation, dip in degrees

$^{12}\!\diagup$ Inclined foliation related to shearing or faulting, dip in degrees

$^{6}\!\diagup$ Plunging lineation, plunge in degrees

86

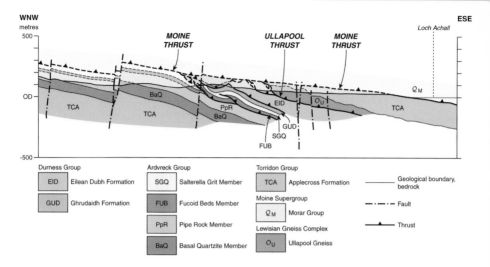

Fig. 43 Cross-section through Glen Achall, along the line indicated on Fig. 42, after British Geological Survey (2008).

overlain by immature arkosic sandstone that is presumed to belong to the Torridon Group (Fig. 42). This thrust sheet is displaced on the Ullapool Thrust (cf. Coward, 1988). The footwall to the Ullapool Thrust comprises a number of localised imbricate stacks composed of a folded succession of the An t-Sròn, Ghrudaidh and Eilean Dubh formations (Fig. 43).

The thrust sequence cannot be interpreted as a straightforward foreland propagating sequence. Folding that pre-dates the generation of the An t-Sròn, Ghrudaidh and Eilean Dubh imbricates locally allows younger strata to be thrust over older, with resultant loss of parts of the succession. The Moine Thrust clearly truncates thrusts in its footwall, as does the Ullapool Thrust in turn. As elsewhere, the Moine Thrust is a composite structure with earlier development of several tens of metres thickness of psammitic ductile mylonite, and then a later brittle to brittle/ductile movement which truncates earlier thrusting in the footwall.

Locality 5.1 [NH 1490 9535]

Torr an Eas quarries.

Park in Ullapool and walk to the cross-roads by the Ullapool River at [NH 1290 9490], then follow the track north-east up Glen Achall and past the quarry buildings. The normal foreland succession, with Torridon Group sandstones overlain by rocks of the Eriboll and An t-Sròn formations, can be seen in the hills to the north and also in outcrops along the track side. The sequence is locally disrupted by later faulting. The normal succession is maintained as far as the Ghrudaidh Formation dolostones, and above this the local Sole Thrust emplaces Eilean Dubh Formation dolostones. Continue along the track as far as [NH 1490 9535], where a view can be obtained into the quarry exposures in Eilean Dubh Formation dolostone (Fig. 44).

The exposures in the quarry walls demonstrate that the sequence has been folded into upright folds with amplitudes of several tens of metres. Thrusting superimposed on these fold patterns has created younger over older thrust relationships in a number of places; folding of the dolostone succession suggests movement along a concealed lower (blind?) thrust, but the fact that thrusts cut the folded succession implies that thrust deformation is out of sequence. A higher quarry to the south-west is in felsic gneisses which have been carried over the dolostones by the Ullapool Thrust.

Continue along the track, taking the left-hand fork to cross the bridge over the Ullapool River, and then walk northwards to outcrops around [NH 1550 9560].

Locality 5.2 [NH 1550 9560]

Lithologies in the Ullapool Thrust Sheet.

The Ullapool Thrust Sheet comprises two components, which can be easily studied in these outcrops on the north side of the Ullapool River. Pale pinkish red to pale brown, rather massive immature arkosic sandstones are unconformable over metagranitoid rocks (the Ullapool Gneiss). The sandstones comprise angular pink feldspar and grey quartz clasts typically

1–3mm in grain size; pebbly lags are developed in places with individual sub-rounded matrix-supported clasts up to 1–2cm in size. Bedding tends to be rather indistinct, usually 20–60cm in scale and tabular to lenticular in form. A distinctive spidery network of fine, <1mm thick, quartz veins is typically seen and in places serves to help distinguish the sandstone where its massive nature tends to blur the distinction with the underlying meta-granitoid rock. At [NH 1561 9565], metre-scale erosive channel bases are preserved in 20–40cm thick beds of coarse 'gritty' sandstone. The sandstone maps out as unconformable patches deposited on an irregular erosion surface with a relief of a few metres [NH 1518 9551]; the preserved total thickness of sandstone within the Ullapool Thrust Sheet is of the order of a few hundred metres. The sandstones have been interpreted as part of the Torridon Group, although they cannot be directly correlated with any specific formation.

Locality 5.3 [NH 1510 9550]

Ullapool gneiss in the Eas Dubh Waterfall.

The Ullapool gneisses are best examined in the exposures north of the Eas Dubh waterfall, (around [NH 1510 9550]). The dominant lithology is a metagranitoid, which comprises quartz and pink feldspar with minor biotite. It is typically massive with only a weakly defined foliation. Coarser-grained quartz-poor areas of syenitic rock are commonly associated with the metagranitoids. This variety comprises pink alkali feldspar and horn-blende crystals up to 1cm; the rock is typically massive and unfoliated, but in places the amphiboles show a mineral lineation plunging gently east.

The metagranitoid rocks are intruded by mafic, originally doleritic to gabbroic sheets at a variety of scales (5cm- to 20m-thick sheets are seen) and orientations (N–S to E–W). The mafic rocks are recrystallised and grano-blastic, massive and unfoliated; they now comprise plagioclase and horn-blende, but in places these minerals seem to be mimetic upon an original igneous texture. The syenites are not seen to be invaded by the mafic rocks and so may also be a younger intrusive phase, but could simply be a locally developed coarser variant of the metagranitoid rock.

The Ullapool Gneiss is interpreted as part of the Lewisian Gneiss Com-plex and known to be Archaean in protolith age (R. R. Parrish, pers. comm.),

89

but its relationship to the surrounding Lewisian terranes is unclear. The mafic sheets most probably represent part of the Scourie Dyke Swarm.

Continue downstream along the northern side of the Ullapool River. The Ullapool Thrust places the gneisses over Eilean Dubh Formation dolostone at [NH 1505 9550]. Below there, the local 'Sole Thrust', defining the boundary between the Ghrudaidh and Eilean Dubh formations, is clearly seen in the river at [NH 1496 9549]. The Eilean Dubh Formation dolostone in the hangingwall of this thrust typically dips at 40–45° ESE whereas the footwall succession dips at $c.10$–15° to the ESE. The thrust itself dips at $c.20°$ to the ESE. From there, walk north-west towards Creag nam Broc, over outcrops of dolostone.

Locality 5.4 [NH 1480 9580]

Creag nam Broc.

At Creag nam Broc the Ullapool Thrust is seen again, emplacing Ullapool Gneiss and the overlying sandstone onto dolostones of the Durness Group (Fig. 45). Imbrication of the lower levels of the Ullapool Thrust Sheet is seen at [NH 1483 9583], with small scale thrusts climbing upwards off the basal Ullapool Thrust to place lenses of gneiss up to a few metres in thickness over sandstone.

North of Creag nam Broc [NH 1476 9604], the Ullapool Thrust apparently cuts up section and has sandstone in its hangingwall (thrust over Cambro-Ordovician rocks), a relationship maintained to the north towards [NH 1480 9670] where the Moine Thrust apparently cuts downwards onto the Ullapool Thrust terminating the Ullapool Thrust Sheet. Note that the point at which the Ullapool Thrust ramps up through the metagranitoid rocks to have sandstone in its hangingwall now coincides with a later steep south-east-dipping brittle reverse fault.

Along the Sole Thrust, Eilean Dubh Formation dolostone is juxtaposed on Salterella Grit Member north of Creag nam Broc, around [NH 1475 9638], and at Creagan na t-Uamha [NH 1460 9680]. Dips in the dolostone are $c.40$–45° in the hangingwall of the thrust; dips in the footwall are $c.20°$. A steeply dipping thrust slice of Eilean Dubh Formation dolostone is emplaced over Salterella Grit Member at [NH 1464 9602], but is itself overthrust by a further thrust slice comprising An t-Sròn and Ghrudaidh formations [NH 1466 9607].

The relationship of the Ullapool Thrust to these underlying dislocations is not clear. Individual thrusts in the imbricate system in the footwall of the Ullapool Thrust are never clearly truncated by the higher thrust and could be interpreted as merging upwards with the Ullapool Thrust. At [NH 1493 9593], the Ullapool Thrust does 'overstep' the thrust which emplaces Eilean Dubh Formation dolostone over Ghrudaidh Formation dolostone (succession already folded pre-thrusting to allow younger over older relationships). The separate thrust traces map out at right angles, but the geometry of the intersection is not exposed and could easily be a convergence upwards rather than truncation.

The Moine Thrust runs to the north-east of Creag nam Broc and can be seen to be an abrupt brittle discontinuity with finely laminated (1–2mm) pale to dark grey mylonitic psammite in the hangingwall. Brittle displacement on the Moine Thrust clearly truncates the underlying thrust structures;

Fig. 44 Deformed Eilean Dubh Formation dolostones in the Torr an Eas quarry. (BGS photograph P596832, © NERC)

Fig. 45 The Ullapool Thrust at Locality 5.4, Creag nam Broc, with Torridon Group sandstone thrust over Ghrudaidh Formation dolostone. (BGS photograph P596850, © NERC)

Fig. 46 Sill of the Nordmarkite Swarm, with abundant pink feldspars, intruded into pale grey Moine mylonites near the summit of Meall Mór (Locality 5.5). (BGS photograph P595828, © NERC)

91

both the Ullapool Thrust and lower imbricates of the foreland succession are truncated by the Moine Thrust to the east of Creag nam Broc.

From Creag nam Broc, return to the bridge across the Ullapool River. At the track junction turn left, and then shortly afterwards take a path off to the right. This path runs above the quarries, and scattered outcrops of Ullapool Gneiss can be seen. Continue on the path as it swings south-east round the slopes of Meall Mòr, ignoring paths off on the right.

Locality 5.5 [NH 1430 9470]

The Moine Thrust at Meall Mòr.

Around [NH 1425 9500] the path dips below the Ullapool Thrust and passes outcrops of the An t-Sròn and Ghrudaidh formations of the foreland sequence. Outcrops just above the path are of Ullapool Gneiss in the Ullapool Thrust Sheet, with good examples of the mafic sheets that are considered to correlate with the Scourie Dyke Swarm.

Take the path that turns off to the left to climb towards Meall Mòr. The Ullapool Thrust Sheet is only about 20 m thick in this area, and consists only of gneiss with no overlying sandstones. The path soon crosses the Moine Thrust, and good examples of finely-laminated Moine mylonites can be seen in numerous outcrops. Both the mylonitic foliation, and the associated lineation, dip gently south-eastwards.

At the summit of Meall Mòr is a pink-weathering, $c.2$ m-thick intrusive igneous sheet, belonging to the 'Nordmarkite Swarm' (Goodenough et al., 2004). This intrusion is formed of abundant pink feldspar phenocrysts, up to one centimetre across, in a darker-coloured quartzofeldspathic matrix (Fig. 46). The core of the sill is undeformed, but the margins show some evidence of grain size reduction and shearing of the matrix. Similar intrusions are found at a number of locations to the north of here, both close to the Moine Thrust and farther east in the Moine.

From Meall Mòr, retrace your steps down to the main path, and then pick up the path that runs almost directly west across outcrops of the foreland succession, to bring you back to Ullapool.

Excursion 6

Knockan Crag and the Knockan Klippen

Kathryn Goodenough and Maarten Krabbendam

Purpose: To study the late, brittle Moine Thrust, where rocks of the Moine Supergroup are brought almost directly above undisturbed Cambro-Ordovician sedimentary rocks, and to see the Moine mylonites. The second part of the excursion looks at the relationships between the Moine Thrust and klippen of underlying thrusts.

Aspects covered: The Cambro-Ordovician sedimentary sequence, thrust geometries and mylonites.

Maps: OS: 1:50,000 Landranger sheet 15 Loch Assynt; 1:25,000 Explorer sheet 439 Coigach and Summer Isles. BGS: 1:50,000 special sheet, Assynt district.

Terrain: The first part of the excursion concentrates on Knockan Crag, the location of a SNH visitor centre and walking trail. The excursion follows a short circular route from the Knockan Crag car-park, along a well-built path, the lower part of which is suitable for wheelchairs. The Knockan Crag visitor centre is targeted at the general public and provides some interesting exhibits.

The second part of the excursion involves a walk over open moor-land, much of which is rather boggy. Up to 100 m of ascent on rough ground is involved and, in poor weather, careful navigation may be required.

Time: First part of the excursion, the trail at Knockan Crag, will occupy most groups for 1–2 hours. The second part of the excursion requires around half a day.

Access: The Knockan Crag trail is open to visitors all year round. The second part of the excursion crosses crofted land; it is important that parked vehicles in this area do not block gates or tracks, and that all gates are left as they are found. Dogs should be kept firmly under control, or ideally left at home. Knockan Crag is a National Nature Reserve and there should be no hammering or sampling at out-crops in this excursion.

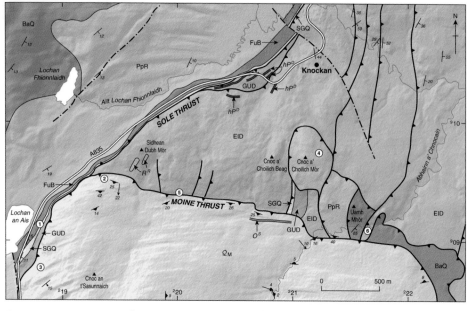

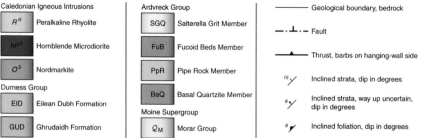

Caledonian Igneous Intrusions

R^R	Peralkaline Rhyolite
hP^D	Hornblende Microdiorite
O^S	Nordmarkite

Durness Group

EID	Eilean Dubh Formation
GUD	Ghrudaidh Formation

Ardvreck Group

SGQ	Salterella Grit Member
FuB	Fucoid Beds Member
PpR	Pipe Rock Member
BaQ	Basal Quartzite Member

Moine Supergroup

Q_M	Morar Group

———————	Geological boundary, bedrock
—·—⊥·—	Fault
▲▲▲▲	Thrust, barbs on hanging-wall side
^{15}⟋	Inclined strata, dip in degrees
^{8}⟋	Inclined strata, way up uncertain, dip in degrees
^{6}⟋	Inclined foliation, dip in degrees

Fig. 47 Simplified geological map of the Knockan area, after British Geological Survey (2007), showing the localities described in Excursion 6.

Fig. 48 The Moine Thrust at Knockan Crag, placing Moine mylonites over fractured dolostones of the Eilean Dubh Formation. (BGS photograph P531955, © NERC)

94

Excursion 6a: Knockan Crag

Locality 6.1 [NC 188 092]

Knockan Crag visitor centre and Moine Thrust trail.

Park in the Knockan Crag car-park, which has toilet facilities, and follow the waymarked trail to the visitor centre. The trail starts with the 'Knockan Puzzle', a wall illustrating all the rock-types of the Assynt region. The puzzle is, of course, how the metamorphosed, Proterozoic Moine psammites have come to lie on top of the younger, unmetamorphosed, Cambro-Ordovician sedimentary rocks. Continue along the trail as it passes through the small SNH visitor centre, which is always open.

The lowest exposures on the trail above the visitor centre are good outcrops of the orange-brown weathering Fucoid Beds Member in a small quarry (Fig. 47). Boulders of Pipe Rock are on display here, but the best outcrops of this rock-type occur lower down the slope, in the road cut by the car-park entrance. The Fucoid Beds are followed in upward sequence by thin layers of the Salterella Grit Member, which can be seen where the trail crosses a small bridge. Just above here, in a mossy waterfall, the Fucoid Beds are repeated by a minor thrust.

The trail continues upwards to the Moine Thrust plane, a striking feature at which dark-grey, fractured Moine mylonites rest on top of brecciated, buff-coloured dolostones of the Eilean Dubh Formation (Fig. 48). Steps have been built up to allow visitors to 'bridge' the thrust with their hands; continuing a few metres along the trail from this point actually allows access to a better exposure of the thrust. The thrust forms a clear plane, which is inclined towards the south-east at an angle of 8–10°. A thin breccia, containing fragments of mylonite, occurs along the thrust.

Although the Moine Thrust here at Knockan is a very clear plane, it actually only represents the last part of a complex sequence of deformation. The Moine Thrust was initiated as a ductile structure, which formed the mylonites in the cliff. However, the thrust that is seen here is a later, brittle fault. Evidence for this comes from the intense fracturing of the mylonites and from the presence of breccia, and locally fault gouge, along the thrust plane, which formed during the late-stage movements. The exact nature of the late, brittle movement is rather uncertain. Coward (1985) argued that the brittle movement was related to extensional movement as the thrust pile collapsed. An alternative explanation is that the brittle movement is simply the latest part of progressively colder and shallower level movements in the thrust zone. The ductile and brittle movements at Knockan would all work along the same plane, whereas in the Assynt Culmination the movements were partitioned along different thrust planes. Freeman *et al.* (1998) have suggested that ductile deformation on the Moine Thrust at Knockan ended at *c.*430 Ma (latest Llandovery, early Silurian).

Locality 6.2 [NC 194 094]

Viewpoint at top of Knockan Crag.

From the thrust plane exposures, follow the trail northwards up onto the top of the crag where mylonites are well-exposed, and take a short spur off to a viewpoint on the left. On a fine day there is a wonderful view from here of the peaks to the west, with Cùl Beag and Cùl Mòr prominent in the foreground and Stac Pollaidh protruding beyond. Canisp and Suilven can also be clearly seen to the north-west. The double unconformity, with pale grey quartzites of the Eriboll Formation overstepping well-layered Torridon Group sandstones which lie on hummocky Lewisian gneisses, can be seen particularly well on the slopes of Cùl Mòr and Canisp.

To the north, the view extends across Cam Loch to the peaks of Conival and Ben More Assynt beyond (Fig. 49). The quartzite-dominated Breabag Dome lies in front of Ben More Assynt. In the foreground, immediately in front of the viewpoint, are peat hags with scattered outcrops of Moine mylonite. Beyond these is a green, grassy knoll with outcrops of pale grey dolostone of the Eilean Dubh Formation. The Moine Thrust runs between these two contrasting areas of ground.

Locality 6.3 [NC 188 086]

Eagle Rock.

Continue southwards along the cliff-top path over exposures of finely banded, grey-weathering Moine mylonites. It is worthwhile taking the short detour to Eagle Rock, where particularly good mylonite exposures

Fig. 49 View north over the Assynt Culmination from the top of Knockan Crag (Locality 6.2). In the foreground, pale grey dolostones of the Eilean Dubh Formation lie immediately beneath the Moine Thrust. In the distance are the prominent quartzite ridges of Conival, Ben More Assynt and Breabag. (BGS photograph P667671, © NERC)

Fig. 50 Moine mylonites at Eagle Rock, Locality 6.3. (BGS photograph P512960, © NERC)

can be seen in the low cliffs (Fig. 50). With careful examination of faces parallel to the ESE–WNW transport direction, shear-sense indicators can be seen in the mylonites. After studying the outcrops, return from here along the path to the car-park.

Excursion 6b: The klippen at Knockan

Drive some two kilometres north-east from Knockan Crag to the hamlet of Knockan, and park in a large lay-by on the left of the road [NC 212 106]. Walk about a hundred metres south-east along the road, and then follow a narrow tarred road towards the east, passing some crofts. At a sharp bend,

97

go through a gate and continue for about 500m along a track that runs south-east across grazing lands. Where the track crosses a small stream, leave the track and follow the stream in a south-easterly direction to a low hill, Cnoc a'Choilich Mhor [NC 2056 0962].

Locality 6.4 [NC 2056 0962]

Cnoc a'Choilich Mhor Klippe.

The low hill of Cnoc a'Choilich Mhor is composed of quartz arenites of the Eriboll Formation (mainly Pipe Rock Member, although pipes can be difficult to find). These outcrops represent a small klippe of a thrust, which carries the Eriboll Formation over the imbricated Durness Group carbonate that underlies all the surrounding low ground to the north and east. The carbonates in this area are characterised by the presence of sink holes.

From here, walk in a WSW direction towards a stream valley south of Druim Poll Eòghainn, passing outcrops of Eilean Dubh Formation dolostones. Variations in the dip of the dolostones indicate that they are part of an imbricate stack, known as the Elphin imbricates.

Locality 6.5 [NC 200 093 to NC 204 094]

Moine Thrust exposures.

The east-west stream section here follows the Moine Thrust, and the thrust can be studied at several places in the stream valley. At [NC 201 094], easterly dipping beds of Eilean Dubh Formation dolostone form the bed of the burn, and are overlain by mylonites which are well exposed in a low cliff (Fig. 51). The thrust plane itself is not actually exposed, but the ground immediately above the stream contains some excellent outcrops in which small-scale structures associated with the Moine Thrust can be seen. The mylonites commonly contain strung-out quartz ribbons, and close to the thrust the mylonitic fabric is locally overprinted by a fracture cleavage or dense fracturing (e.g. at [NC 2069 0927]). The dolostones close to the thrust are fractured and locally show incipient brecciation. The fabric in the mylonitic Moine psammite dips south here and strikes parallel to the

Fig. 51 The Moine Thrust in the area of Locality 6.5, with Moine mylonites resting on dolostones of the Eilean Dubh Formation. (BGS photograph P537568, © NERC)

outcrop of the (brittle) Moine Thrust itself. This shows that the later, brittle Moine Thrust does not cross-cut the ductile, mylonitic Moine Thrust (cf. Coward, 1985).

Locality 6.6 [NC 213 092 to 217 092]

Uamh an Tartair Klippe.

From the thrust exposures, walk eastwards to the prominent right-angle bend in the Abhainn a'Chnocain (the Knockan Burn) at [NC 213 092]. Here the outcrops change from carbonate into quartz arenite as the unexposed Uamh an Tartair thrust is crossed. At [NC 2153 0911] Basal Quartzite Member can be recognised within the Uamh an Tartair Klippe. The Moine Thrust occurs only just to the south and must decapitate this klippe.

Continue along the stream to the east to [NC 2164 0912], taking great care as you approach an abrupt small gorge and a large sinkhole, which betray the presence of Durness Group carbonate, lying beneath the thrust.

However, the small hillock 50m to the east is again composed of quartz arenite. Several explanations, including normal faulting, could explain this apparent repetition of the thrust. However, on the south side of the stream it can be demonstrated that the carbonate overlies the Basal Quartzite Member to the west (i.e. young over old). This arrangement is best explained by breaching, in that a thrust within the underlying carbonate breached the Uamh an Tartair Thrust and emplaced carbonate over quartz arenite.

The overall sequence of events that can be established from Localities 6.4–6.6 is as follows:

(1) Ductile movement along the Moine Thrust, forming mylonitic fabric;
(2) Movement along the Uamh an Tartair Thrust, emplacing quartz arenite over Durness Group carbonate;
(3) Imbrication within the Durness Group carbonate, forming the Elphin imbricates, with some thrusts breaching the overlying Uamh an Tartair Thrust;
(4) Decapitation of the Uamh an Tartair Thrust Sheet and the breaching thrusts by the (reactivated) brittle Moine Thrust.

From Uamh an Tartair it is best to go north, passing two large sinkholes along the way, to pick up the track back to Knockan and the main road.

Excursion 7

Traligill and
Bealach Traligill

Maarten Krabbendam

Purpose: To study the thrust structures of the Traligill and Breabag imbricate systems and the Ben More Thrust ramp below Conival, in the Assynt Culmination.

Aspects covered: Thrust exposures, lateral ramps, klippen, large-scale thrust structures in the Breabag Dome and the Ben More Thrust, late faults.

Maps: OS: 1:50,000 Landranger sheet 15 Loch Assynt; 1:25,000 Explorer sheet 442 Assynt and Lochinver. BGS: 1:50,000 special sheet, Assynt.

Terrain: The first part of the excursion follows a good path to Cnoc nan Uamh. To the top of Cnoc nan Uamh and beyond to Bealach Traligill, the route goes over rough and boggy ground, generally.

without a path. To appreciate the geology and to navigate, good visibility is required for the part of the excursion beyond Cnoc nan Uamh.

Time: The excursion all the way to Bealach Traligill involves some 15km of walking, much of it over rough ground, and is a full day for a fit group. In poor weather, only the half-day excursion as far as Cnoc nan Uamh (Locality 7.5) is recommended.

Access: There are no constraints on access for this excursion, but during the stalking season (July to November) it is advisable to contact Assynt Estates before setting out. Localities 7.1 and 7.2 can also be visited as part of Excursion 8 (Conival).

Park in the large public car-park at the Inchnadamph Hotel [NC 251 216], with an interpretation panel pointing to the Peach and Horne monument on the far side of the road. From the car-park, turn right onto the main road and then right again on a track past Inchnadamph Lodge and a group of cottages. Pass through a gate and continue along the track to a dry-stone wall.

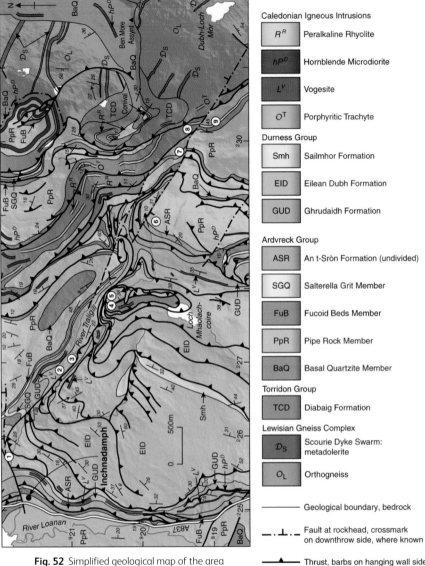

Fig. 52 Simplified geological map of the area around Glen Traligill, after British Geological Survey (2007), showing the localities described in Excursion 7.

Caledonian Igneous Intrusions

R^R	Peralkaline Rhyolite
hP^D	Hornblende Microdiorite
L^V	Vogesite
O^T	Porphyritic Trachyte

Durness Group

Smh	Sailmhor Formation
EID	Eilean Dubh Formation
GUD	Ghrudaidh Formation

Ardvreck Group

ASR	An t-Sròn Formation (undivided)
SGQ	Salterella Grit Member
FuB	Fucoid Beds Member
PpR	Pipe Rock Member
BaQ	Basal Quartzite Member

Torridon Group

TCD	Diabaig Formation

Lewisian Gneiss Complex

$\mathcal{D}_S$	Scourie Dyke Swarm: metadolerite
O_L	Orthogneiss

──────── Geological boundary, bedrock

─·─⊥─·─ Fault at rockhead, crossmark on downthrow side, where known

───▲─── Thrust, barbs on hanging wall side

$^{45}\diagup$ Inclined strata, dip in degrees

$^{44}\diagup$ Inclined gneissose foliation, dip in degrees

$^{6}\diagdown$ Plunging lineation, plunge in degrees

102

Locality 7.1 [NC 2561 2189 to NC 2671 2140]

Durness Group dolostone outcrops.

Around [NC 2561 2189] the track passes outcrops of pale grey dolostone of the Eilean Dubh Formation, with well-developed clints and grykes formed by karstic weathering. The beds here have a dip of *c.*35° to the east, much steeper than the 'Foreland dip' of 10–12° west of Inchnadamph. In this area the dolostones have been deformed by thrusting into a series of imbricates, recognisable by the presence of repeated ridges and hollows that strike roughly north–south (Fig. 52). The Sole Thrust is situated just west of Inchnadamph Lodge, but is not exposed.

Continue eastwards along the track, which crosses the stream, and then climbs up to the cottage at Glenbain. Between Glenbain and a shed at [NC 2671 2140] the path follows NW–SE striking, steeply dipping beds of the Ghrudaidh Formation. The heather-covered slopes above and to the left of the path are underlain by the Pipe Rock Member with the same orientation. These beds form the steep limb of the NW–SE striking Poll an Droighinn Anticline (Bailey, 1935), which was probably formed above a zone of imbricate thrusting that is not exposed.

Locality 7.2 [NC 2693 2112]

View of the Traligill Thrust.

Continue up the track to the corner of the conifer plantation, where NW–SE-striking beds of Eilean Dubh Formation crop out. The main interest of this stop is the view across the (usually dry) River Traligill to the south. Just above the river-bed, on its south side, is a long continuous cliff of dark grey dolostones of the Ghrudaidh Formation, passing up into pale grey outcrops of the Eilean Dubh Formation on the slope above. However, pale grey Eilean Dubh Formation dolostones are also exposed on the slope between the track and the river-bed, dipping down beneath the dark grey cliffs. The Ghrudaidh Formation in the cliffs is thrust over the Eilean Dubh Formation along the Traligill Thrust, which follows the river-bed in this area and is exposed at Locality 7.3. The Traligill Thrust is an oblique lateral ramp (roughly parallel in strike to the WNW transport direction) that also serves as the floor thrust of the Stronchrubie imbricates to the south (Fig. 52).

Continue up the path, and to continue with Excursion 7 keep right at the path junction at [NC 2706 2104]. Rather than crossing the small footbridge, turn right and follow the river bank downstream for about 100m to the Lower Traligill Cave.

Locality 7.3 [NC 2706 2089]

Lower Traligill Cave.

Lower Traligill Cave is one of the major sinks within the Traligill drainage system, and thus the river-bed below it is usually dry, providing excellent exposures of the Traligill Thrust. Dark grey dolostones of the Ghrudaidh Formation to the south-west are thrust over pale grey rocks of the Eilean Dubh Formation to the north-east (Fig. 53). The thrust plane is exposed in the river-bed as a weathered dipslope of Eilean Dubh Formation dolostone. The Lower Traligill Cave itself is developed in the Ghrudaidh Formation above the Traligill Thrust, and exhibits some hangingwall folding. In very wet weather this sink becomes a resurgence, draining part of an underground plumbing system between the Traligill and the Cnoc nan Uamh caves (see below).

Return to the footbridge, noting the occurrence of duplex structures in Durness Group dolostones in the tributary stream that feeds the River

Fig. 53 The Traligill Thrust in the river-bed below Locality 7.3. Dark grey Ghrudaidh Formation dolostones are thrust over pale grey Eilean Dubh Formation dolostones. (BGS photograph P530634, © NERC)

Fig. 54 Cnoc nan Uamh from the west. On the lower slopes are caves formed in Durness Group carbonates; the crags on the top of the hill are exposures of the Ardvreck Group within the Cnoc nan Uamh Klippe (Locality 7.4). (Photograph: © K. M. Goodenough)

Traligill. Cross the footbridge and follow the path towards Cnoc nan Uamh. Around the base of this low hill are further examples of caves (Fig. 54) developed in the Ghrudaidh Formation just above the Traligill Thrust plane, one of which has a partially collapsed roof; great care should be taken around these caves. Brick-red intrusions of peralkaline rhyolite can be seen within the dolostones in this area. After visiting the caves, leave the path and climb the steep north-western slopes of Cnoc nan Uamh.

Locality 7.4 [NC 2765 2047 to NC 2767 2046]

Cnoc nan Uamh Klippe.

The low hill of Cnoc nan Uamh represents a small klippe, floored by the Cnoc nan Uamh Thrust. Approximately 10m below the top of the Cnoc nan Uamh plateau, on the north-western side, is a small, 1m-high outcrop of the Salterella Grit Member, dipping at about 35° to the east. Above it on the slope is a small outcrop of the Fucoid Beds Member, and above that a small cliff of the Pipe Rock Member. The Fucoid Beds are locally folded. Further left (to the north-east) another east-dipping layer of Fucoid Beds can be seen, on a steep and rather treacherous slope. These outcrops form part of a set of imbricate thrusts involving the Pipe Rock, Fucoid Beds and Salterella Grit members, which root into the Cnoc nan Uamh Thrust. This thrust in turn overlies the Durness Group dolostones, exposed at the caves below, which lie within the Traligill–Stronchrubie thrust system (Fig. 52). As a multitude of thrusts involving Pipe Rock occur further east, it is un-clear as to which main thrust the Cnoc nan Uamh Thrust can be linked.

Continue climbing upward and eastward to the summit plateau of Cnoc nan Uamh.

Locality 7.5 [NC 2778 2048]

The summit of Cnoc nan Uamh.

The summit of Cnoc nan Uamh offers an excellent viewpoint from which to study the thrust systems of central Assynt, including the Ben More Thrust and the thrusts underneath it. To the north is a frontal view of the Beinn an Fhurain Thrust, which emplaces Basal Quartzite Member over Pipe Rock

105

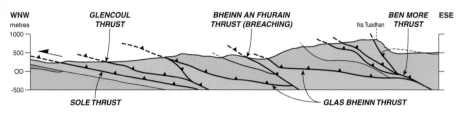

North of the Traligill Fault

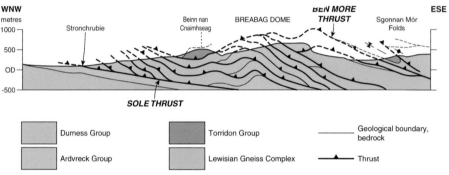

South of the Traligill Fault

Fig. 55 Simplified cross-sections showing the structures to the north and south of the Traligill Fault.

Member. Higher up on the slope, the Beinn Uidhe Thrust emplaces Basal Quartzite over Basal Quartzite.

To the east is the west face of Conival, with its dark, castellated south ridge composed of Torridon Group sandstone, which is underlain by the Ben More Thrust.

To the ESE is Bealach Traligill, with north-dipping slabs of quartz arenite on its south side. These are part of the gently north-plunging Breabag Dome, which can be seen to the south-east. It consists of thick slabs of Pipe Rock Member (with minor Basal Quartzite Member) that have been thrust over each other to form a broad dome. To the south, on Cnoc Eilid Mhathain, are white dip slopes of Eilean Dubh Formation dolostone, which dip east towards the foreland. These form the frontal part of the Breabag antiformal thrust stack (Fig. 55).

To the SSW is the broad, brown hill of Beinn nan Cnaimhseag. The top part of this hill is composed of Torridon Group sandstone; this hill is interpreted to be a klippe of the Ben More Thrust Sheet, which was folded over the Breabag Dome.

On a large scale, Glen Traligill separates two very different areas within the Assynt Culmination. To the north are thick thrust sheets containing Lewisian gneisses, whereas to the south are thinner thrust sheets of Ardvreck and Durness groups. The Traligill Thrust functions as an oblique transverse zone between these two domains (Krabbendam and Leslie, 2010).

If a shorter excursion is required, the summit of Cnoc nan Uamh is the best place to turn back and retrace your steps. Otherwise, to continue the excursion, cross the boggy summit plateau of Cnoc nan Uamh in a south-easterly direction, passing scattered outcrops of Pipe Rock Member, towards a dry river-bed at [NC 2799 2020]. Follow the stream-bed upstream towards the south. At a junction in the stream, follow the left-hand fork, the Allt a' Bhealaich. Continue past a waterfall at [NC 2829 1984]. As the valley becomes steeper and narrower, climb onto the left (north) bank and continue over boggy ground. Keep the stream on your right hand until a dog-leg in the stream is reached.

Locality 7.6 [NC 2895 1995]

Pipe Rock Member in the Breabag Dome.

Around the sharp dog-leg in the Allt a'Bhealaich are good outcrops of the Pipe Rock Member, which dip $c.40°$ to the WNW. In contrast, some 50m to the north, the Pipe Rock dips gently northwards. These outcrops are in the north-plunging hinge zone of the Breabag Dome, which plunges underneath the Beinn an Fhurain Thrust further north. Above here, the deep NW-SE trending cleft of the Allt a' Bhealaich follows the later Bealach Traligill Fault. Despite this impressive topographical expression, the Bealach Traligill Fault only has some 100–120m sinistral displacement, and the higher thrusts can be relatively easily traced across the fault.

Continue on a bearing of 80° (aiming towards the summit of Conival), climbing steps of Pipe Rock and crossing a grassy area, keeping boggy ground to your right hand side. Follow a small stream as far as [NC 2914 2002] where a faint path crosses the stream, about 50m before a dog-leg. Turn right (south-east) and follow the faint path in the direction of the Bealach Traligill, with a bog to the right and a steep slope of Basal Quartzite to the left. In front is a vast dip slope of Pipe Rock, gently curved around the north-plunging hinge zone of the Breabag Dome. The steeper cliff above, forming the top of Breabag Tarsuinn, is composed of Pipe Rock and Basal Quartzite members, with a thrust beneath.

Keep following the path to the south-east until the Allt a' Bhealaich is reached again near [NC 2967 1946]. Follow the path up along the stream and through the impressive cleft of the Bealach Traligill Fault. Note the fractured quartz arenites on either side of the gorge (Fig. 56). Keep climbing until the path levels out on the north-west side of the Bealach Traligill.

Locality 7.7 [NC 2992 1937]

Outcrops on the north-east side of the Bealach Traligill Fault.

To the left of the stream, and north-east of the Bealach Traligill Fault, are outcrops of steeply north-west-dipping Fucoid Beds Member, overlying Pipe Rock Member. Dolostone of the Ghrudaidh Formation is exposed some 60 m further to the north-east; the intervening Salterella Grit Member is not exposed here, but can be seen further north. Continue towards the Bealach Traligill to a large boulder of conglomerate.

Locality 7.8 [NC 3018 1921]

Bealach Traligill.

A number of interesting features can be seen at this usually very windy locality.

A large (5 m) boulder of coarse conglomerate attests to the presence of basal Torridon Group sandstone (Diabaig Formation) on the castellated south ridge of Conival, from whence it has fallen. Note the large proportion of clasts of vein quartz, which reflect the very long period of weathering of the Lewisian landscape, prior to deposition of the Diabaig Formation.

Just to the south-west of the boulder are outcrops of the Fucoid Beds Member, dipping steeply to the north-west. These can be correlated with the Fucoid Beds on the other side of the Bealach Traligill Fault at Locality 7.7, thus constraining the movement along the fault to c. 120 m of sinistral displacement.

Looking back to the NNW, a shallow hollow can be seen on the slope of Conival, just above Locality 7.7. This hollow marks the position of the Beinn an Fhurain Thrust, which emplaces Pipe Rock Member on Conival over the Ghrudaidh Formation of Locality 7.7.

From here, leave the path and climb the slope obliquely due south to a viewpoint on the slopes of Breabag Tarsuinn.

Locality 7.9 [NC 3020 1904]

Breabag Tarsuinn.

At this point, steeply dipping Salterella Grit Member is exposed. To the north is the south ridge of Conival, composed of Torridon Group conglomerate and sandstone. Below that ridge, in the Garbh Coire, is the unconformity between Torridon Group sandstones and Lewisian gneiss.

The Ben More Thrust runs below the ridge and dips steeply towards the east (Fig. 57). Note that the Ben More Thrust descends steeply from a height of about 900 m, almost at the top of Conival, to the Bealach Traligill at about 500 m. A thin sliver of pale-weathering, highly sheared Lewisian gneiss occurs just above the Ben More Thrust and below the Torridon Group. This occurrence can be explained in two ways. Butler (1997) argued that the bedding in the Torridon Group abuts against the Lewisian gneiss at a high angle, and that the contact is a Precambrian normal fault. An alternative view is constrained by the fact that just above the Lewisian gneiss–Torridon Group contact there is a tight anticline-syncline pair within the Torridon Group, similar to folds that occur further south on Sgonnan Mòr (Johnson and Parsons, 1979). This would suggest that the Lewisian gneiss–Torridon Group contact is an unconformity, highly modified by thrusting and associated folding and shearing along the Ben More Thrust.

To the ESE, note the deep cleft of the Bealach Traligill on the south-east side of Garbh Coire. To the south is the glacially gouged Glen Oykel. On the east side of Glen Oykel are low cliffs of Torridon Group sandstone and Basal Quartzite Member, in the hangingwall of the Ben More Thrust. The Ben More Thrust crosses the valley and reappears on Sgonnan Mòr to the south. Part of the western side of Glen Oykel is formed of large east-dipping dip slopes of quartz arenite, which form the trailing edge of the Breabag Dome. Some of these dip slopes show spectacular landslips.

From here, retrace your steps to Inchnadamph. Do not be tempted to take a shortcut toward the upper part of the Traligill River; the descent is steep and dangerous.

Fig. 56 View west along the gorge formed by the Traligill Fault from the approach to Locality 7.7, with cliffs of fractured quartz arenite. (BGS photograph P702205, © NERC)

Fig. 57 View of the south face of Conival from Locality 7.9, showing the main thrust structures. (BGS photograph P531829, © NERC)

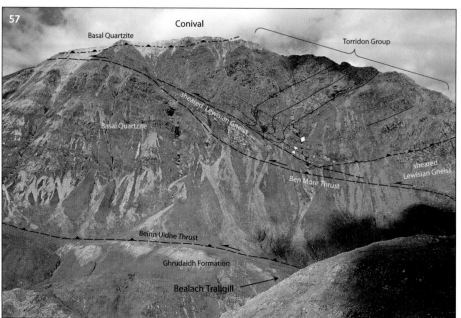

Excursion 8

Conival and Ben More Assynt

Kathryn Goodenough and Maarten Krabbendam

Purpose: To study the Ben More Thrust Sheet, including outcrops of the thrust plane, together with large-scale folding and structures such as the 'double unconformity' within the thrust sheet. On a clear day, an excellent overview of the Assynt region can be obtained from the summit of Conival.

Aspects covered: Ben More Thrust, minor intrusions, the double unconformity in the thrust sheet, and superb views of Assynt.

Maps: OS: 1:50 000 Landranger sheet 15 Loch Assynt; 1:25,000 Explorer sheet 442 Assynt and Lochinver. BGS: 1:50,000 special sheet, Assynt.

Terrain: This is a strenuous excursion, involving a climb of

some 900m and a walk of around 16km. It should only be undertaken in good weather, by well-equipped and well-prepared parties. In low cloud there is little geological point in any party ascending beyond the Coire a' Mhadaidh outcrops (Locality 8.4). Localities 7.1 and 7.2 can be taken in as part of an excursion to Conival.

Time: This excursion requires a full day and is one of the longest routes in this guide.

Access: There are no constraints on access for this excursion at most times of the year, but during the stalking season (July to November) it is advisable to contact Assynt Estates before setting out.

Park at the large public car-park at the Inchnadamph Hotel [NC 251 216], with an interpretation panel pointing to the Peach and Horne monument on the far side of the road. From the car-park, turn right onto the main road and then right again on a track past Inchnadamph Lodge and a group of cottages. Pass through a gate and follow the path up Gleann Dubh, passing abundant Durness Group dolostone outcrops in the valley of the River Traligill. Excursion 7 (Localities 7.1 and 7.2) contains descriptions of some of the features en route. Follow the path as far as a wooden footbridge [NC 2713 2098]. Do not cross the bridge but take the left-hand path, which continues along the left (northern) bank of the Traligill River.

Locality 8.1 [NC 2734 2093]

Traligill River.

Along the path and in the Traligill River are outcrops of Eilean Dubh Formation (pale grey dolostone) succeeded by Ghrudaidh Formation (dark grey dolostone). The strata dip steeply to the south-west. Farther to the north-east, and higher up, are dip slopes of Eriboll Formation, also south-west dipping (Fig. 58). The dolostone lies structurally above the Eriboll Formation quartz arenite (in stratigraphical order) and all strata here form part of the south-west limb of the Poll an Droighinn Antiform.

Locality 8.2 [NC 2794 2064] to [NC 2800 2061]

Traligill River.

The stream here cuts obliquely through the strata and progressively lower units are encountered. On the right-hand (south-west) side of the stream are poor outcrops of Fucoid Beds Member, typified by brown-weathering dolomitic siltstone and lush vegetation. To the left are outcrops of quartz arenite of the Pipe Rock Member, although *Skolithos* pipes are difficult to discern.

Locality 8.3 [NC 2867 2039]

Traligill River.

Here the path turns left. The outcrops around this junction of stream valleys are of steeply eastward-dipping dolostone on the north-east limb of the Poll an Droighinn Antiform (Fig. 58). The antiformal trace strikes NW–SE, oblique to the thrust direction. Rocks underneath this antiform are not exposed, but it is likely the antiform is an anticlinal stack, pushed up by the formation of imbricates below. Composition of these imbricates is unknown.

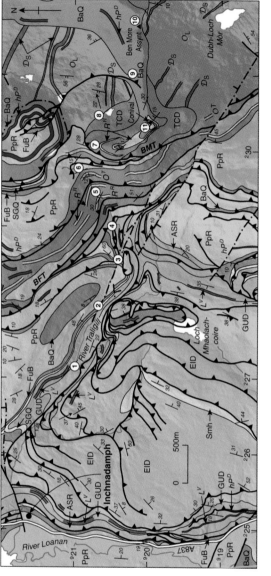

Fig. 58 Simplified geological map of the area around Glen Traligill and Conival, after British Geological Survey (2007), showing the localities described in Excursion 8.

BFT – Beinn an Fhurain Thrust
BMT – Ben More Thrust

Caledonian Igneous Intrusions

R^R	Peralkaline Rhyolite
hP^D	Hornblende Microdiorite
L^V	Vogesite
O^T	Porphyritic Trachyte

Durness Group

Smh	Sailmhor Formation
EID	Eilean Dubh Formation
GUD	Ghrudaidh Formation

Ardvreck Group

ASR	An t-Sròn Formation (undivided)
SGQ	Salterella Grit Member
FuB	Fucoid Beds Member
PpR	Pipe Rock Member
BaQ	Basal Quartzite Member

Torridon Group

TCD	Diabaig Formation

Lewisian Gneiss Complex

$\mathcal{D}_S$	Scourie Dyke Swarm: metadolerite
O_L	Orthogneiss

———— Geological boundary, bedrock

—.⊥.— Fault at rockhead, crossmark on downthrow side, where known

—▲—— Thrust, barbs on hanging wall side

$^{45}\diagup$ Inclined strata, dip in degrees

$^{44}\diagup$ Inclined gneissose foliation, dip in degrees

$^{6}\diagdown$ Plunging lineation, plunge in degrees

113

Follow the path, which is very boggy for some distance above here, and climbs fairly steeply in an ENE direction.

Locality 8.4 [NC 2894 2049]

Path west of Allt a'Choinne Mhill.

Stop where the path becomes blocky and offers a wide view (in good weather!). To the left (north-west) is a large-scale nick in the slope below the plateau of Beinn an Fhurain. This marks the position of the Beinn an Fhurain Thrust, which emplaces Eriboll Formation rocks over the Poll an Droighinn Antiform and the Traligill thrust system (see Excursion 7). To the east is the steep east face of Conival. This 400m-high face is mainly composed of Eriboll Formation quartz arenite, almost tripled in thickness by thrust repetitions on the Beinn an Fhurain Thrust and subsidiary thrusts.

Keep following the path upwards.

Locality 8.5 [NC 293 206] to [299 212]

Path west of Allt a'Choinne Mhill.

The rocks exposed along the path are mainly eastward-dipping quartz arenites of the Basal Quartzite Member within the Beinn an Fhurain Thrust Sheet. At [NC 2927 2057], the Basal Quartzite Member dips more steeply to the north-east, indicating the presence of a subsidiary thrust.

The quartz arenites are cut by a variety of prominent intrusive sheets. A yellow-brown weathering sill of hornblende microdiorite occurs on the path at [NC 2948 2075]. A more conspicuous, brick-red intrusive sill occurs at [NC 2968 2083], where the path crosses the stream. This intrusion is a porphyritic trachyte; similar intrusions elsewhere can be seen to cut across foliations associated with the Ben More Thrust, and so are considered to post-date movement on the thrusts. They are chemically similar to some of the rocks of the Loch Borralan Pluton to the south. Some other red sills that outcrop on these slopes are peralkaline rhyolites; these are difficult to distinguish from the porphyritic trachytes in the field, but are actually part of a slightly earlier phase of magmatism (Goodenough et al., 2004).

114

Locality 8.6 [NC 297 208 to NC 300 210]

Pipe Rock steps and the upper corrie.

The path climbs up some steep rock steps adjacent to a waterfall. As one climbs the rock steps, it can be clearly seen that these are composed of Pipe Rock, with distinct vertical *Skolithos* burrows (Fig. 59). Above the steps, the path flattens out and skirts a small corrie. Look out for clear glacial striae on some of the quartzite slabs in this area. At [NC 2992 2090] the Basal Quartzite Member is encountered again, and has been emplaced over the Pipe Rock Member by another thrust.

At [NC 2997 2089], not far from the path, is a large blocky outcrop in which Pipe Rock is sheared and folded in west-vergent recumbent folds.

Fig. 59 Typical pitted surfaces of Pipe Rock Member on the slopes around the Allt a'Choinne Mhill, Locality 8.6. (BGS photograph P530557, © NERC)

Fig. 60 Outcrops of Eriboll Formation quartz arenites intruded by brick-red porphyritic trachytes at the col below Conival, Locality 8.6. (Photograph: © K. M. Goodenough)

115

Strained *Skolithos* are seen on open folded bedding surfaces a short distance to the SSE.

Continue upwards towards the prominent col on the ridge. In outcrops just below that col, further intrusive sheets of porphyritic trachyte cut across deformed Pipe Rock in which the pipes have been strongly sheared (Fig. 60).

Locality 8.7 [NC 3005 2080]

Conival–Beinn an Fhurain col.

Climb to the col, and turn right towards low outcrops on the southern side of the col. These outcrops, which are of strongly sheared Basal Quartzite Member, mark the plane of the Ben More Thrust, which has brought the Basal Quartzite over the underlying Pipe Rock. The thrust dips eastwards into Coire a' Mhadaidh, where the lower parts of the succession within the Ben More Thrust sheet can be seen.

Locality 8.8 [NC 302 210] to [306 205]

Coire a' Mhadaidh.

From the Conival–Beinn an Fhurain col, descend south-east across grassy slopes towards the lochan at [NC 305 205]. Care should be taken on these slopes, especially in wet weather. Quartz arenite cliffs tower above the

Fig. 61 View south-east across Coire a' Mhadaidh (Locality 8.8) toward Ben More Assynt. Outcrops of Lewisian gneisses (on the left) and Diabaig Formation conglomerates (on the right) form the rocky pavements around the loch, with NE-dipping Basal Quartzite Member forming the ridge above. (BGS photograph P530369, © NERC)

116

slopes, but the ground around the lochan is underlain by the Torridon Group (Fig. 61). To the east, in the lower part of Coire a' Mhadaidh, the hummocky ground is underlain by Lewisian gneiss. All these rocks lie within the Ben More Thrust Sheet.

To the north and south of the lochan there are good exposures of the Diabaig Formation of the Torridon Group, which here comprises coarse conglomerate with cobbles up to 10cm long. The cobbles are dominated by vein quartz, suggesting long exposure and weathering of the underlying Lewisian gneiss. These conglomerates are deformed, with clasts flattened parallel to a cleavage that dips gently to the ENE.

At [NC 3060 2038] the unconformity between rocks of the Lewisian Gneiss Complex and the overlying rocks of the Diabaig Formation can be seen. The cleavage in the conglomerates of the Diabaig Formation is clearly at an angle to the fabric in the gneisses.

In the cliffs above, on the north ridge of Conival, the unconformity at the base of the Cambrian succession can be seen. At [NC 3079 2021], below the Conival–Ben More Assynt ridge, the Cambrian quartzites overstep the basal Torridon Group unconformity to lie directly on the Lewisian. The broad architecture of this double unconformity is clearly visible from below (Fig. 61), but the actual junction between the two unconformities is not exposed. Butler (1997) suggested that the Torridon Group–Lewisian gneiss contact is, at least in part, a faulted contact. The fault does not appear to cut the sub-Cambrian unconformity and so is considered to be Precambrian in age (but see Locality 7.9 for an alternative interpretation).

From this point, several options are possible. In poor weather and low cloud, many parties may wish simply to retrace their steps to Inchnadamph. Those that wish only to climb Conival may return to the Conival–Beinn an Fhurain col and ascend the north ridge to the summit (Locality 8.7). However, for parties that are comfortable on steep ground, a worthwhile route climbs south-east out of Coire a' Mhadaidh, up boulder scree slopes onto the ridge between Conival and Ben More Assynt. This route is described below, but note that it should not be followed in conditions of poor visibility.

Fig. 62 View north-west from the Conival–Ben More Assynt ridge towards the face of Na Tuadhan, showing large-scale folding in the hangingwall of the Ben More Thrust. (BGS photograph P530512, © NERC)

Locality 8.9 [NC 308 202]

Ben More Assynt–Conival col.

Climb south-east from the lochan up steep slopes of quartzite boulder scree, picking a route around craggy areas, and aiming for the low point on the ridge between Ben More Assynt and Conival.

A short way below the ridge the sub-Cambrian unconformity, running roughly parallel to the ridge-line, transgresses across the Torridon Group–Lewisian gneiss unconformity. Unfortunately this junction is covered in scree. On reaching the col, look back across Coire a' Mhadaidh to the dramatic face of Na Tuadhan. This face clearly displays major large-scale folds in the Cambrian quartzites in the hangingwall of the Ben More Thrust (Fig. 62).

From the col, either continue east along the ridge to the summit of Ben More Assynt (this adds approximately an hour to the excursion), or turn west along the ridge toward Conival.

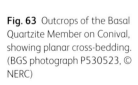

Fig. 63 Outcrops of the Basal Quartzite Member on Conival, showing planar cross-bedding. (BGS photograph P530523, © NERC)

Locality 8.10 [NC 318 203]

Ben More Assynt summit.

The summit of Ben More Assynt consists of twin knolls of coarse-grained, pebbly cross-bedded quartz arenite, belonging to the lowest part of the Basal Quartzite Member. About 50 metres southwards along the south ridge of Ben More Assynt lies the contact between the Cambrian Basal Quartzite Member and the underlying Lewisian Gneiss Complex. Beneath the contact, the gneisses are sheared over a few metres. This shear zone (informally termed the Coire a' Mhadaidh detachment) was formed by deformation along the basal Cambrian unconformity, and can be traced many kilometres to the north and south. Farther north, the Basal Quartzite Member is significantly thinned along the detachment. On the classic 1923 Assynt Map, this shear zone was erroneously mapped as a sill.

From the sheared gneisses, return over the summit of Ben More Assynt and westwards along the ridge of shattered Basal Quartzite Member (Fig. 63) to Conival. The south ridge of Ben More Assynt involves scrambling and is not recommended as a descent route.

Locality 8.11 NC [304 199]

Conival.

From the summit of Conival, the views of Assynt on a clear day are particularly impressive. To the south, a steep ridge descends to the classic glacial valley of Glen Oykel, with the Breabag Dome on its west side. To the north, the southern face of Na Tuadhan dominates the view across Coire a' Mhadaidh, with spectacular large-scale folds in the Cambrian quartz arenites. To the east, a large expanse of undulating boggy ground marks the rocks of the Moine Supergroup; and to the west, the mountains of the foreland can be clearly seen.

From Conival, descend the north ridge over outcrops of Basal Quartzite Member. Close to the summit, note the local presence of agalmatolite, a pale greenish, friable muscovite- and quartz-rich rock that represents a residual saprolitic tropical soil developed locally beneath the base of the Eriboll Formation. Traces of Torridon Group sandstone can be found, suggesting that minor thrusts disrupt the basal Cambrian unconformity in this area.

Rejoin the outward route and retrace your steps back to Inchnadamph.

Excursion 9

Glen Oykel and the Loch Ailsh Pluton

Kathryn Goodenough and Ian Parsons

Purpose: To study the syenites of the Loch Ailsh Pluton and the folded Lewisian Gneiss Complex–Torridon Group unconformity within the Ben More Thrust Sheet.

Aspects covered: Syenites of the Loch Ailsh Pluton; Diabaig Formation conglomerates and Lewisian gneisses in the Ben More Thrust Sheet; folds within the Ben More Thrust Sheet.

Maps: OS: 1:50,000 Landranger sheet 15 Loch Assynt; 1:25,000 Explorer sheets 440 Cassley and Glen Oykel, and 442 Assynt and Lochinver. BGS: 1:50,000 special sheet, Assynt district.

Terrain: The route is a 12km walk up the little-visited valley of Glen Oykel. The first part of the excursion is on good paths, but it then enters some fairly remote country and crosses rough, often wet ground. Many of the outcrops are in stream sections, so this excursion will be most interesting after a period of dry weather.

Time: This excursion requires a full day.

Access: Permission for access to the glen, and for use of the private road, must be obtained from Assynt Estates at any time of the year; and during the stalking season (July to November) it will probably also be necessary to confirm access with the stalker on the day.

Turn off the A837 at [NC 296 083] onto the private track to Ben More Lodge. Vehicular use of this track, and parking of cars at Ben More Lodge, is only by prior permission from the Assynt Estate Office. Use of a mountain bike would provide the best alternative to driving, and bikes could be taken as far as Locality 9.3.

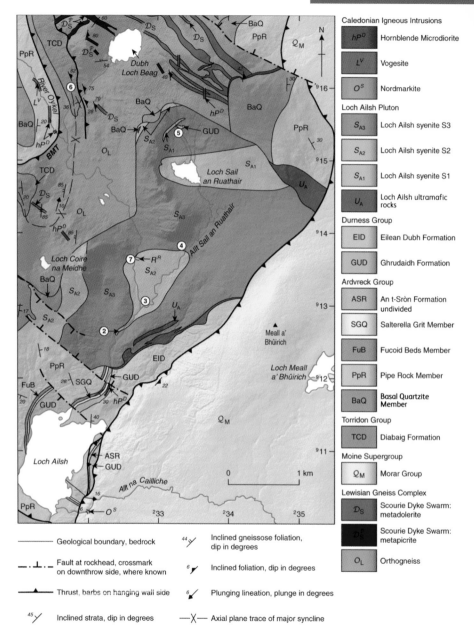

Locality 9.1

Track to Ben More Lodge.

En route along the track there are several exposures of minor intrusions, cutting rocks of the Cambro-Ordovician succession. At [NC 306 092] there are outcrops of pink peralkaline rhyolite, part of a large sill cutting dolostone.

Locality 9.2 [NC 326 127]

Loch Ailsh syenites in the River Oykel.

From Ben More Lodge [NC 323 115], walk up the landrover track along the River Oykel, passing scattered outcrops of Durness Group dolostone. A wide stream, the Allt Cathair Bhàn, can be crossed at a ford or at a small, rickety footbridge just upstream from the track. Further up this stream, exposures of pyroxenite have been found, but the abundant plantations that have grown up in recent years have made the outcrops very inaccessible and not worth visiting. Geophysical studies (magnetic anomalies) have shown that these pyroxenites form a sub-vertical sheet extending along the margin of the Loch Ailsh Pluton (Fig. 64; Parsons, 1965b). The anomaly dies out where the pyroxenites pass beneath the Moine Thrust.

At [NC 324 125] outcrops of coarse-grained syenite are seen in the river and the track. These are typical outcrops of the S3 phase of the Loch Ailsh Pluton. A little distance further up the river, at [NC 326 127], a large area of rock outcrop forms a waterfall, which provides excellent exposures of a variety of different facies of the Loch Ailsh syenites. Here, coarse-grained pyroxene-rich syenites are heavily veined by, and in places enclosed within, grey-pink leucosyenites (Fig. 65). The pyroxene syenites contain abundant diffuse clots of dark green pyroxene, as well as xenoliths of dark green pyroxenite and hornblendite that are typically several cm across and have sharply defined margins. There are at least two generations of later leuco-syenite veins or sheets, which have sharp boundaries with the host pyroxene-rich syenites. These later intrusions include red syenite veins and later, grey leucosyenites that are related to the S3 syenites. Late-stage shear zones run through all the rocks, indicating deformation subsequent to the intrusion of the syenites.

Fig. 65 Outcrops in the waterfall in the River Oykel (Locality 9.2), showing medium-grained grey leucosyenite veins cutting coarse-grained pyroxene syenites. (BGS photograph P506429, © NERC)

Fig. 66 View west across Loch Sail an Ruathair to the dome of S1 syenite surrounded by S3 syenite, after Parsons (1999). (BGS photograph P693860, © NERC)

Locality 9.3 [NC 328 129]

Syenite outcrops at stream confluence.

Return to the track and continue north-east. A few hundred metres further up the river, the confluence of the Allt Sail an Ruathair and the River Oykel is reached. A few scattered outcrops in the stream at this point are of red, pyroxene-bearing S2 syenite, which forms a dome-shaped mass in the centre of the Loch Ailsh Pluton (Fig. 64). Between here and the last locality, the boundary between the S2 and S3 syenites is gradational, with red feldspar xenocrysts from S2 included within grey S3 syenite. Rock exposures in the track are of grey S3 syenite with red feldspar xenocrysts, cut by many narrow shear zones.

Locality 9.4 [NC 332 134]

Allt Sail an Ruathair.

Cross the Allt Sail an Ruathair by the footbridge and then turn right to follow the stalker's path up the stream, crossing again at a ford. A slight diversion from the track can be made to see outcrops of typical coarse-grained, red-weathering S2 syenite in the river at [NC 332 134]. Follow the track to [NC 337 141], where it crosses the river by a ford or a footbridge.

123

Outcrops in the river here are of grey-weathering S3 syenite. An outcrop just above the ford is cut by a 10cm red dyke, probably a peralkaline rhyolite. Carry on along the track until it crosses the outflow from Loch Sail an Ruathair at [NC 337 143], then follow this stream up to the loch and walk round the eastern side. Across the loch, the contact between an early dome of S1 syenite and the later S3 syenite can be seen on the slopes of the Sail an Ruathair ridge (Fig. 66).

Locality 9.5 [NC 334 154]

Metamorphic Burn.

Continue to the north side of the loch, where two sizeable streams flow into it. Follow the more westerly of these two streams, which runs into a narrow gully with good rock exposures. This stream was termed the 'Metamorphic Burn' by Phemister (1926) because it shows grey-brown S3 syenites enclosing metamorphosed blocks of the Cambrian sedimentary succession, which are apparently in correct stratigraphical order, but the wrong way up: *i.e.* with dolostone at the base of the slope. This is because the dip of the sedimentary succession is steeper than the fall of the stream. Screens of the earlier syenites have also been recognised within the S3 syenites in the burn.

Walking up the burn, the first rock exposures are reached about 400m above the loch at [NC 333 154]. These exposures are of grey syenite (reddened in the stream) containing isolated, altered xenoliths of dolostone, which have been converted to diopside- and phlogopite-bearing calc-silicate rocks. These xenoliths are most easily recognised by the abundant flakes of phlogopite mica. In places the syenite enclosing the calc-silicate rocks shows signs of alteration, and mafic pyroxene-rich patches are common.

Continue upstream past syenite outcrops. After a short gap in exposure, more calc-silicate xenoliths are seen at [NC 3334 1546]. Syenites with white-weathering calc-silicate xenoliths, some up to a metre across, continue upstream. Within this succession is a roughly 20m-thick sheet of red S1 syenite, which has sharp upper and lower contacts with the surrounding S3 syenites.

Further up the stream, at [NC 3330 1558], is a smooth, slabby exposure of hard grey quartzite, taken to be a xenolith of the Salterella Grit Member. This is in contact with a layer of fine, flinty, dark-green rock with conspicuous pink feldspars. Slightly above, about midway up the steep section of the stream, is a thick layer of baked grey shale (the Fucoid Beds Member) with black streaks and folded and fractured bedding. Immediately above the Fucoid Beds is a 2 m-thick body of dark green pyroxenite, which is in sharp contact with grey S3 syenite above. From here upwards, the rocks in the burn are pale grey S3 syenites, enclosing massive tabular quartzite xenoliths [NC 3351 1573] that have been fenitised. Xenoliths of red syenite (probably S2) are also present.

The xenoliths in the Metamorphic Burn are considered to represent remnants of an undisturbed, southerly dipping Cambrian succession into which the Loch Ailsh syenites were intruded. The preservation of the sequence suggests that the mode of intrusion of the syenites was relatively passive. However, the country rocks nearby are Lewisian gneisses, suggesting that these sedimentary xenoliths must have moved from their original position.

From the top of the Metamorphic Burn, walk roughly north-west over the peaty ridge towards the stream flowing out of Dubh Loch Beag, passing scattered outcrops of Lewisian gneiss. Across the glen, Eriboll Formation quartzites thickened by thrusting can be clearly seen on the slopes of Breabag. In places, major rockfalls have occurred where large slabs of quartzite have slipped downwards along thrust and bedding planes.

Locality 9.6 [NC318 158]

Sgonnan Mòr Syncline and basal Torridon Group.

Follow the outflow stream of the loch downhill into Glen Oykel, past outcrops of Lewisian gneiss. At [NC 3187 1584] the gneiss overlies sheared Torridon Group sandstone along the Oykel Thrust. This thrust was first identified by Milne (1978) and considered to cut the Loch Ailsh Pluton, but is now thought to be of limited extent, representing the sheared-out common limb between the Sgonnan Mòr Syncline and Anticline (British Geological Survey, 2007). There is no evidence that this thrust actually cuts the Loch Ailsh Pluton.

A little further downhill, just above the path, are excellent ice-polished outcrops of the basal Torridon Group conglomerate and sandstone, with a distinct near-vertical to north-easterly-dipping cleavage (Fig. 67). The bedding and cleavage are at roughly right angles to each other; these basal Torridon Group rocks lie in the broad fold-hinge of the Sgonnan Mòr Syncline.

Fig. 67 Diabaig Formation conglomerate with a strong cleavage, in the core of the major syncline in Glen Oykel, Locality 9.6. (BGS photograph P693864, © NERC)

Fig. 68 Peralkaline Rhyolite dyke cutting fractured and quartz-veined syenites of the Loch Ailsh Pluton in the River Oykel at Locality 9.7. (BGS photograph P693870, © NERC)

Locality 9.7 [NC 327 136]

Peralkaline rhyolite dykes.

From the Dubh Loch Beag outflow, follow the path down Glen Oykel, noting a brick-red rhyolite dyke which cuts Lewisian gneisses just above the path at [NC 3195 1570]. The route crosses back into the Loch Ailsh Pluton at about the point where the path rejoins the river bank. At [NC 3270 1360], another *c.*4m-thick dyke of reddish-brown, fine-grained rhyolite cuts reddish, coarse-grained S2 syenites (Fig. 68). These dykes are members of the Peralkaline Rhyolite Swarm. These intrusions are found as dykes and sills throughout the Assynt Culmination, although concentrated in the Ben More and Glencoul Thrust sheets. In some localities (such as on Cnoc an Droighinn above Inchnadamph) they have been deformed by thrust related folds, and thus they are considered to have been intruded during or prior to movement on the thrusts in the Moine Thrust Zone. The cross-cutting evidence here in Glen Oykel shows that these dykes are clearly younger than the Loch Ailsh Pluton, which has been dated as 430.6 ± 0.3 Ma (Goodenough *et al.*, 2011). Thus movements in the thrust belt must have occurred after *c.*430.6 Ma. This is one of the few constraints in existence on the age of movement on the thrusts, making this an important location.

Follow the track down Glen Oykel to return to Ben More Lodge.

126

Excursion 10

Cam Loch, Ledmore and the Loch Borralan Pluton

Kathryn Goodenough and Ian Parsons

Purpose: To study the Loch Borralan Pluton and its contact relationships with the structures of the Moine Thrust Zone.

Aspects covered: The Cam Loch Klippe, syenites of the Loch Borralan Pluton, contact relationships of the pluton, and the Loch Urigill carbonatite.

Maps: OS: 1:50,000 Landranger sheet 15 Loch Assynt; 1:25,000 Explorer sheet 439 Coigach and Summer Isles. BGS: 1:50,000 special sheet, Assynt.

Terrain: The excursion comprises a series of stops linked by short drives. The longest walking distance at any stop is about 5km, mostly on paths and tracks, although some rough and boggy ground is covered, particularly around Cam Loch and Loch Urigill.

Time: The whole excursion will take a full day, but most of the localities can be visited separately.

Access: Localities 10.1, 10.2, 10.4, 10.5 and 10.6 should have no problems with access at most times of the year; for Locality 10.3 (Ledmore Marble Quarry) the quarry manager (Tel: 01854 666241) should be contacted before visiting. Hard hats and high visibility jackets will be required, and all instructions from the quarry manager should be followed.

Locality 10.1 [NC 230 121] to [NC 224 140]

Cam Loch Klippe.

The first stop is a walk over the Cam Loch Klippe, which will take 3–4 hours and involves some steep and rough ground. This klippe comprises two fairly significant thrusts (the Cam Loch and Leathaid Bhuidhe thrusts) that

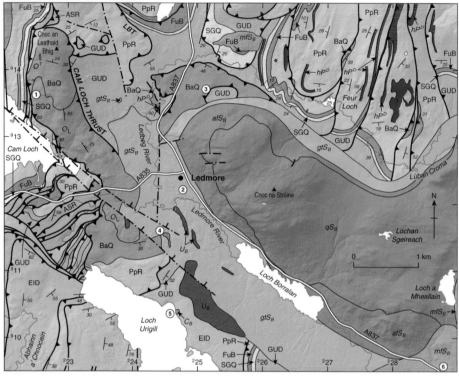

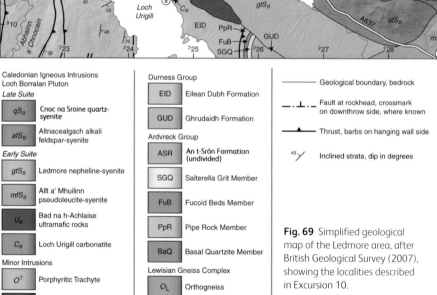

Caledonian Igneous Intrusions
Loch Borralan Pluton

Late Suite

qS_B	Cnoc na Sroine quartz-syenite
afS_B	Altnacealgach alkali feldspar-syenite

Early Suite

gtS_B	Ledmore nepheline-syenite
mfS_B	Allt a' Mhuilinn pseudoleucite-syenite
U_B	Bad na h-Achlaise ultramafic rocks
C_B	Loch Urigill carbonatite

Minor Intrusions

O^T	Porphyritic Trachyte
hP^D	Hornblende Microdiorite

Durness Group

EID	Eilean Dubh Formation
GUD	Ghrudaidh Formation

Ardvreck Group

ASR	An t-Sròn Formation (undivided)
SGQ	Salterella Grit Member
FuB	Fucoid Beds Member
PpR	Pipe Rock Member
BaQ	Basal Quartzite Member

Lewisian Gneiss Complex

O_L	Orthogneiss

——————— Geological boundary, bedrock

—·—⊥—·— Fault at rockhead, crossmark on downthrow side, where known

———▲——— Thrust, barbs on hanging wall side

^{45}∕ Inclined strata, dip in degrees

Fig. 69 Simplified geological map of the Ledmore area, after British Geological Survey (2007), showing the localities described in Excursion 10.

LBT = Leathaid Bhuidhe Thrust

128

Fig. 70 The overturned, steeply dipping unconformity between Lewisian gneiss and Basal Quartzite Member in the Cam Loch Klippe. The geologist's hand is resting on Lewisian gneisses, but immediately to his left is the weathered-out unconformity, with Basal Quartzite outcrops further left. (BGS photograph P693882, © NERC)

Fig. 71 Red Porphyritic Trachyte dyke, cutting Basal Quartzite Member in the Cam Loch Klippe. (BGS photograph P693883, © NERC)

carry Lewisian gneiss and Eriboll Formation over rocks of the Sole Thrust sheet (Fig. 69). It is not certain how these thrusts relate to other thrusts to the east, although it has been suggested in the past that the Cam Loch Thrust can be equated to the Ben More Thrust.

Park on the A835 about 1.5 km west of Ledmore Junction, at [NC 234 122], where there is a small car-park with a footpath signpost saying 'Lochinver 19km. Follow the path round the eastern side of the Cam Loch. At the easternmost tip of the loch [NC 233 126], quartzites of the Pipe Rock Member are exposed near the shore, with Lewisian gneisses slightly higher up the slope to the north. The Cam Loch Thrust lies in the unexposed ground in between these outcrops, and has carried the gneiss over the quartzite. Follow the path along the north-eastern side of the loch for approximately a kilometre. Just after a gate in a deer fence, the path runs over an exposure of Lewisian gneiss; at this point you are above the Cam Loch Thrust, which here dips eastward fairly steeply.

Follow the path along the loch shore until it ascends a low ridge at [NC 222 135], and then walk up that ridge towards the cliffs that form the eastern side of Cnoc an Leathaid Bhig. The Cam Loch Thrust runs at the base of these cliffs, carrying Lewisian gneisses over Durness Group dolostones in the Sole Thrust Sheet, but the thrust itself is not exposed here. Scramble up steep slopes to a rowan tree growing out of a fallen boulder at [NC 224 137]. Here, the rocks above the thrust belong to the Basal Quartzite Member, and dip beneath the Lewisian gneisses (Fig. 70); the rocks of the thrust sheet here are inverted by a major anticline. The steeply-dipping unconformity can be seen in the cliffs about 20 m south-east of the rowan tree.

129

Continue northwards along the foot of the cliffs and ascend a broad heathery gully. At the top of this gully [NC 2244 1384], a conspicuous fine-grained red dyke, about 1 m thick and striking roughly NNE–SSW, cuts the Basal Quartzite Member (Fig. 71). This dyke is a member of the Porphyritic Trachyte Swarm, and is among the later intrusions in the area. It has similar mineralogy and chemistry to the syenites of the late suite of the Loch Borralan Pluton. Several smaller dykes of this swarm occur around the Cam Loch Klippe.

Continue upwards to the summit of Cnoc an Leathaid Bhig, which is an excellent viewpoint. To the east, the hill of Cnoc na Stròine is formed of quartz syenites of the late suite of the Loch Borralan Pluton; the topography of the hill reflects the stock-like nature of this late suite intrusion (Fig. 72). To the north-east, darker-coloured Torridon Group rocks form klippen of the Ben More Thrust Sheet on the hills of Beinn an Fhuarain and Beinn nan Cnaimhseag, in front of the quartzites of the Breabag Dome and Conival. Beyond Breabag darker-coloured rocks are seen above the Ben More Thrust on Sgonnan Mòr. To the north-west, the double unconformity is clearly visible on Canisp, with the distinctive profile of Suilven to the west. Directly to the north, the hill of Cnoc an Leathaid Bhuidhe consists of Pipe Rock that has been thrust over Durness Group dolostones. To the south, the green fields around Elphin indicate the presence of dolostone in the Sole Thrust Sheet.

Fig. 72 View east from Cnoc an Leathaid Bhig. The low, dark hill slightly right of centre in the image is Cnoc na Stròine, formed of quartz-syenites of the late suite of the Loch Borralan Pluton. The early suite syenites outcrop in the poorly exposed lower ground around Loch Borralan on the right of the photograph. Some of the main thrusts in the area are indicated (BMT= Ben More Thrust). At a large scale these thrusts are cross-cut by the Loch Borralan Pluton; poor exposure obscures the detailed relations between the early suite syenites and the thrusts. (BGS photograph P693885–P693889, © NERC)

Return to the car-park down the south ridge of Cnoc an Leathaid Bhig, recrossing the (poorly exposed) folded unconformity between Lewisian gneisses and the Basal Quartzite Member. Descend slopes alongside the deer fence to return to the lochside path.

Locality 10.2 [NC 247 120]

Loch Borralan syenites at Ledmore.

Drive to the hamlet of Ledmore, turning off on a track on the right (east) just before the road junction, and park near the end of the track at [NC 247 121]. Walk down to the river, where there are scattered outcrops of the Ledmore nepheline-syenites ('ledmorites'). These medium-grained, purple-grey melanite-pyroxene nepheline-syenites make up a major part of the early, undersaturated suite of the Loch Borralan Pluton. In places the syenites are cut by sheets of white aegirine-aplite.

Slightly downriver, at [NC 246 120], there is a rather rotten exposure of pyroxene-rich syenite with many leucocratic veins. Pyroxenites have been recorded at this locality in the past, but are no longer exposed. However, geophysical methods and borehole drilling have indicated that these ultramafic rocks extend over a wide area on the south-western side of the intrusion.

Locality 10.3 [NC 252 137]

Ledmore Marble Quarry.

From Ledmore, turn left at Ledmore Junction and drive along the road for a little over 1 km to the entrance to the Ledmore Marble Quarry. Access permission to visit this quarry should be confirmed with the quarry manager (Tel: 01854 666241); hard hats and high-visibility jackets may be required.

This quarry cuts through a thrust that has carried Basal Quartzite Member over dolostones of the Ghrudaidh Formation, and which may be tentatively correlated with the Cam Loch Thrust. The cross-bedded quartz arenites are exposed in a low cliff just to the left of the quarry entrance. In the main body of the quarry, Ghrudaidh Formation dolostones of the Sole Thrust Sheet have been intruded and metamorphosed by coarse-grained, irregular sheets of melanite-biotite-pseudoleucite nepheline-syenite ('borolanite'). The 'borolanites' are recognisable by their distinctive texture, with white pseudoleucite 'spots' in a dark grey matrix (Fig. 73). The dolostones have been melted, metamorphosed and metasomatised by the intrusive sheets, producing a variety of interesting patterns in the rock faces. Of particular interest are cross-cutting carbonate sheets, which have been shown to have formed through melting of the local dolostones, in the presence of high temperatures and a fluid flux. These are the best available exposures of the contacts of the Loch Borralan Pluton with the country rocks, but unfortunately the quarry exposures at the time of writing do not provide clear evidence of the relationship between the intrusive rocks and the thrust. However, the field relationships of the area in general indicate that the late suite of the Loch Borralan Pluton does indeed cut, and therefore post-date, thrusts in this area.

Locality 10.4 [NC 245 115]

Bad na h'Achlaise.

Return to the vehicles and drive eastwards, carrying straight on at Ledmore Junction, to park at the bridge over the Ledmore River at [NC 254 116]. Walk south over the bridge, go through the gate into the forestry plantation and follow the track uphill for about 800m, until it descends slightly to a stream which passes underneath the track through a conspicuous culvert (large pipe). This area is known as Bad na h'Achlaise, and contains some small but very important outcrops of the Loch Borralan intrusion.

Just before reaching the stream, on the south side of the track [NC 2462 1139], there is a small quarry, much of it cut in drift. On the left, at the entrance, there is a substantial pile of large, angular fragments of various types of nepheline-syenite. They are not erratic blocks and appear to have been broken from an exposure during road or quarry construction.

Most blocks are grey, medium grained, meso- to leuco-cratic nepheline-syenite (alkali feldspars 1–5mm), but there are also pink variants which locally occur as veins cutting the grey varieties. There are mafic inclusions with sharp margins, some of which are foliated or layered, and locally veined by nepheline-syenite. In addition, there are diffuse, mafic patches in the syenites. Drilling work south and south-east of Bad na h'Achlaise has shown that rocks of these types are abundant under the now forested Mointeach na Totaig, although there are no exposures.

Fig. 73 'Borolanite' in Ledmore Marble Quarry (Locality 10.3), with the characteristic spotted appearance due to the presence of white pseudo-leucites. (BGS photograph P531474, © NERC)

Fig. 74 Pegmatitic syenite in the Bad na h-Achlaise excavation, Locality 10.4. (BGS photograph P530690, © NERC)

In the back left corner of the quarry there are exposures of jointed, fine-grained more melanocratic syenite similar in appearance to the Ledmore nepheline-syenites. This type is also cut by pink, leucocratic syenite veins.

Leave the forestry track at the culvert [NC 2458 1140] and walk down the right (east) bank of the stream. On a steep grassy bank overlooking the forest, which is about 150m ahead, there is a small exposure of pink nepheline-syenite [NC 2455 1150]. Immediately after the brow in front there is an outcrop of rusty-weathering, carbonated biotite pyroxenite [NC 2455 1152].

During the 1980s, the Nature Conservancy Council opened up a series of excavations running along the top of the slope to the west of the stream, to investigate the relationships between the igneous rocks and the rocks of the Cam Loch Klippe (Parsons and McKirdy, 1983). These exposures are becoming overgrown, but are still worthy of investigation. The smallest of the new exposures, some 12m west of the stream in Bad na h'Achlaise at [NC 2453 1151], consists of pyroxenite cut by an inclined sheet of nepheline-syenite. The pyroxenite is soft and highly weathered, but can be seen to be cut by cm-thick syenite veins.

Some 40m due west at [NC 24485 11506] a larger excavation, with a number of large loose blocks, revealed extremely coarse grained pegmatitic nepheline-syenite and some finer leucocratic variants (Parsons and McKirdy, 1983, loc. 2). At the top of the exposure there is a southward-inclined sheet of zoned pegmatite with striking euhedral, dark grey feldspars up to 20 centimetres in length (Fig. 74). The host rock is finer-grained, more mafic, pink nepheline-syenite.

133

Continue west for 60m along a conspicuous excavated terrace to a large (20m long) excavated exposure at [NC 24411 11514 to NC 24432 11513] (Parsons and McKirdy, 1983, loc. 3). This is an important exposure which shows unequivocally that igneous rocks of the Loch Borralan Pluton were intruded into the Basal Quartzite Member, considered to be part of the Cam Loch Klippe. Since intrusions belonging to this pluton also cut rocks of the Sole Thrust sheet in Ledmore Marble Quarry, it is clear that the pluton cuts across the Cam Loch Thrust. It also shows that the pyroxenites are intrusive rocks, not metasomatic skarn rocks at the contact of intrusion with dolomite.

The pyroxenite occurs at the extreme west of the exposure, near the base. It is now more restricted in exposure than shown by Parsons and McKirdy (1983), and is very soft, but has clearly been injected into quartzite. The quartzite is fenitised, with rosettes of pale blue amphibole. The main face of the exposure is now cleaner than in 1983, and a number of pink syenite veins, typically around 30cm wide, are visible, forming a network in quartzite. There is a 10cm vug in the quartzite close to one of these veins, lined by euhedral quartz. The eastern end of the exposure is entirely pink, fine to coarse grained nepheline-syenite, with tight angular jointing.

Locality 10.5 [NC 247 104]

The Loch Urigill carbonatite.

Return to the forest road above Bad na h'Achlaise and follow it westwards until a Y-junction; take the left-hand (uphill) fork and continue to the end of the track. From here a path continues downhill to the shores of Loch Urigill. Do not cross the deer fence, but follow it round the east side of the small bay to [NC 247 104]. The carbonatite exposure, the only known example of this rock-type in the British Isles, lies in an excavated hollow (Young *et al.*, 1994). The carbonatite outcrops are dark grey on weathered surfaces, but fresh surfaces are white, crystalline and coarse-grained. These are sövites (calcite-carbonatites), with xenoliths of nepheline-syenite and pyroxenite from the Loch Borralan intrusion. Also found in the area, chiefly as blocks, are phlogopite sövites, which have an orange weathered colour due to the presence of plates of phlogopite within the calcite matrix of the rock. One of the sövite outcrops shows layering, brought out by the mineral

134

chondrodite, and brecciated carbonatites are also present. The carbonatite was actually intruded into dolostones of the Durness Group, and is not an integral part of the Loch Borralan Pluton, but it is considered to be associated with it.

Locality 10.6 [NC 287 096]

Allt a'Mhuillin Quarry.

Return to the cars; drive south-east along the A837, past the Altnacealgach Motel, to where the road crosses the Allt a'Mhuillin stream at [NC 287 096]. Park at the roadside, and walk through tussocky grass just to the west of the forest, to reach the prominent quarry at [NC 287 097].

This quarry is the type locality for the Allt a'Mhuilinn pseudoleucite-syenite ('borolanite'), part of the early suite of the Loch Borralan Pluton. These rocks are melanite-biotite-pyroxene nepheline-syenites which contain white spots that are pseudomorphs after leucite, now made up of an aggregate of K-feldspar, white mica and nepheline. These pseudoleucites show varying degrees of flattening, from near-spherical to highly flattened white streaks, but other minerals in the rock appear euhedral. The pseudoleucite-syenites contain numerous xenoliths of darker-coloured rock types, including a more mafic melanite-pyroxene-biotite syenite. Many fresh samples can be found among the fallen blocks that litter the quarry floor.

The pseudoleucite-syenites in the quarry are cut by a set of undeformed pegmatite veins that contain an unusual mineral assemblage: feldspar, nepheline, biotite, melanite, magnetite, titanite, allanite, zeolite and blue cancrinite. Later shear zones cut all the rock-types.

The earliest workers interpreted the relationships in this quarry as proof that the intrusion of the Loch Borralan Pluton must have overlapped movements on the Ben More Thrust, with the 'borolanites' being deformed by thrusting prior to the intrusion of the pegmatites. The flattening of the pseudoleucites has been interpreted as of igneous origin (Elliott and Johnson, 1980) or as a tectonic fabric (Searle, *et al.*, 2010), with different implications for the relative timing of intrusion and thrusting. This controversy has not yet been fully resolved; it is most likely that intrusion of the rocks of the early suite was broadly contemporaneous with thrusting, and that the late suite syenites were intruded after thrust movement had ceased (Woolley, 1970; Goodenough *et al.*, 2011).

135

Excursion 11

Glencoul

Rick Law, Rob Butler, Kathryn Goodenough
and Maarten Krabbendam

Purpose: To see the classic exposure of the Glencoul Thrust, and the ductile mylonite zone that forms the Moine Thrust on the Stack of Glencoul.

Aspects covered: Glencoul Thrust exposure, Moine mylonites.

Maps: OS: 1:50,000 Landranger sheet 15 Loch Assynt; 1:25,000 Explorer sheet 442 Assynt and Lochinver. BGS: 1:50,000 special sheet, Assynt district.

Terrain: If done entirely on foot, this excursion represents a serious day out, with around 16km of walking and 600m of climbing, through remote and largely pathless country. In particular, around the Glencoul Thrust exposure at Tom na Toine it is necessary to traverse steep grassy slopes above a high cliff. This section of the route can prove treacherous, especially in wet conditions, and serious injuries have occurred here. Only experienced, well-equipped parties should take this route. At the time of writing, the Stack of Glencoul (Localities 11.2 and 11.3) can also be reached during the

summer as part of a trip on the MV *Statesman*, from Kylesku – it should be possible to walk to the Stack from the Glencoul landing between the morning and afternoon sailings (Tel: 01971 502345 for information). It may also be possible to take the boat in and walk out, although this involves arranging for a vehicle pick-up on the A894 or a long, tiring tramp back along the tarmac road to Kylesku.

Time: The entire excursion represents a full day out, and is one of the most strenuous routes in this guide. If the boat trip is available, the walk from the boat landing at Glencoul to the Stack of Glencoul will take around 4–5 hours there and back.

Access: There should be no significant problems with access, although during the stalking season (July to October), phoning Westminster Estates in advance is advised. The excursion is not recommended in poor weather, and after a period of heavy rain the river crossings below the Stack may prove difficult.

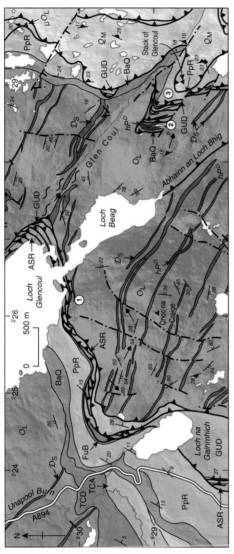

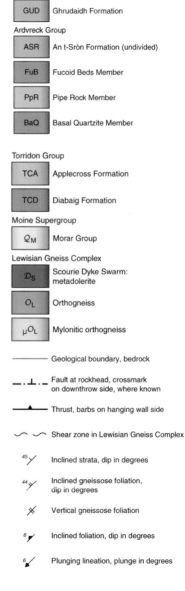

Caledonian Igneous Intrusions

| hP^D | Hornblende Microdiorite |

Durness Group

| GUD | Ghrudaidh Formation |

Ardvreck Group

ASR	An t-Sròn Formation (undivided)
FuB	Fucoid Beds Member
PpR	Pipe Rock Member
BaQ	Basal Quartzite Member

Torridon Group

| TCA | Applecross Formation |
| TCD | Diabaig Formation |

Moine Supergroup

| Q_M | Morar Group |

Lewisian Gneiss Complex

$\mathcal{D}_S$	Scourie Dyke Swarm: metadolerite
O_L	Orthogneiss
μO_L	Mylonitic orthogneiss

——————— Geological boundary, bedrock

— · ⊥ · — Fault at rockhead, crossmark on downthrow side, where known

——▲——— Thrust, barbs on hanging wall side

⌒⌒ ⌒⌒ Shear zone in Lewisian Gneiss Complex

⁴⁵⟋ Inclined strata, dip in degrees

⁴⁴⟋ Inclined gneissose foliation, dip in degrees

⤬ Vertical gneissose foliation

⁶⟋ Inclined foliation, dip in degrees

⁶⟋ Plunging lineation, plunge in degrees

Fig. 76 Simplified geological map of the Glencoul area, after British Geological Survey (2007), showing the localities described in Excursion 11.

137

Fig. 75 View of the Stack of Glencoul from the boat up Loch Glencoul, with the stalkers' path visible on the left. The grassy areas on the shore are underlain by imbricates of the An t-Sròn and Ghrudaidh Formations, overlain by craggy Lewisian gneisses in the Glencoul Thrust Sheet. The cliffs forming the prominent summit of the Stack of Glencoul are composed of Moine mylonites in the Moine Thrust Sheet. (BGS photograph P531993, © NERC)

For the Stack of Glencoul only, take the MV *Statesman* morning sailing and ask to be landed at the Glencoul jetty. From there, make your way to where the stalkers' path (Fig. 75) comes down to the loch side at [NC 271306], using the wooden bridge. Walk up this path for approximately 2km to where the path begins to climb steeply at [NC 285 295]. Find a convenient place to cross the river and then head SSE up the boulder-strewn and grassy hillside towards the skyline ridge, in order to join the excursion at Locality 11.2.

If instead you wish to complete the entire excursion, park at a lay-by on the A894, at the mouth of a gorge cutting through the escarpment of Cambrian quartzites [NC 240 295]. Walk along the road and follow the foot of the escarpment north, then east to the shores of Loch Glencoul. This route starts on Torridon Group sandstones, but crosses onto Lewisian gneisses beneath the sub-Cambrian unconformity (Fig. 76). There are good views back to Quinag and the double unconformity from the ridge just north of the A894 [NC 239 300] and north onto the Glencoul Thrust on the Aird da Loch peninsula from the slopes above the loch, around [NC 249 303]. Once at the shore, walk east, taking in good outcrops of Basal Quartzite Member with 0.5–1.5 m sets of planar cross-bedding, e.g. at [NC 255 304], and then excellent examples of *Skolithos* in the Pipe Rock Member, e.g. at [NC 258 303]. These outcrops are worth examining for they show undeformed pipe geometries, perpendicular to bedding, for comparison with the strained pipes at the Stack of Glencoul.

Follow the loch shore to a point where steeper slopes rise in front of you, with a line of small trees marking the outcrop of imbricated repetitions of Fucoid Beds and Salterella Grit. Ascend via narrow sheep tracks onto a grassy bench, where a series of inclined panels of Salterella Grit can be found, e.g. at [NC 258 301]. These imbricate slices are capped by the

138

Glencoul Thrust. The main cliff line above the shelf is formed by Lewisian gneisses of the Glencoul Thrust Sheet.

Locality 11.1 [NC 2570 3000 to 2600 3010]

Glencoul Thrust Plane at Tom na Toine.

The thrust itself is exposed in a few sites along the back of the shelf. If time permits, it is worth visiting the western exposure [NC 257 300]. Here the gneisses are strongly deformed into mylonites within a metre of the thrust plane, resting on a few centimetres of strongly sheared, buff-coloured carbonates of the Durness Group. These lie in turn on Salterella Grit underlain stratigraphically by Fucoid Beds.

Although it is possible to follow the Glencoul Thrust along the shelf towards Loch Glencoul, this ground is steep and the sheep trails particularly tenuous. A better alternative is to return to the gentle slopes at the foot of the escarpment and the shore line of Pipe Rock. The way ahead is now guarded by the Tom na Toine escarpment of imbricated An t-Sròn Formation, but a faint sheep path climbs a steep grassy slope to above the sea cliffs. Great care should be taken, especially in damp weather, as serious accidents have resulted from slips here.

The path leads up to a grassy amphitheatre defined by steep dark cliffs of Lewisian gneisses of the Glencoul Thrust Sheet. The Glencoul Thrust Plane is very well exposed at the base of the overhanging cliffs (Fig. 77). Above the thrust lies Lewisian gneiss of the Glencoul Thrust Sheet, and beneath lies buff-coloured Durness Group dolostone, presumably from the Ghrudaidh Formation. The thrust plane itself is very sharp and marked by a discrete gouge zone. The Lewisian gneiss above is strongly deformed into mylonite within a few metres of the thrust plane. Closest to the thrust is a 10cm-thick zone of very fine chloritic mylonite, followed by 30–50cm of chloritic mylonite with small feldspar porphyroclasts. The feldspar porphyroclasts increase in size upwards, and a metre above the thrust plane there are lenses of fractured feldspar in a matrix of chloritic mylonite to protomylonite. The carbonate below is strongly recrystallised and shows fractures at right angles to the thrust plane

From here, a narrow path follows the shelf below the Glencoul Thrust eastwards, with cliffs both above and below; this eventually picks its way between boulders back down to the loch shore, which should then be followed south-eastwards. Much of this ground is rough and progress is commonly rather slow. At the head of Loch Beag, continue up the Abhainn an Loch Bhig, crossing it where possible; fording this river may be very difficult, if not impossible, after heavy rain. At [NC 280 284], leave the valley floor and climb north-east along a stream to a small lochan at [NC 283 288], passing outcrops of Lewisian gneiss.

Locality 11.2 [NC 283 288 to 288 289]

Imbricates below the Stack of Glencoul.

The hillside to the east of the lochan is formed of Eriboll Formation quartz arenites, here downthrown by a fault to lie adjacent to the Lewisian gneisses of the Glencoul Thrust Sheet. The geology of this area is best investigated by continuing north a short distance from the lochan onto a ridge, which overlooks the river valley of Glen Coul, and then turning to climb south-east towards the Stack of Glencoul. The ridge, which provides an entertaining scramble with plenty of outcrops to be seen, straddles an oblique fault that juxtaposes Lewisian gneisses on the lower slopes to the north, against the Cambrian quartz arenites on the ridgeline.

On the lower parts of the ridge, the Basal Quartzite Member is imbricated with Lewisian gneisses. Within the quartz arenites are sills of hornblende microdiorite; these are part of a large swarm of intrusions that occur throughout Assynt, and were emplaced into the quartz arenites shortly before the onset of thrusting. Good examples can be seen around [NC 2860 2905].

Fig. 77 The Glencoul Thrust exposure at Tom na Toine (Locality 11.1), with dark grey, mylonitic Lewisian gneisses thrust over buff-coloured Durness Group carbonates. (BGS photograph, © NERC)

Continuing up the ridge, careful observation will allow the stratigraphic transition from Basal Quartzite Member up into Pipe Rock Member to be identified and then, near the top of the ridge, the top of the Pipe Rock Member. A grassy terrace obscures Fucoid Beds, Salterella Grit and a few metres of Durness Group carbonates. These units are capped tectonically by Pipe Rock Member quartz arenites that continue on to the east, towards the Stack of Glencoul. A well-exposed portion of the base of the upper Pipe Rock Member, thrust onto Durness Group carbonates, occurs around [NC 288 287] and can be found by tracing a grassy shelf above cliffs to the south, about 80m from the crest line that overlooks Glen Coul. The thrust contact forms a 2m-wide overhang, a feature that provides the only shelter from bad weather hereabouts. The fault is strongly cataclastic and decorated with cemented gouges derived from Pipe Rock Member. The Durness Group carbonates in the footwall are strongly fractured and veined. Notwithstanding these classic faulting characteristics, it is the base of the carbonates here that is especially interesting. At the overhang outcrop, the carbonates rest directly on Pipe Rock – the expected Fucoid Beds and Salterella Grit members are missing. This omission implies the local action of extensional tectonics.

After debating the significance of the outcrops at the overhang, walk up onto the plateau above [NC 288 289], overlooked by the Stack of Glencoul. This site provides spectacular views south onto the NE slopes of Beinn Uidhe, dominantly formed of folded Pipe Rock and Basal Quartzite. These quartz arenites overlie Lewisian gneisses of the Glencoul Thrust Sheet, which form the steep cliffs crossed by Eas a' Chual Aluinn, Britain's highest waterfall.

The outcrops on the plateau are of Pipe Rock Member. With care, examples of *Skolithos* can be found, with moderately elliptical sections on bedding planes. In profile the burrows are inclined with respect to bedding, implying shear strains of about one. These values are intermediate between the undeformed examples found below the Glencoul Thrust on the shores of the loch, and the strongly deformed examples that can be found on the slopes of the Stack of Glencoul.

Cross the shelf and ascend the lower slopes of the Stack of Glencoul to Locality 11.3.

Locality 11.3 [NC 2888 2876]

Stack of Glencoul.

This classic locality offers opportunities to examine the mylonitic Moine psammites and Cambrian quartz arenites in the hangingwall and footwall to the Moine Thrust at the Stack of Glencoul. These mylonites belong to a belt of high strain plastically deformed Neoproterozoic and Cambrian rocks that are variably preserved along much of the length of the Moine Thrust. Arguably the Stack of Glencoul provides the most spectacular exposures of mylonite anywhere along the length of the Moine Thrust. This is a Site of Special Scientific Interest (SSSI), and is a frequently visited site for undergraduate teaching, so please do not hammer or collect any samples.

The high western cliffs of the Stack of Glencoul itself are largely composed of mylonites derived from Moine metasedimentary rocks. However, in the flatter, peaty ground beneath the cliffs, exposures are of deformed quartz arenites of the Pipe Rock Member with highly sheared pipes. Strain in these quartz arenites increases upwards, so that at the base of the cliffs the mylonites are actually derived from quartz arenite. This has led to significant controversy over the tectonic junction that should be taken to represent the Moine Thrust (*sensu stricto*). The gently ESE dipping, foliation-parallel ductile contact (Fig. 78) between the mylonitic Cambrian quartz arenite and similarly deformed overlying Moine metasedimentary rocks (and possible Lewisian gneisses) was regarded by C. T. Clough (in Peach *et al.*, 1907) as marking the position of the Moine Thrust. This theory has been supported since by a number of workers, including Christie (1963, 1965), Coward (1983), Law *et al.* (1986), and Law (1987, 1998). However, Johnson (1965) and others, including Elliott and Johnson (1980), considered the Moine Thrust (*sensu stricto*) to be a late brittle feature (as seen at Knockan Crag). In this case, the thrust would be placed at the base of the mylonitic Cambrian quartz arenites (Johnson 1967) in the unexposed ground between these strongly deformed tectonites and the underlying, relatively weakly deformed, Cambrian quartz arenites. Here, we adopt the former (and historically earlier) definition of the Moine Thrust at the Stack of Glencoul.

The macroscopic and microscopic features associated with these intensely deformed rocks were first described and interpreted by Callaway (1884). Of particular importance are: the horizon of intensely deformed

Fig. 78 The Moine Thrust at the base of the Stack of Glencoul cliffs (Locality 11.3). The scale marker rests on pale grey mylonitic Cambrian quartz arenite, which is overlain by darker grey Moine mylonites at the top of the photograph. (BGS photograph, © NERC)

Pipe Rock Member at the base of the Stack; metre-scale foreland-dipping extensional faults (or shear bands) and cm-scale back thrusts cutting the mylonitic foliation in the Cambrian quartz arenites; and isoclinally folded quartz veins in the platy pelitic Moine rocks.

The microstructures of these greenschist facies, mylonitic Cambrian quartz arenites and Moine rocks at the Stack of Glencoul were first comprehensively described by Christie (1956, 1963). The mylonites are characterised by a strongly developed foliation, which dips gently to the ESE, and a rather weak grain shape stretching lineation which plunges down the dip of the foliation planes parallel to the transport direction inferred from thrust geometries. At the Stack of Glencoul these mylonites are typically S>L tectonites. Christie recognised that the intense internal straining and ribbon-grain development of quartz grains in these mylonites was due to crystal plastic processes, and he was also amongst the first geologists worldwide to recognise that the small (<10 micron) equant quartz grains in such rocks were due to dynamic recrystallization rather than cataclasis (Christie 1960).

Quartz crystal fabrics are exceptionally well developed at the Stack of Glencoul, particularly in the mylonitic Cambrian quartz arenites. Optically measured c-axis fabrics from the mylonitic quartz arenites were first described by Christie (1956); these fabrics later became internationally renowned following publication of his seminal paper (Christie, 1963). These c-axis fabrics were famous for their high degree of symmetry relative

143

to foliation and lineation, and were regarded by Christie (1963) as indicating a relatively late stage period of vertical coaxial shortening (pure shear) overprinting asymmetric fabrics (simple shear) produced during thrust-related shearing. Unfortunately, no records were kept of the outcrop positions of these Cambrian quartz arenite samples relative to the position of the Moine Thrust at the Stack of Glencoul (J. Christie, pers. comm. to R. D. Law in 1988).

Resampling of the Cambrian quartz arenites at the Stack of Glencoul (Law *et al.*, 1986, 2010b) led to recognition of a major change in quartz fabrics with depth beneath the Moine Thrust, demonstrating that formation of asymmetric fabrics (top to the WNW shear sense) in the hangingwall and immediate footwall to the Moine Thrust must either be contemporaneous with, or later than, formation of the symmetrical fabrics at greater distances beneath the thrust. This interpretation, which is based on spatial variation in fabric symmetry, is in marked contrast to the original interpretation by Christie (1963) that the symmetric fabrics at the Stack of Glencoul indicated a relatively late stage of vertical coaxial shortening over-printing asymmetric fabrics produced during thrust-related shearing. Quantitative vorticity analysis (Law *et al.*, 2010b) indicates that flow in both the Moine and Cambrian mylonites exposed at the Stack involved a significant (45–50%) pure shear component, with only mylonites at less than 15 cm beneath the thrust being dominated by simple shear deformation (less than 30% pure shear). Integration of vorticity and 3D strain data indicates a vertical shortening of approximately 50–75% (assuming constant volume deformation) perpendicular to thrust plane/foliation in these gently dipping mylonites, with along-strike stretches of 30–50% and stretches of approximately 100–130% parallel to the thrust transport direction. These data indicate that extrusional flow was an important tectonic process during thrusting at the base of the Moine nappe.

From the Stack of Glencoul, the only reasonable return is by retracing one of the routes detailed above.

Excursion 12

Scourie Mòr

Clark Friend

Purpose: To study aspects of the Lewisian Gneiss Complex of the Assynt Terrane, including the classic Scourie Dyke.

Aspects covered: Granulite-facies felsic and mafic gneisses, Scourie Dykes.

Maps: OS: 1:50,000 Landranger sheet 9 Cape Wrath; 1:25,000 Explorer sheet 445 Foinaven, Arkle, Kylesku and Scourie. BGS: 1:50,000 Sheet 107, Glencoul.

Terrain: This excursion incorporates a number of stops around Scourie Bay, mostly involving short walks over some rough and rocky ground.

Time: The whole excursion is likely to occupy most of a day.

Access: There are no known problems with access to these sites, but please ensure that all gates are closed and that dogs are kept on leads.

Locality 12.1 [NC 148 448]

Scourie Graveyard.

Turn off the A894 at a minor junction in Scourie village, on the south side of the bay, and park just before the graveyard. Go through the gate in the north-west wall of the graveyard and walk onto the gneiss outcrops north of the main beach, Port an Tagail. These outcrops include one of the classic examples of a Scourie Dyke (Fig. 79). Because the dykes in the Scourie area are relatively little deformed, an estimate of the amount of crustal extension that this segment of continental crust underwent may be made here. This locality is best visited at low tide, but outcrops can be reached at any tide state.

The gneisses on the headland of Meallan an Tiodhlacaidh [NC 149 449] are typical tonalitic, granulite-facies gneisses that have suffered intense ductile strain, reflected by a strong compositional banding comprising

145

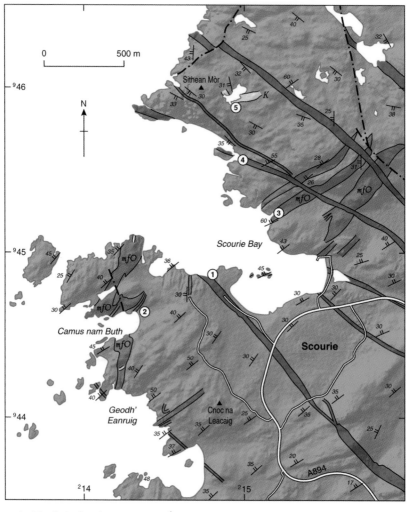

Lewisian Gneiss Complex

$\mathcal{D}$	Scourie Dyke Swarm: metadolerite
K	Metasedimentary gneisses
O	Orthogneiss
mfO	Mafic and ultramafic orthogneiss

——— Geological boundary, bedrock

—·—·— Fault

44 ⤢ Inclined gneissose foliation, dip in degrees

Fig. 79 Simplified geological map of the Scourie area, after Mendum, *et al.* (2009), showing the localities described in Excursion 12.

finely interbanded orthopyroxene-bearing tonalitic layers and thin, discontinuous, plagioclase-rich leucocratic layers. Because the gneisses are essentially unretrogressed, these events appear to be pre- or syn-granulite facies metamorphism and prior to dyke emplacement. No distinct lithological boundaries are evident in the gneisses, due to extensive granulite-facies recrystallisation and ductile deformation. Scattered throughout the gneisses are numerous small, dark green to black, lens-shaped, hornblendite pods up to ~1 m across. These are contained within the structure and larger pods preserve the process of break-up, demonstrating stages in the formation of the smaller hornblendite pods that appear to be derived from larger mafic-ultramafic bodies. In a few places orthopyroxene is patchily absent from the quartzo-feldspathic gneisses owing to a greater degree of late hydrous retrogression.

Several Scourie dykes in the vicinity are relatively little deformed, preserving discordant relations with structures in the host gneisses. Between Port an Tagail and Meallan an Tiodhlacaidh are two sub-parallel dykes, both trending roughly ESE. The southern, larger, dyke belongs to the ophitic-textured, quartz-bearing, microgabbroic type (Tarney and Weaver, 1987) and is one of the most studied in the suite. Whilst little deformed, both dykes have been variably sheared and hydrated to amphibole-bearing assemblages ± garnet demonstrating that they were subject to amphibolite-facies (Laxfordian) metamorphism (e.g. O'Hara, 1961a).

The thinner dyke ($c.0.75$ m) is exposed on the rock platform $c.50$ m north of the thicker dyke, and has a contact displaced by numerous small faults that appear to be related to joints in the host gneisses. On the basis of the textures, most of these faults do not appear to go through the dyke and displace it. These joints could be interpreted to have been active during dyke emplacement indicating a brittle regime. However, there is still debate as to whether the dykes were emplaced into hot or cold rocks. The whole of this dyke has been hydrated and no remnants of igneous minerals occur, though small, granular aggregates of plagioclase appear to retain a texture resembling igneous domains in a microgabbro. Small (<5 mm) garnet porphyroblasts are present amongst dark greenish amphibole and plagioclase (± quartz).

The thicker dyke is sub-vertical, $c.55$ m thick, and forms a distinct gully on the shoreline north of the graveyard. This dyke has a Rb-Sr whole rock isochron age of 2390 ± 20 Ma (Chapman, 1979). It is asymmetrically zoned across its width and shows several different internal responses to later deformation and metamorphism, which in part depend upon distance from the margin of the dyke. At its northern contact a zone of about 1–2 m of variably foliated and sheared amphibolite occurs with small, rounded garnet porphyroblasts, resembling the thinner dyke, and probably representing a chilled margin. A transition zone follows from the foliated margin through a zone of decreasing strain into areas that are essentially undeformed. Within this zone, thin (*c.* 1–2 mm), cross-cutting, discontinuous garnet veinlets can be found. These veinlets appear to be late, as they cross the weak shear fabric. Traversing southwards, the shear foliation continues to decrease in intensity and a relict, ophitic igneous texture becomes apparent with relict igneous ortho- and clinopyroxene, mainly replaced by amphibole and some biotite. Towards the centre of the dyke, the amount of amphibole decreases and garnet coronas between plagioclase and pyroxenes give the rock a pinkish colour. This zone extends towards the southern contact where there is a thin zone of foliated, amphibolitised material against the host gneiss.

The gneisses on the southern contact are typically more mafic than on the north side, and spectacular coronitic garnets including reaction relations with ortho- and clinopyroxene can be found. The state of the tide will dictate how far north-west along the contact can be reached.

Locality 12.2 [NC 143 443]

Scourie Mòr [NC 144 446] to Geodh' Eanruig.

Drive back to the A894, turn south and take the next turning on the right at [NC 153 440] towards Scouriemore, and park close to the primary school. Walk up the Scouriemore road to its end, and just before the last house, turn left and go out through a gate onto open moorland. Walk towards the low hills on the north side of the bay of Camas nam Buth [NC 143 447].

The outcrops in the area immediately west of the road are fairly typical felsic gneisses of the Assynt Terrane. These gneisses are broadly tonalitic or dioritic in composition and are typically dark grey-brown when fresh. They are commonly banded, with layers of felsic gneiss alternating with more mafic gneiss, frequently foliated and in some places lineated, though outcrop-scale fold structures are uncommon. Orthopyroxene, commonly associated with garnet, is extensive and provides evidence for granulite-facies metamorphic conditions. The lithological layering is mostly foliation-parallel and any original relations between the slightly different acid

Fig. 80 View north across Camas nam Buth, Locality 12.2. The low hills on the north side of the bay are largely made up of mafic to ultramafic layered gneisses with sheets of felsic gneiss. (BGS photograph P706764, © NERC)

Fig. 81 Outcrop of layered mafic-ultramafic gneiss on the north side of Camas nam Buth at Locality 12.2. These outcrops have suffered generally low strain, so that this layering is thought to be igneous in origin. (BGS photograph P593099, © NERC)

lithologies have largely been obliterated due to extensive recrystallisation during high strain under granulite-facies conditions. Syn-granulite facies deformation appears to have occurred in a ductile environment because orthopyroxene commonly defines a lineation and, together with discontinuous quartz ribbons, is found parallel to the banding and foliation.

On the low hills around [NC 143 447] are outcrops of layered mafic-ultramafic gneisses. These are part of a large mafic-ultramafic body (hundreds of metres across) that outcrops on the north side of Camas nam Buth (Figs 80, 81), and is part of a suite of similar bodies scattered around Scourie Bay. Some of these mafic-ultramafic bodies outline map-scale folds. The ultramafic bodies display a variety of lithologies that are commonly inter-layered, grading from pure dunite through clinopyroxene- and/or orthopyroxene-rich varieties into spinel-lherzolites and peridotites. Common mineral assemblages at Scourie Mòr are opx-cpx-olivine in the peridotites and opx-cpx-pargasite ± spinel ± olivine in the pyroxenites. The mafic rocks are generally more homogeneous, commonly with two pyroxenes + plagioclase + garnet with accessory spinel, sulphides and FeTi oxides. There are some layers in which prominent garnet porphyroblasts, up to 5cm diameter, have grown; good examples can be seen at [NC 1436 4470]. These normally have plagioclase-rich, symplectic decompression coronas around them that, where the garnets are small, completely replace them. The decompression symplectites vary according to the FeO:MgO ratio of the rock and have been used to constrain a *PT* path (Savage and

149

Sills, 1980; Rollinson 1981). That these delicate granulite-facies textures survive demonstrates the general lack of later, hydrous deformation.

Along the north shore of Camas nam Buth, where overall strain appears to have been relatively low, sheets and sub-parallel masses of felsic gneiss are interleaved with some of the ultramafic/mafic rocks, and veins of felsic material intrude the more mafic gneisses, clearly cross-cutting the mineral layering. This relationship is consistent with similar instances on the north side of Scourie Bay (e.g. Friend and Kinny, 1995), but does not fit with dating studies from the area. An early Sm/Nd study of Scourie Mòr peridotites gave an age of 2670 ±110 Ma (Whitehouse, 1989), and this emplacement age for the mafic-ultramafic bodies has been supported by Re-Os studies which suggested that emplacement occurred at 2687 ± 15 Ma (Burton *et al.*, 2000). These dates apparently conflict with 2960–3030 Ma U-Pb ages for the protoliths of the felsic gneisses (Friend and Kinny 1995; Kinny and Friend 1997). Possible explanations for this include: (a) the felsic gneisses are indeed older, and the apparently cross-cutting sheets are rheomorphic veins formed when the magmas were emplaced at *c.*2687 Ma; or (b) the mafic-ultramafic bodies are older, but their isotopic systems have been disturbed during their long and complex history.

At Camas nam Buth the mafic-ultramafic bodies have been shown to represent fragmented layered complexes, through extensive geochemistry that demonstrated cryptic layering and established a consistent geochemical way up, which could be traced over two sets of fold hinges (Sills *et al.*, 1982). It is now accepted that the ultramafic and mafic rocks have suffered the same metamorphic history as the gneisses, but the survival of any remnants of the primary igneous minerals is still debated.

From the head of Camas nam Buth, pick up a rough path that winds along the south side of the bay just above the shoreline. Continue SSW, over a low col between two rocky knolls, towards Geodh' Eanruig [NC 142 442]. Here, mafic-ultramafic gneisses similar to those at Camas nam Buth can be seen, including some pyroxene-rich varieties with large garnet porphyroblasts. Also in this area are examples of cross-cutting, broadly ESE-trending, narrow Scourie Dykes as at [NC 1412 4418], mostly with microgabbroic texture and essentially undeformed but amphibolitised. The area is cut by hydrous shear zones, many of which coincide with the margins of parts of the dykes. As these shears and associated metamorphism affect the Scourie Dykes, they are of presumed Laxfordian age.

The gneisses at Geodh' Eanruig [NC 142 442] are cut by a largely undeformed sheet of pegmatitic granite (Fig. 82), with spectacular crystals of pink alkali feldspar, showing graphic texture on a very coarse scale. With some searching, it is possible to find outcrops in which a Scourie Dyke cuts across this pegmatite (e.g. [NC 1415 4418]), and the pegmatite is thus considered to be Inverian in age. From Geodh' Eanruig, return eastwards across moorland to the road.

Locality 12.3 [NC 152 453]

First Inlet.

Drive back onto the A894 and turn north; just beyond the caravan site, at [NC 1550 4460], turn left and park before the pier. From the pier, climb a steep path up the slope to the north and then follow a field wall in a north-west direction until it abruptly turns north [NC 1535 4520]. If the path appears very overgrown or parking is difficult, it is also possible to park at the public toilets on the main road through Scourie and follow the minor road that turns into a track through a farm at [NC 1570 4510], then walk west through the fields beyond the farm to reach the same point.

Continue north along the wall to cross a small stream and then descend steeply to the beach at First Inlet. This locality can be visited at any state of the tide, but is better with low water.

Layered ultramafic and mafic bodies, which have been interpreted to

Fig. 82 View of the outcrops at Geodh' Eanruig, with a prominent pink pegmatitic granite sheet in the foreground. This intrusion cuts the local mafic gneisses, but is in turn cut by a Scourie Dyke. (BGS photograph P667680, © NERC)

151

belong to the same supracrustal suite exposed on Scourie Mòr, are contained in granulite-facies gneisses and form a distinct ridge in the middle of the inlet. The clear peridotite-pyroxenite layering appears to outline the nose of a fold that possibly links south to those on Scourie Mòr. On the north side of the inlet, boulders often obscure the relationships with mafic rocks that contain spectacular decompression textures. Good examples can be found in the loose blocks and there is a very complex prograde and retrograde metamorphic history preserved in these textures. On a gross scale the ultramafic body appears to be concordant within the gneisses. However, the internal layering is cross-cut by sheets and veins of tonalite that have bluish quartz on fresh surfaces and carry orthopyroxene with the same linear fabric as the gneisses outside. Zircons from one sheet have a maximum age of ~2960 Ma, which matches the age of a gneiss sample from the ridge above the bay to the north, and is interpreted as the igneous age of the sheet, not the age of an inherited component (Friend and Kinny, 1995).

On the south side of the inlet, a prominent, thin layer of pyroxene + quartz + magnetite (+ minor garnet) rock is interpreted as an ironstone and thus considered to represent sedimentary material (Barnicoat and O'Hara, 1979). This unit contains manganiferous pigeonitic pyroxene from which exsolution lamellae compositions suggest temperatures of at least 1000°C were attained.

If time permits, in the next inlet to the north-west ('Second Inlet') good exposures of the relationships between ultramafic and gabbroic lithologies are seen, again with intercalated gneiss sheets. Thin, rusty, brown-weathering sulphide bands that are garnetiferous may be sedimentary in origin.

Locality 12.4 [NC 150 456]

Poll Eòrna.

Climb out of First Inlet on the north side and then head north between two knolls to the foot of a prominent rise. Turn north-west along a grassy gully (in fact the trace of a Scourie Dyke) to a small raised beach that slopes down to the present beach (Fig. 83). The rocky beach is eroded into a *c.*35 m-thick WNW–ESE Scourie Dyke that emerges on the shore at [NC 149 456]. Best visited at low tide, this dyke dips *c.*80° northwards and can be seen to continue on the same strike across the bay to the north-west where it occurs

Fig. 83 The Scourie Dyke at Poll Eòrna. The figures on the beach are standing on the Scourie Dyke, which forms a weathered gully that is also traceable on the far headland. (BGS photograph P593100, © NERC)

in a marked notch through the headland of Creag a' Mhàil. It is considered to be the type Scourie Dyke, first described by Teall (1885) and later by O'Hara (1961b), and cuts granulite-facies quartzo-feldspathic gneisses that can be examined along either contact.

The felsic gneisses contain, and appear to break up, layers and lenses of mafic to ultramafic gneisses, which are locally interlayered with brownish-weathering, biotite-rich rocks interpreted to be of metasedimentary origin (O'Hara, 1960, 1961b). These latter rocks probably represent a continuum with those recognised on Sìthean Mòr [NC 150 460] about 350m to the north. The host gneisses demonstrate a variable degree of retrogression and associated shear fabric development. In some places on the dyke contact discordances are still preserved, but most frequently there are sections where a completely new amphibolite-facies fabric parallel to the dyke margin has developed.

Whilst the Scourie Dyke is essentially undeformed on a large scale, it has suffered much internal deformation and metamorphism, assumed to be Laxfordian, and is now amphibolitised. The centre still preserves a relict ophitic texture, with variably amphibolitised pyroxene still visible.

The dyke is cut by many amphibolite-facies shear zones that have two dominant directions; sub-parallel to the margins of the dyke, and at a high angle across the dyke. Inspection of these shears suggests that they are linked and the new fabrics indicate a dominantly dextral sense of movement. The NE–SW shear zones cause a marked dextral displacement by some 2m of the contact on the north side of the beach, interpreted as consistent with development by simple shear deformation (Ramsay and Graham, 1970). The shear zones become much wider in the gneisses outside

153

the dyke and two main hypotheses have been debated. Were there two shearing episodes? Was the dyke emplaced towards the end of the shearing event? As at Scourie Graveyard 1–2 mm straight to highly irregular veinlets of garnet cross-cut the late shear foliation in the dyke. Some of the straight veins may be developed in conjugate sets with SE and SSE directions, whilst the more irregular ones have random orientations. Obviously all of this metamorphism and deformation is post-shearing and clearly indicates that the metamorphic history of the Assynt Terrane is not as straightforward as it might appear.

Locality 12.5 [NC 150 461]

Sìthean Mòr.

From the beach, ascend steeply northwards following the eastern side of a small stream up to a lochan and pass round to the north shore.

Here brown-weathering granulite-facies gneisses are interlayered with garnetiferous metabasic rocks, interpreted as a sediment-lava supracrustal succession. The most abundant lithologies are quartz-plagioclase-garnet-biotite gneisses. These rocks commonly appear in the field as rusty brown weathering gneisses, probably because of a small but significant sulphide content. These rocks are described as being traversed by slightly paler-coloured Laxfordian shear zones (Beach, 1973) in which small blades of kyanite occur. Monazites from these rocks have been dated by Zhu *et al.* (1997), who found evidence for two episodes of granulite-facies meta-morphism at *c.*2760 Ma and *c.*2526 Ma, followed by Laxfordian metamor-phism at 1750 Ma, during which the kyanite formed.

From here, retrace your steps back to the vehicles.

Excursion 13

Tarbet

Kathryn Goodenough and Maarten Krabbendam

Purpose: To study the rocks around the Laxford Shear Zone, a probable terrane boundary in the Lewisian Gneiss Complex.

Aspects covered: Lewisian ortho- and paragneisses, large mafic bodies within the Lewisian, a Precambrian shear zone, Laxfordian granites.

Maps: OS: 1:50,000 Landranger sheet 9 Cape Wrath; 1:25,000 Explorer sheet 445 Foinaven, Arkle, Kylesku and Scourie. BGS: 1:50,000 Sheet 107, Glencoul.

Terrain: This excursion involves a relatively short walk (5 km), but it is strenuous in that it crosses rough, undulating, heathery and locally boggy ground without a clear path. Some steep, rocky and vegetated slopes must be ascended and descended.

Time: The excursion will occupy most of a day.

Access: There should be no problems with access to this area, but please ensure that you leave all gates as you find them on this crofting land, and keep dogs on leads.

Park just above the pier at Tarbet, where there are abundant parking spaces. Go through the gate behind and to the right of the public toilets, and walk through the field behind the Shorehouse Restaurant to reach the rocky knoll immediately on the north side of the bay. These outcrops lie on the south side of the Laxford Shear Zone, and are thus within the Assynt Terrane. However, this area has been largely retrogressed to amphibolite-facies during the Laxfordian event. The excursion represents a traverse north-eastwards, towards and across the Laxford Shear Zone (Fig. 84).

155

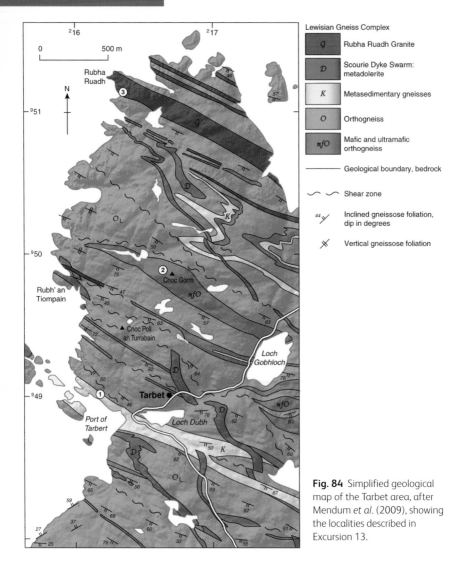

Lewisian Gneiss Complex

g	Rubha Ruadh Granite
D	Scourie Dyke Swarm: metadolerite
K	Metasedimentary gneisses
O	Orthogneiss
mfO	Mafic and ultramafic orthogneiss
———	Geological boundary, bedrock
⌒ ⌒	Shear zone
44 ⤢	Inclined gneissose foliation, dip in degrees
✕	Vertical gneissose foliation

Fig. 84 Simplified geological map of the Tarbet area, after Mendum *et al.* (2009), showing the localities described in Excursion 13.

Locality 13.1 [NC 1615 4902]

North side of Port of Tarbet.

Outcrops on both sides of the low fence are of mafic and felsic gneisses with bands of rusty-weathering, medium- to coarse-grained garnet-biotite-plagio-clase-quartz schist (Fig. 85). These 'brown schists' are interpreted as being

Fig. 85 Outcrops of brown-weathering metasedimentary rocks on the north side of Port of Tarbet, Locality 13.1. (BGS photograph P593106, © NERC)

Fig. 86 (below) Schematic cross-section through the Laxford Shear Zone, showing the major structures, after Goodenough *et al.* (2010).

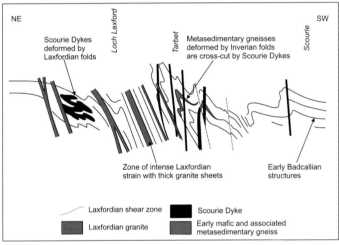

metasedimentary. They form a unit running along the southern side of the Laxford Shear Zone, and along strike to the south-east they are associated with large meta-mafic bodies. Their age is not known, though they are cross-cut by, and thus undoubtedly pre-date, the Scourie Dykes. The foliation in this unit dips steeply toward the south-west; the rocks are strongly lineated. Discontinuous outcrops of coarse-grained, foliated pink-weathering rock containing quartz, K-feldspar and biotite may represent a deformed granite sheet within the metasedimentary rocks.

From there, walk north-east across strike of the gneisses, crossing rocky knolls and gullies that are typically eroded along narrow, discrete Laxfordian shear zones. The second gully [NC 1615 4915] separates the metasedimentary gneisses from more typical quartzofeldspathic Lewisian gneisses of the Assynt Terrane to the north-east. These gneisses have a strong, steeply-dipping foliation and an intense lineation, which are considered to be the

157

Fig. 87 Thin, pink granitic sheets cutting amphibolitic gneisses, strongly foliated and tightly folded by Inverian deformation, [NC 1638 4932]. (BGS photograph P618228, © NERC)

Fig. 88 Coarse-grained, essentially undeformed Laxfordian granite sheet cutting across gneisses with a strong Inverian foliation, [NC 1635 4940]. (BGS photograph P593114, © NERC)

Fig. 89 View from south to Cnoc Gorm (Locality 13.2), showing the distinctive dark-coloured mafic gneiss which gives the hill its name. (BGS photograph P593116, © NERC)

products of Inverian deformation, whilst Laxfordian deformation is concentrated in the discrete shear zones (Fig. 86).

Some layers and lenses of more mafic hornblende-rich gneiss are seen within the felsic gneisses. Around [NC 1638 4932], on the sides of a shallow valley, amphibole-rich gneisses are cut by thin, pink-weathering, medium-grained, strongly foliated granitoid sheets (Fig. 87). The south-west-dipping foliation is defined principally by elongated 'ribbons' of quartz. Both gneisses and granitoid sheets are folded into tight, upright folds that are axial planar to the main Inverian foliation. Across the valley at [NC 1635 4940], relatively undeformed Laxfordian pegmatitic granite sheets cut the deformed lithologies (Fig. 88); this is essentially the most southerly extent of the Laxfordian granites, and provides clear evidence that they cut the Assynt Terrane (Goodenough *et al.*, 2010).

Continue northwards along that shallow valley past further tightly folded gneiss outcrops, and then drop down a steep scarp to a flat area with several lochans. Beyond this flat area are the steep slopes of Cnoc Gorm.

Locality 13.2 [NC 1675 4985]

Cnoc Gorm.

The hill of Cnoc Gorm (blue hill) is composed of coarse-grained, dark grey weathering garnet-bearing metagabbro (Fig. 89). This is part of a large-scale belt of Archaean meta-mafic bodies, locally associated with meta-sedimentary rocks, which extends south-east along the southern side of the Laxford Shear Zone. The Cnoc Gorm metagabbro is characterised by areas with dark red garnet crystals up to 5 cm across, which are commonly surrounded by albitic rims formed during decompression. The metamafic bodies in this zone show a range of mineral assemblages; granulite-facies (Badcallian) mineral assemblages (cpx + plagioclase ± garnet ± opx) are locally preserved, although parts of the unit have been retrogressed, with the growth of amphibole. The metamafic rocks are veined by a number of tonalite sheets, up to about a metre in thickness. The metagabbros show a strong south-west dipping foliation and south-east plunging lineation, and the foliation can be seen to wrap round the garnets. The metagabbro is cut through, and bounded by, a number of narrow, curving shear zones of Laxfordian age.

From the summit of Cnoc Gorm, continue northwards over more rocky knolls towards Rubha Ruadh. The outcrops in this area are of tightly folded gneisses, cut by scattered pegmatitic granite sheets. A north-west trending Scourie Dyke can be shown to cut across the folds, constraining them to be Inverian rather than Laxfordian in age. However, the Scourie Dyke itself is locally folded. This area thus shows evidence for reactivation of an Inverian shear zone during the Laxfordian.

Descend down a heathery gully towards the coast, and then walk west towards Rubha Ruadh.

Locality 13.3 [NC 1650 5115]

Rubha Ruadh.

Rubha Ruadh (Red Point) is formed of a sheet of coarse-grained, foliated pink Laxfordian granite, about 1 km in width and north-west to south-east trending. Within the granite sheet are abundant pegmatitic patches. The

159

mafic minerals in this thick granitic sheet include a blue-green alkali amphibole and grass-green aegirine-augite; this contrasts with the thinner granitic sheets and pegmatitic granites occurring in this area, in which biotite is the main mafic mineral. An example of a biotite-bearing granitic sheet from near Laxford Bridge has been dated at 1854 ± 13 Ma (Friend and Kinny, 2001).

The southern margin of the Rubha Ruadh granite sheet is sharp and broadly parallel to the gneissic banding in the host rocks. This margin has been considered by some authors to represent the boundary between the Assynt and Rhiconich terranes at this point. In this area there are a number of schistose, ultramafic lenses, consisting mainly of biotite with subsidiary hornblende, formed by metasomatism of mafic bodies along the shear zone that represents the terrane boundary.

On the north side of the granite sheet, the gneisses of the Rhiconich Terrane (exposed to the east of Rubha Ruadh) are biotite- and hornblende-bearing quartzofeldspathic gneisses. The gneisses are foliated, but lack the distinct lineation seen in many outcrops to the south. These gneisses are typically migmatitic, with abundant patches and irregular sheets of granite and granitic pegmatite. Geochemical analyses have shown that the gneisses of the Rhiconich Terrane have higher average K_2O, Rb, Th and U contents than the gneisses of the Assynt Terrane (Sheraton et al., 1973).

From Rubha Ruadh, one possibility is to retrace your steps to Tarbet. A diversion can be taken on the way to see an interesting example of a wide composite Scourie Dyke on the coast at Poll an Turrabain [NC 161 495], which thins rapidly inland. This spectacular dyke was described by Beach (1978) as a complex mixture of three rock types: felsic, mafic and 'normal' dolerite. It has a discordant contact with the host rock gneisses, of which it contains a number of xenoliths. It shows variable Laxfordian deformation that ranges from a marginal strong penetrative foliation to anastomosing shear zones and areas that retain an igneous texture. From the south end of the dyke follow a rough path up the obvious gully south-east and rejoin the outwards route.

Alternatively, walk along the coast from Rubha Ruadh as far as [NC 175 503], then turn south to join the road to Fanagmore and return along the road.

160

Excursion 14

Durness, Balnakeil Bay and Faraid Head

Robert Raine, Paul Smith,
Bob Holdsworth and Rob Strachan

Purpose: To examine the carbonate rocks of the Durness Group and the faulted exposures of the Moine Thrust Sheet.

Aspects covered: Carbonate sedimentology and sequence stratigraphy, Cambro-Ordovician stratigraphy, Moine and basement-derived mylonites, Caledonian thrusts, and post-Caledonian faults.

Maps: OS: 1:50,000 Landranger sheet 15 Cape Wrath; 1:25,000 Explorer sheet 446 Durness and Cape Wrath. BGS: Scotland sheet 114W Loch Eriboll.

Terrain: Coastal paths and wave-cut platform.

Time: The main part of the excursion (Localities 14.1–14.13), around Balnakeil Bay, including Durness Group and Moine litho-logies and Caledonian structures, will take a full day. The additional localities (14.14–14.18) can be visited separately, depending on the interests of the party. An alternative day is to combine Localities 14.1–14.10 with 14.14, 14.15 and 14.17; in this way a complete review of the foreland carbonates of the Durness Group can be undertaken in the type area, in ascending stratigraphic order.

Access: This excursion largely comprises coastal outcrops and no access problems are known. The first part of the excursion is adjacent to Durness golf course, and care should obviously be taken in this area. All the outcrops in this excursion lie in Sites of Scientific Interest, and thus hammering should be avoided.

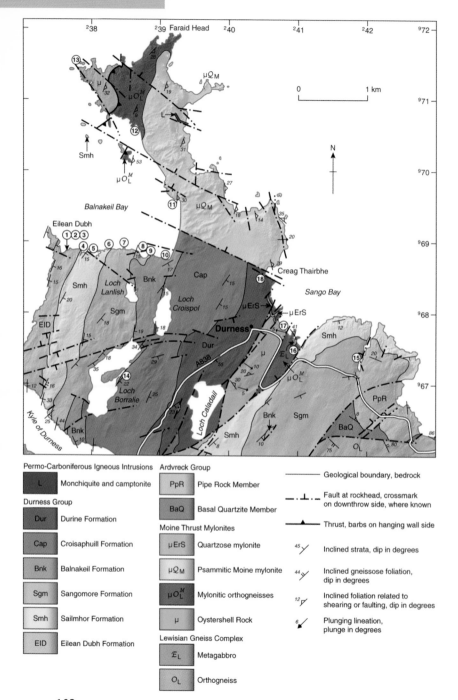

Permo-Carboniferous Igneous Intrusions

L Monchiquite and camptonite

Durness Group

Dur Durine Formation

Cap Croisaphuill Formation

Bnk Balnakeil Formation

Sgm Sangomore Formation

Smh Sailmhor Formation

EID Eilean Dubh Formation

Ardvreck Group

PpR Pipe Rock Member

BaQ Basal Quartzite Member

Moine Thrust Mylonites

μErS Quartzose mylonite

μQM Psammitic Moine mylonite

μOLM Mylonitic orthogneisses

μ Oystershell Rock

Lewisian Gneiss Complex

ƐL Metagabbro

OL Orthogneiss

——— Geological boundary, bedrock

─··┴··─ Fault at rockhead, crossmark on downthrow side, where known

──▲── Thrust, barbs on hanging wall side

⁴⁵⟋ Inclined strata, dip in degrees

⁴⁴⟋ Inclined gneissose foliation, dip in degrees

¹²⟋ Inclined foliation related to shearing or faulting, dip in degrees

⁶⟋ Plunging lineation, plunge in degrees

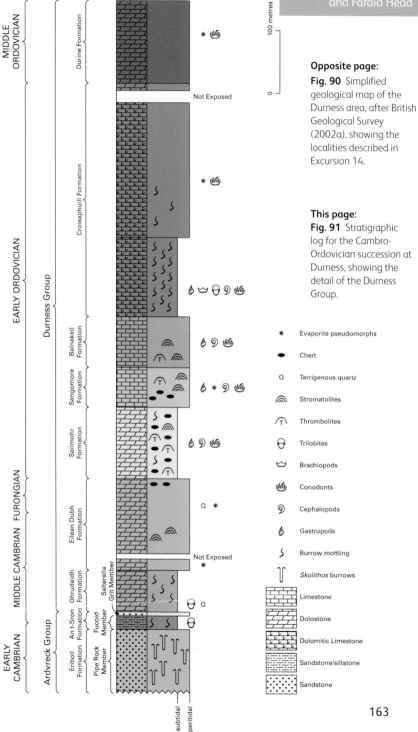

Opposite page:

Fig. 90 Simplified geological map of the Durness area, after British Geological Survey (2002a), showing the localities described in Excursion 14.

This page:

Fig. 91 Stratigraphic log for the Cambro-Ordovician succession at Durness, showing the detail of the Durness Group.

* Evaporite pseudomorphs
● Chert
Q Terrigenous quartz
🝆 Stromatolites
⊤ Thrombolites
Ɵ Trilobites
🝑 Brachiopods
🌿 Conodonts
𝓰 Cephalopods
𝓫 Gastropods
𝑆 Burrow mottling
𝕌 *Skolithos* burrows

Limestone
Dolostone
Dolomitic Limestone
Sandstone/siltstone
Sandstone

163

Excursion 14A: Balnakeil Bay and Faraid Head

In the centre of Durness village, turn left at Mackay's Hotel, signposted to Balnakeil. After 2km Balnakeil Church is reached, where there is a public car-park. To the west are exposures of carbonates of the Durness Group, which will be visited first; to the north is the Faraid Head outlier of the Moine Thrust Sheet, which constitutes the second part of the excursion (Fig. 90).

From the car-park, walk along the continuation of the road to the golf club and then walk west across the golf course to the head of a small bay to the east of Eilean Dubh, adjacent to the deserted village of Solmar [NC 735 686]. The beach sand at the head of the bay is a mixture of quartz sand and a typical foramol carbonate assemblage, with abundant bryozoa, calcareous algae and some forams.

The carbonates of the Durness Group contain a particularly diverse range of sedimentary rocks generated and/or mediated by bacteria (Fig. 91). These are collectively termed microbialites and include stromatolites (with a laminated fabric), thrombolites (with a clotted mesofabric) and leiolites (internally structureless). Although sediments of this type originated in the Palaeoproterozoic, the Early Ordovician represents the final major flourish of this distinctive type of biogenic sediment. From the mid-Ordovician onwards, microbialites are restricted to a range of niche environments rather than constituting the dominant components of continent-scale sedimentary systems.

Locality 14.1 [NC 3762 6878]

Type sequence of the Eilean Dubh Formation.

The coast eastwards from the small bay exposes the upper part of the Eilean Dubh Formation (minimum exposed thickness 120m). Walk northwards along the eastern edge of the bay, climbing over small ledges to the base of a small cliff [NC 3762 6878]. The Eilean Dubh Formation here comprises typical peritidal facies, with well-developed ripple and parallel lamination and flaser bedding overlying structureless microbial domes, indicating a muddy tidal flat environment. Thin beds and laminae of millet seed quartz sand and brown siliciclastic silts, of probable aeolian origin, punctuate the laminated facies. At the foot of the main cliff, *c.*5 m below the top, is a horizon containing distinctive gutter casts, with axes slightly less than perpendicular to the cliff face, which have been accentuated by compaction and pressure solution. The orientation of these is consistent with them being developed perpendicular to the shoreface. Forty centimetres above the gutters is a distinctive flake conglomerate containing reworked intraclasts of local carbonate material that is overlain by hackly weathering, crinkly laminated microbialite (Fig. 92). The development of metre-scale shallowing upwards units (parasequences) is here characterised by an alternation of stromatolites with a variety of microbial and current-laminated dolostones.

Locality 14.2 [NC 3765 6879]

Stromatolites in the Eilean Dubh Formation.

Return to the head of the bay and walk back along the cliff top to a point directly above the last locality. Spectacular 1–2 m wide domed and columnar stromatolites rest on top of a flake conglomerate and possible thrombolites that mark the base of the parasequence. The stromatolites are draped by fine-grained peritidal dolostones that cap the parasequence and contain ripple lamination, contorted lamination, laminae of millet seed sand grains and acicular cavities left after the dissolution of evaporates (Fig. 93); there are also occasional halite pseudomorphs. Laminites above this horizon are contorted and contain well-developed tepee structures and irregular quartz nodules, the latter probably representing pseudomorphed anhydrite.

Fig. 92 Flake conglomerate comprising reworked intraclasts of local carbonates within the Eilean Dubh Formation at Locality 14.1, [NC 376 687]. The brown weathering of the clasts indicates a component of detrital quartz silt within the early cemented carbonates, derived from supratidal flat facies. (Photograph: © R. J. Raine)

165

Locality 14.3 [NC 3769 6880]

Walk east over rock ledges at a level a few metres beneath the base of the grass slope to the next locality. Locality 14.3 shows further details of microbialite–sediment relationships. A vuggy but otherwise structureless, microbialite mound is flanked by a breccia with angular clasts composed of peritidal laminites. Other mounds occur at the same horizon, some of which show faint stromatolitic lamination and irregular mottling. Beds composed of millet seed quartz grains drape the mound horizon and pass upward into peritidal dolostones with tepee structures. Farther eastwards, across a small fault that throws down to the north, is a spectacular flake conglomerate with large but relatively thin, red-weathering intraclasts. Mudstone intra-clasts such as these result from desiccation and subsequent reworking during storm or flooding events on supratidal flats.

Locality 14.4 [NC 3782 6878]

Eilean Dubh–Sailmhor Formation boundary.

Walk up the grass bank and eastwards along the cliff top to the next promontory of pale grey Eilean Dubh Formation, immediately before a dark cliff farther to the east. Descend the steep grass bank with care and then walk across the wave-cut platform to the foot of the black cliff. The upper Eilean Dubh Formation comprises pale grey weathering dolostones with ripple lamination; cherts preserve ooids, which must have been more common prior to diagenesis and dolomitisation of these sediments. The abrupt change from pale to dark dolostones at around 1 m above the base of the cliff marks the Eilean Dubh–Sailmhor formation boundary. Cono-dont collections (Huselbee, 1998) indicate that the Cambro-Ordovician boundary lies in the upper few metres of the Eilean Dubh Formation. The boundary marks a major facies change from peritidally dominated dolostones of the Eilean Dubh Formation to the dark, subtidal Sailmhor Formation. This coincides with a major eustatic shift that is seen globally at the base of the Ordovician, and in north-east Laurentia a similar transition is seen at the same level in North Greenland, East Greenland and New-foundland.

Fig. 94 Dark grey dolostones of the Sailmhor Formation at Locality 14.5 [NC 3788 6881]. The 1 m yellow rule marks the boundary between two shallowing upward parasequences. The lower part comprises lighter grey, finer grained intertidal dolostones with domal stromatolites, commonly with prominent cherts between stromatolite mounds; the cherts preserve stromatolite laminae as pale–dark alternations. Above the rule, darker subtidal dolostones show characteristic 'leopard rock' texture. (Photograph: © M. P. Smith)

Fig. 93 Cavities formed from the dissolution of evaporite pseudomorphs in Eilean Dubh Formation dolostone [NC 376 687]. The euhedral crystal shape indicates that the mineral was originally gypsum or anhydrite, but the cavities are now filled with non-ferroan calcite in unweathered material. (Photograph: © R. J. Raine)

Locality 14.5 [NC 3788 6881]

Face in Sailmhor Formation.

Return to the top of the cliff and walk around to a point directly above the last locality. Prominent pinnacles of dark Sailmhor Formation carbonates adorn the top of the cliff, and around 20 m farther east is a face with prominent white chert nodules. **BEWARE – there are deep shafts (blowholes) immediately in front of this face.** The cherts are laminated and pillow- or balloon-shaped (Fig. 94), and lie in the depressions between large stromatolite domes. The dark host rock is distinctively mottled, and has often been informally termed 'leopard rock'. The origins of the mottling have been much debated and variously attributed to bioturbation, diagenetic artefact, or thrombolites. Although bioturbation with superficially similar patterns does occur in the Durness Group, it is not likely to be the cause here since burrow junctions are not seen on bedding surfaces. The mottling is here considered to be thrombolitic in origin, with each individual thrombolite body being rather biostromal or tabular in form, although a degree of diagenetic modification as a product of dolomitisation is recognised. Parasequences are well-developed, with biostromal thrombolites at the

167

bases overlain by the large domal stromatolites. Increased sediment accommodation space at the base of the next parasequence, created by a rise in relative sea-level, is recorded by the small, chert-replaced columnar stromatolites that frequently occur on top of the domal forms.

Regain the coastal path and continue to walk eastwards to where a prominent deep geo lies on a fault plane. Inland, farther along the fault, a fenced-off blowhole is seen [NC 3813 6869]. The top of the blowhole reveals collapsed sections through the superficial deposits overlying the Sailmhor Formation; a thin till with clasts predominantly composed of Eriboll Formation quartz arenites and Lewisian Gneiss Complex lithologies is overlain by the base of the blown sand unit that dominates the landscape in Balnakeil Bay. Carry on eastwards along the coastal path across a bare landscape of winnowed tills with quartzite and gneiss clasts overlying fractured carbonates of the upper Sailmhor Formation. Continue until the cliff path ascends a marked change in slope, with a cairn to the left at the base of the slope. Leave the path and descend towards the sea, bearing right towards the foot of a cliff with a prominent notch at the base.

Locality 14.6 [NC 3836 6885]

Sailmhor–Sangomore Formation boundary.

The notch at the base of the cliff marks the Sailmhor–Sangomore Formation boundary (Fig. 95). The uppermost part of the Sailmhor Formation contains coarsely crystalline dolostones, which in places contain preserved ooids (one well-preserved horizon lies 1.5m below the top of the formation).

Abundant coast-parallel fractures that cross the upper Sailmhor Formation are deeply eroded by karstic weathering and commonly contain a partial fill of cemented beachrock. The fissures continue westwards across the bare ground and were mistaken as an intra-Ordovician unconformity by Palmer et al. (1980). The existence of the unconformity has been questioned on the basis of Sr isotope geochemistry (Nicholas 1994) and there is no evidence for a significant gap in the conodont record (RJR/MPS unpublished collections).

The formation boundary is marked by a distinctive dolostone bed that when hammered reveals only dolomite cleavage planes. However, close inspection of weathered surfaces reveals that the bed is a coarse- to very coarse-grained sandstone composed almost entirely of reworked clasts of dolomite. The base of the Sangomore Formation contains thrombolites and is paler weathering than the Sailmhor Formation; there are also thick chert beds in the lower few metres. It is not clear what criteria were used by Peach *et al.* (1907) for differentiating the two units, though it was probably a combination of colour and the grain size of the dolomite. However, the colour contrast of the dolostones is not always reliable, and the colour of the cherts in the two units is a more distinctive character, with white cherts in the Sailmhor Formation abruptly giving way to orange-brown cherts in the Sangomore Formation.

Return to the cliff path via the cairn and follow the path to a gate. After passing through the gate, cut down to the left towards the cliff top.

Fig. 95. View of the Sailmhor–Sangomore formation boundary at Locality 14.6 [NC 3836 6885], looking NE towards the head of Balnakeil Bay. The formation boundary occurs at the prominent notch, which contains a distinctive sandstone composed entirely of reworked dolomite crystals. The overlying Sangomore Formation is characterised by being paler than the Sailmhor Formation and by the presence of orange-brown cherts and chert breccias. (Photograph: © M. P. Smith)

169

Locality 14.7 [NC 3860 6886]

Sangomore Formation.

The locality illustrates typical lithologies in the Sangomore Formation. Peritidal laminites with possible quartz-pseudomorphed chicken-wire anhydrite nodules occur in an area of small faults. The parasequences comprise a thin, subtidal unit of peloidal grainstone and/or thrombolite overlain by a thicker peritidal succession of stromatolites, microbial laminites and ripple lamination.

Locality 14.8 [NC 3864 6885]

Continue east along the cliff to the next small headland. Walk down a bedding plane ramp to the foot of the small cliff with pale/dark bedding alternations, which constitute well-developed parasequences. The bases of the parasequences are developed in dark burrow-mottled facies with very dark grey limestones containing silicified burrows. The parasequence tops comprise pale laminated dolostones, some of which have well-developed tepee structures. The bedding plane used for descent contains oncoids.

The uppermost bed, a dark parasequence base, forms a limestone pavement at the north-western tip of the distinctive horseshoe-shaped bay. The bed contains silicified burrows and a moderately abundant fauna of gastropods together with rare cephalopods.

Locality 14.9 [NC 3887 6876]

Sangomore–Balnakeil formation boundary.

Walk around the horseshoe bay to the final green of the golf course. Keep to the left of the green and descend the steep grassy slope to the wave-cut platform, then walk eastwards at the foot of the low cliff. This is still within the Sangomore Formation and at [NC 3883 6876] there are well-developed thrombolite heads with cherts lying between each head (Fig. 96). Farther on, large structureless microbial bioherms are developed. Proceed to where a fence stops at the top of the low cliff, with wire stays attached to the dolostones.

Fig. 96 Columnar branching thrombolite–stromatolite interactions forming small bun-shaped mounds at the base of the figure. With continued growth, these coalesced to form an over-arching large stromatolite with crinkly lamination, reflecting the control of microbialite growth by sediment supply and relative sea-level. Uppermost Sangomore Formation, Locality 14.9 [NC 3887 6876]. (Photograph: © M. P. Smith)

Just before the fence, the extensive microbialite facies are overlain by *c.* 5 m of peritidal laminites, which are in turn overlain by a distinctive oncoidal pebble bed that marks the Sangomore–Balnakeil Formation boundary. The pebble bed is best seen close to the base of the stays that anchor the final fence post and can be traced from there onto the foreshore. The basal metre of the Balnakeil Formation also contains a series of erosional surfaces, dolostone breccias and chert breccias, and marks a major shallowing event that may correlate with the pebble bed horizon within the upper Boat Harbour Formation in western Newfoundland.

Locality 14.10 [NC 3903 6872]

Balnakeil Formation.

Proceed eastwards across darker microbialitic limestones of the Balnakeil Formation to a small bay and continue beyond the bay to a point around 30 m before the beach armour below the road begins, at the point where the road bends seawards and the beach becomes sandier.

Limestones typical of the Balnakeil Formation are present here, with large thrombolite domes draped by 'ribbon rock' lithofacies (centimetre-scale alternations of ripple laminated dolostone and darker siltstone). Good silicified burrows are present in places, but most commonly the burrow fills are dolomitised. The 'ribbon rock' lithofacies is characterised by the reworking of penecontemporaneously dolomitised burrow fills into parallel

171

and ripple lamination. The lithofacies is considered indicative of a shallow subtidal depositional environment above storm wave base.

The overlying beds a few metres farther eastwards include large stromatolites with smaller conical 'egg-carton' forms on the top surface and a shallow channel filled with edgewise intraclast conglomerates.

Walk northwards across the beach, aiming for outcrops close to the track marked on the OS map.

Locality 14.11 [NC 3925 6965]

Moine psammites in the Faraid Head outlier.

At this locality there are exposures of Moine psammites that carry a strong mylonitic fabric, which dips shallowly to the ESE and is associated with a down-dip mineral and extension lineation. The mylonitic fabric is axial-planar to rare isoclinal folds that plunge ESE sub-parallel to the mineral lineation. Thin layers of garnetiferous semi-pelite contain shear bands that indicate a top-to-the-WNW sense of displacement parallel to the lineation. Rare lenticular bands of garnetiferous pelite up to 10cm thick carry a quartz segregation fabric that is folded around the hinges of minor folds; garnets up to 7–8mm in diameter are strongly wrapped by the mylonitic fabric that is axial planar to these folds.

These outcrops are part of the Faraid Head outlier (Holdsworth *et al.*, 2007), a segment of the Moine Thrust Sheet that was down-faulted during the late Palaeozoic and/or the Mesozoic. These outcrops are of historical importance because Peach *et al.* (1907) were able to deduce from them a minimum displacement of *c.* 15km along the Moine Thrust – one of the first times that this approach had been used to constrain large-scale horizontal movements in an orogenic belt.

Locality 14.12 [NC 3855 7070]

Gneissic mylonites in the Faraid Head outlier.

Walk northwards to beach outcrops at [NC 3855 7070]. If the tide is high, good outcrops are also present nearby above the high-water mark. The

Fig. 97 Typical acid Lewisianoid mylonite in the Faraid Head outlier, with asymmetric S-C fabrics giving top-to-the-WNW (left) senses of shear consistent with Caledonian thrusting. Note the asymmetric sigma-shaped wrapping of the pegmatitic pod in the centre of the image. Viewed looking to the NNE, in a vertical section sub-parallel to the mineral lineation, Locality 14.12. (Photograph: © R. E. Holdsworth)

spectacular exposures here are of Lewisianoid basement-derived mylonites that exhibit a wide variety of features typical of mid-crustal shear zones. The mylonites vary from creamy-pink types derived from acid gneiss (Fig. 97) to strips and pods of chlorite-actinolite schist that may represent boudinaged and highly retrogressed amphibolites. Relict gneissic layering is represented by colour banding in the acid types. The mylonite fabric dips to the ESE and a strong lineation plunges down-dip. Classic examples of shear criteria such as shear bands, asymmetrically-wrapped porphyroclasts and boudins, all indicate a top-to-the-WNW sense of displacement parallel to the lineation. Locally, centimetre-scale, close to tight minor folds are present, plunging at low to moderate angles to the mineral lineation. Numerous quartz-chlorite veins are preserved; early types are concordant and mylonitic, later types cross-cutting, often in boudin necks, and little deformed. In more feldspathic units, mylonite is associated with pale yellow-green cataclasite seams, many of which are concordant with the foliation. These are examples of semi-brittle behaviour typical of greenschist-facies fault rocks in which feldspar-rich layers deform in a brittle fashion whilst adjacent quartz and phyllosilicate-rich layers undergo dynamic recrystallization (White *et al.*, 1982). In places just above the high-water mark to the west, strain is less intense and the mylonites resemble more closely the Lewisianoid rocks that lie at the same structural level at Sango Sands (Locality 14.17). These basement mylonites are thus considered to have a Lewisianoid protolith; that is, they formed part of the basement to the Moine psammites.

Traverse inland to [NC 3825 7084], a series of crags composed of the Oystershell Rock just below the unexposed trace of the Moine Thrust. The Oystershell Rock is a mottled, dark grey-green, fine-grained phyllonite which is rich in chlorite and white mica; it is considered to be derived from

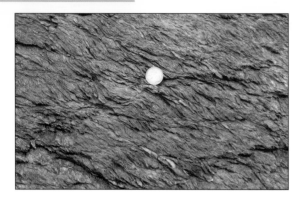

Fig. 98 Flat lying shear bands cutting ESE-dipping mylonitic foliation in chlorite-muscovite phyllonite unit (Oystershell Rock). Consistent with top-to-the-WNW (left) Caledonian thrusting. Viewed in vertical face looking NNE, Locality 14.12. (Photograph: © R. E. Holdsworth)

a (foreland) Lewisian gneiss protolith (Holdsworth *et al.*, 2001, 2007). The Moine Thrust has therefore been mapped at the boundary between the Lewisianoid basement mylonites and the Oystershell Rock. Gently-dipping Oystershell Rock includes numerous deformed quartz veins; a strong lineation plunges to the ESE. Pervasive shear bands and 10cm-scale shear zones again indicate a top-to-the-WNW sense of displacement (Fig. 98). The Oystershell Rock is notable here for the presence of 10–15cm thick bands of brown-weathering marble that are continuous for several metres in some cases. F_3 S-folds of the mylonite fabric verge north-west to north, and hinges are markedly curvilinear, plunging between the north-east and east; eye-structures consistent with sheath fold development are locally present. A 10cm-thick east–west-trending, steeply-dipping basic dyke of possible Permo-Carboniferous age cross-cuts the upper part of these crags at [NC 3828 7093].

Locality 14.13 [NC 3785 7135]

Moine Thrust viewpoint.

Walk 700m north-west across the raised beach, in which isolated crags of Oystershell Rock are exposed, until the far end of the headland is reached at [NC 3785 7135]. Look ENE towards the Ministry of Defence buildings and the steep cliffs on the northern coast of Faraid Head to view the ductile Moine Thrust. This is the flat-lying boundary exposed in the western cliffs of Poll a' Geodha Bhain that separates stripy, multicoloured Lewisianoid mylonites in the hangingwall from more uniform dark-green-grey Oystershell Rock in the footwall (Fig. 99).

Moine Thrust

Fig. 99 View east towards
the cliffs of Poll a' Geodha
Bhain from Locality 14.13,
showing the ductile Moine
Thrust separating striped
Lewisianoid mylonites in
the hangingwall from dark
green Oystershell Rock
in the footwall. (Photo-
graph: © R. E. Holdsworth)

Return to the vehicles, noting the excellent views to the west of Cape
Wrath, and to the south of the east-dipping Durness Group succession on
the south side of Balnakeil Bay.

Excursion 14B: additional localities

Locality 14.14 [NC 384 670]

The Croisaphuill Formation at Loch Borralie.

The upper part of the Durness Group is not visible in Balnakeil Bay, and the
Croisaphuill Formation, which overlies the Balnakeil Formation, is best
examined on the east side of Loch Borralie. Park at the Cape Wrath Hotel
[NC 380 662] and cross the field to the north, towards Loch Borralie.
Proceed along the eastern side of the lake, crossing the end of one wall that
descends to the loch, until a second wall in poorer repair is met where the
strait between island and shore is at its narrowest [NC 3844 6709]. This
point is very close to the base of the Croisaphuill Formation, which extends
down-dip for over half a kilometre to the east.

The lower part of the Croisaphuill Formation comprises burrow-
mottled limestones with abundant brown cherts. The burrow fills were penecontemporaneously dolomitised (Morrow, 1978), and in places evidence of
this can be seen where dolomite burrow-fills are reworked into parallel
and ripple lamination (as in the ribbon-rock lithofacies of the Balnakeil
Formation). Following the wall up to the cairned summit of the small hill

175

provides a discontinuous but representative section through the lower 90m of the formation. Cherts become less abundant, but otherwise this part of the Croisaphuill Formation is remarkably uniform. This is the most macro-fossil rich part of the Durness Group, and close searching will reveal a variety of dolomitised and silicified gastropods, several species of the silici-fied snail operculum *Ceratopea* and a moderately diverse cephalopod fauna, including both coiled and orthoconic forms. Conodonts indicate that the unit is of basal Arenig age, and the base of the formation marks a major shift away from the microbially dominated Middle Cambrian–Tremadocian part of the group. This change in depositional architecture was caused by a eustatic rise in sea-level that flooded most of Laurentia and which consti-tutes one of the highest sea-level stands in the Phanerozoic.

There are excellent views from the summit cairn of the down-faulted outlier of Durness Group that constitutes the east side of the Kyle of Durness, surrounded by Precambrian and Lower Cambrian rock units.

Locality 14.15 [NC 418 671]

Smoo Cave.

Smoo Cave, a short distance east of the main village of Durness, is well signposted and has a small car-park. Walk eastwards from the car-park through the picnic area and down the slope to a series of swallow holes. At the top of the opposite slope, turn left at the T-junction and turn north-wards along the cliff top on the east side of Smoo inlet. The path doubles back and descends into the inlet, affording an excellent view of the large entrance (approximately 40m wide and 15m high) – the cave results from the interaction of coastal processes with a karst drainage system. At the rear of the entrance chamber is a large fan of vegetated flowstone (undated) and there is some flowstone on the walls. A covered walkway leads to a second chamber where Allt Smoo descends a shaft into a large pool. Boat trips into a third chamber are sporadically available.

The accessible part of Smoo Cave is developed entirely within the Sangomore Formation, but the inlet shows good sections across the Sailmhor–Sangomore formation boundary (Fig. 100). Two prominent chert bands run down the length of the inlet, offset half-way down by a small fault, and the formation boundary lies 3 metres above the base of the lower

Fig. 100 A stack of shallowing upward parasequences in the upper Sailmhor Formation at Pocan Smoo, Locality 14.15. Within each parasequence there is a thick dark grey subtidal base overlain by a thin lighter grey peritidal cap. The Sailmhor–Sangomore formation boundary is marked by the prominent white chert at the cliff top, adjacent to the fence. (Photograph: © M. P. Smith)

Fig. 101 Roadside exposure of sub-vertical carbonate-cemented red breccia-sandstone (?Permo-Trias) and white carbonate vein infill of cavity in Durness Group dolostone oriented parallel to the Sangobeg Fault, Locality 14.16. View looking north. (Photograph: © R. E. Holdsworth)

chert. The upper part of the Sailmhor Formation comprises a series of parasequences that consist of dark, burrow-mottled subtidal carbonates overlain by thin, pale, laminated peritidal carbonates. The shallowing-upward parasequences form part of a classical, lower order, shallowing upward succession in which the subtidal portions of the parasequences progressively thin upwards, and there is a concomitant decrease in the subtidal-peritidal balance of each parasequence. This aspect is clearly illustrated from a distance by the proportion of dark subtidal to pale peritidal carbonate. A closer view of these parasequences can be safely gained by following the cliff top path to the end of the inlet on the northern side.

Locality 14.16 [NC 4100 6740]

Sangobeg Fault.

Park at the Tourist Information Centre in Durness [NC 4070 6775] overlooking Sango Sands. From the car-park, view the steep wall of Durness

177

Group dolostone *c.*400m to the SE; this lies along the Sangobeg Fault, one of the main bounding normal faults of the Durness outlier of the Moine Thrust Sheet (Holdsworth *et al.*, 2006). Walk *c.*300m east along the road to roadside exposures in the Durness Group at [NC 4100 6740], which lie in the immediate footwall of the Sangobeg Fault. Here, a series of carbonate-cemented red sandstone-breccia infills and carbonate veins are preserved in sub-vertical fractures trending NNE–SSW, approximately parallel to the trend of the adjacent normal fault (Fig. 101). The sedimentary material – which is most likely to be of Permo-Triassic age – is thought to have infilled tectonically active open fractures in the limestone that formed synchronously with normal faulting activity. This suggests that this phase of extension was associated with sedimentation, although most of the basin infills have subsequently been eroded. Similar red-bed infills are common in the region between Durness and Cape Wrath. Clast types are mainly Durness Group, but isolated examples of mylonite and Cambrian quartz arenite are also preserved (see Wilson *et al.*, 2010 for details).

Locality 14.17 [NC 4080 6770 to 4070 6800]

Sango Bay.

Return to the car-park and walk down onto the beach via the wooden steps. East of the base of the steps is a prominent headland, which comprises outcrops of banded quartzo-feldspathic and amphibolitic Lewisianoid basement gneisses. These are thought to lie close to the base of the Moine Thrust Sheet (Holdsworth *et al.*, 2006). Creamy-pink acidic gneisses and dark green metabasic sheets are cut by pegmatitic and quartz veins. The gneisses contain greenschist-facies mineral assemblages (chlorite, actinolite, epidote) indicative of retrogression; the dominant banding dips east and carries an ESE-plunging mineral and extension lineation.

The gneisses are probably bounded to the west by a normal fault that separates them from upstanding outcrops in the central part of the bay of a green chlorite phyllonite. These phyllonites are correlated with the 'Oyster-shell Rock' identified within the mylonite belt of the Moine Thrust Zone at Loch Eriboll (see Localities 14.12–14.13, and Excursion 15). They contain numerous lunate quartz segregations and pervasive shear bands that indicate a top-to-the-west sense of displacement parallel to an E–W-trending lineation that is particularly well developed in the lenticular quartz-bearing layers.

Walk towards the rocky headland at the north-western limit of the beach. Look up towards the cliffs to the left to see further outcrops of the Oystershell Rock. These contain thin mylonitized pegmatitic veinlets; a set of intrafolial isoclinal folds can be identified, as well as later folds that deform the mylonite fabric. The structurally lowest rock unit on the headland is rather fractured, pink-purple weathering recrystallised dolostone of the Durine Formation, the youngest unit of the Durness Group. This is separated by a gently-inclined thrust from a 2–3 m-thick slice of quartz mylonite, which is itself overlain by another thrust above which is a more coherently laminated group of mylonites (derived from both the Oystershell Rock and, locally, Lewisian gneiss). Walk up onto the headland to examine these thrust contacts in detail, and then follow them around to the west into the next bay. Note that the continuity of the thrust contacts is very much disrupted by the effects of later carbonate veining, located mainly in the footwall of the lowermost thrust, and also due to offsets along numerous, steeply-dipping normal faults (Hippler and Knipe 1990; Holdsworth *et al.*, 2006). Care should be taken on this path if conditions are wet. An alternative route into this bay is to retrace the route back to and up the wooden steps, and walk westwards along the main cliff top, parallel to the boundary fence of the campsite.

One interpretation of these outcrops is that the lowermost thrust corresponds to the Lochan Riabhach Thrust, which was thought by Holdsworth *et al.* (2006) to underlie the mylonite belt at Loch Eriboll (see Excursion 15) and interpreted by them as a separate structure from the Moine Thrust, which is exposed at a higher structural level at Faraid Head (see above). The alternative view is that the lowermost thrust does in fact correspond to the Moine Thrust (Peach *et al.*, 1907; Butler 2009).

Locality 14.18 [NC 4040 6850]

Creag Thairbhe.

Return to the top of the cliff and, following the fence, walk approximately 500 m north-west along the cliffs of Durness Group towards the cliffs extending inland from Creag Thairbhe [NC 4040 6850]. The steep cliffs here define the trend of the WNW–ENE-trending Faraid Head Fault that down-faults the main Faraid Head outlier of Moine rocks and the Moine Thrust Zone mylonites that outcrop to the north (Holdsworth *et al.*, 2007; Wilson *et al.*, 2010). Most of the cliff comprises variably brecciated carbonate, but at its western end where the upper parts of the cliff can be accessed from the sand dunes, carbonate-cemented red sandstone-breccia infills are preserved in a series of sub-vertical fractures trending parallel to the main fault. These are virtually identical to those exposed at Locality 14.13, and are also thought to represent sedimentary material that has infilled tectonically open fractures in the limestone formed synchronously with normal faulting activity. The dominant clast types are Durness Group carbonates, but clasts of Moine psammite, mylonitized Lewisian gneiss and quartzite mylonite are also present. At least two units of infill are recognised based on differences in grain-size and sorting.

The ages of the sedimentary infills at Localities 14.13 and 14.15 – and hence the age of extension – are uncertain, but a Permo-Triassic age seems likely given the timing of sedimentary basin formation in the West Orkney Basin that lies immediately offshore and to the north (see Wilson *et al.*, 2010, and references therein). Detailed studies of the normal faulting along the north coast in the Durness–Cape Wrath area (Wilson *et al.*, 2010) suggests that the NNE- and WNW-trending normal faults are likely to be contemporaneous, forming a complex transfer zone that defines the southern margin of the West Orkney Basin. Return to the vehicles, retracing your steps along the cliff top.

Excursion 15

The Moine Thrust Zone at Loch Eriboll

Rob Butler, Robert Raine and Paul Smith

Purpose: To examine aspects of thrust belt geometry and the evolution of fault rocks, including the classic outcrops where Lapworth worked in the 1880s, demonstrating the repetition of rock sequences by thrusting, and coining the term mylonite.This excursion also contains the type locality for the An t-Sròn Formation.

Aspects covered: Cambro-Ordovician stratigraphy in the Moine Thrust Zone; major and minor thrust structures; thrust systems and their fault rocks (cataclasites and mylonites); recognising imbricate thrust systems; deformation gradients in the thrust zone.

Maps: OS: 1:50,000 Landranger Sheet 9 (Cape Wrath); 1:25,000 Explorer sheets 445, 446 and 447. BGS: 1:50,000 Scotland sheet 114W, Loch Eriboll.

Terrain: The excursion covers a range of terrain types, from rocky coastline to rough moorland. There are no paths and the terrain is rough, which can make progress rather arduous. There are short, steep ascents and descents.

Time: The entire excursion will take a full day, and will be difficult to complete if the group is large and/or unused to walking over rough ground. However, the excursion can be undertaken in two distinct parts, visiting Localities 15.1–15.7 separately from Localities 15.8–15.10.

Access: No access problems are known. However, this excursion is entirely within a Site of Special Scientific Interest and so hammering of outcrops and collection of specimens, even from float, is strictly prohibited.

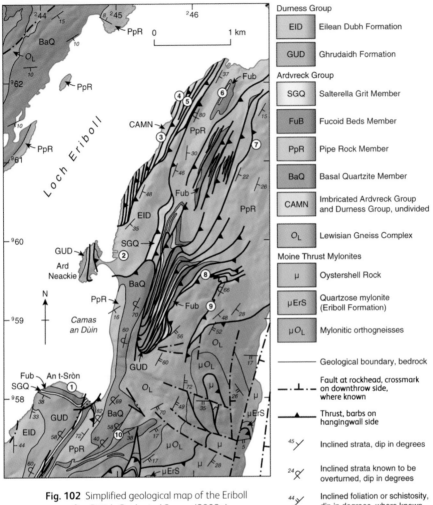

Durness Group

| EID | Eilean Dubh Formation |

| GUD | Ghrudaidh Formation |

Ardvreck Group

| SGQ | Salterella Grit Member |

| FuB | Fucoid Beds Member |

| PpR | Pipe Rock Member |

| BaQ | Basal Quartzite Member |

| CAMN | Imbricated Ardvreck Group and Durness Group, undivided |

| O_L | Lewisian Gneiss Complex |

Moine Thrust Mylonites

| μ | Oystershell Rock |

| μErS | Quartzose mylonite (Eriboll Formation) |

| μO_L | Mylonitic orthogneisses |

——— Geological boundary, bedrock

—·⊥·— Fault at rockhead, crossmark on downthrow side, where known

▲— Thrust, barbs on hangingwall side

⁴⁵⤢ Inclined strata, dip in degrees

²⁴⤫ Inclined strata known to be overturned, dip in degrees

⁴⁴⤢ Inclined foliation or schistosity, dip in degrees, where known

Fig. 102 Simplified geological map of the Eriboll area, after British Geological Survey (2002a), showing the localities described in Excursion 15.

The route starts on the eastern coast of Loch Eriboll, where there is a good section through the Cambrian sedimentary rocks, before heading along the road to the viewpoint over Ard Neackie and thence to Heilam, Lapworth's base for his mapping during the 1882 and 1883 seasons. From Heilam the route goes over rough ground to Ben Arnaboll and then back down to examine the thrusting at Kempie (Fig. 102).

This excursion can be followed in a long day as described, in which case it gives an ideal introduction to how geologists have built an understanding of thrust system architecture in the North-west Highlands. This is where it all began, with the work of Charles Lapworth in 1882–83, followed up by the work of the Geological Survey (Peach *et al.*, 1907). It was on the northeast shores of Loch Eriboll that the tectonic emplacement of Lewisian gneiss and therefore the allochthonous nature of the Moine succession was first unequivocally demonstrated, together with the process of imbrication that caused the multiple repetition of elements of the Cambrian stratigraphy. The outcrops inspired the coining of the terms 'thrust' (Geikie, 1884) and 'mylonite' (Lapworth, 1885). Since the 19th century, the area has continued to inspire research of global interest. The outcrops of the Pipe Rock Member are most instructive because the burrows they contain, both the abundant *Skolithos* and the rarer *Monocraterion*, form ideal strain markers. In undeformed strata these burrows display circular sections on bedding planes and are perpendicular to bedding in profile. Modifications of these geometries can be used to quantify the directions and magnitudes of strains in 3D (Coward and Kim, 1981; Fischer and Coward, 1982), information that bears on the evolution of thrust systems and the localisation of deformation in the continental crust. The quartz arenites were also important for the application of electron microscope techniques to understand mineral physics and rock deformation at the scale of crystal lattices (e.g. White, 1979). Current research is focused on the ways in which basement is incorporated into thrust systems (e.g. Wibberley, 2005; Butler *et al.*, 2006). The route is described to give an insight into how field relationships between the rock units can be used to infer structural geometry and evolution. Some of the outcrops are amongst the most globally important in structural geology.

Locality 15.1 [NC 4440 5798]

An t-Sròn peninsula: a stratigraphic overview.

The coastline at An t-Sròn is one of the localities at which Lapworth constructed his reference stratigraphy in 1882 and the section is illustrated on his field slips (Fig. 103). The section along the coast runs from the Pipe Rock Member of the Eriboll Formation (base not seen) through the Salterella Grit Member (6m) into the Fucoid Beds Member (22m) of the An t-Sròn Formation (Fig. 104). The section continues into the carbonate facies of the

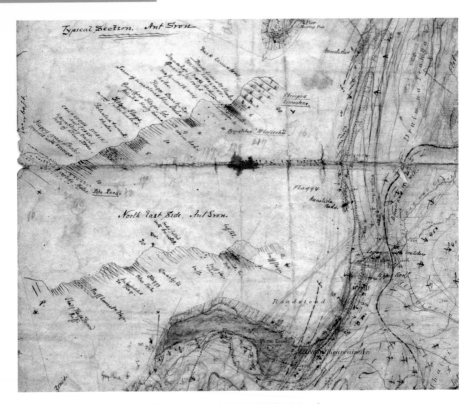

Fig. 103 Extract from Charles Lapworth's 1:10,560 field slip of the An t-Sròn area from the 1882–1883 seasons, incorporating his reference sections for the Cambrian stratigraphy that are the focus of Locality 15.1. (© Lapworth Museum of Geology)

Ghrudaidh Formation (Durness Group; 65 m) and into the paler dolostones of the Eilean Dubh Formation (top not seen).

Park in the large lay-by at [NC 4440 5798]. The instructive outcrops opposite the parking place contain Fucoid Beds Member in the crest of the An t-Sròn anticline, thickened up by minor thrusts of different polarity. The Salterella Grit Member can also be observed. From the lay-by, walk north-west towards the shore of Loch Eriboll [NC 4423 5816], where cream-coloured, fine-grained quartz arenites of the Pipe Rock Member contain well-developed *Skolithos*. The generally low deformation state of the quartz arenites can be established here using the geometry of *Skolithos* burrows, which is useful for comparison with more deformed parts of the thrust belt seen later in the day.

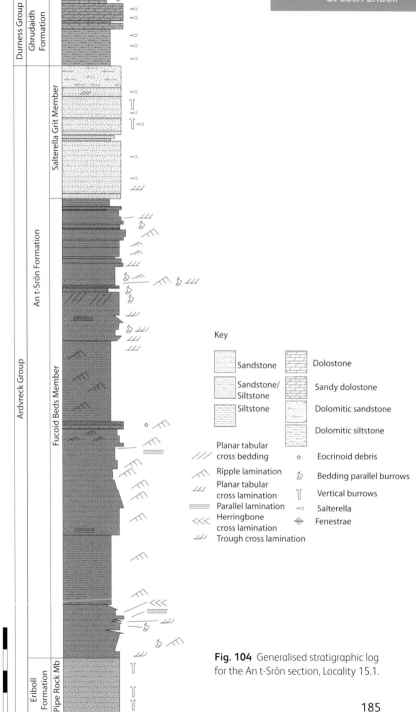

Fig. 104 Generalised stratigraphic log for the An t-Sròn section, Locality 15.1.

Key

Sandstone	Dolostone
Sandstone/Siltstone	Sandy dolostone
Siltstone	Dolomitic sandstone
	Dolomitic siltstone

/// Planar tabular cross bedding
Ripple lamination
/// Planar tabular cross lamination
= Parallel lamination
<<< Herringbone cross lamination
Trough cross lamination

☆ Eocrinoid debris
Bedding parallel burrows
Vertical burrows
Salterella
Fenestrae

185

The boundary with the overlying Fucoid Beds Member is at [NC 4416 5811], where quartz arenites of the Pipe Rock Member are overlain by fine- to medium-grained, carious weathering, orange brown sandstones; small scale hummocky cross stratification is present. These are overlain by moderately bioturbated, very fine- to fine-grained sandstones with burrow mottling and ripple lamination. The ripples are picked out by green-grey siltstone drapes, and display *Planolites* burrows on the underside. There is also some hummocky cross stratification in medium-grained sandstones, and herring bone cross-stratification.

Walk along shore and along the strike to [NC 4408 5811]; a 0.3 m marker bed comprising decimetre-scale tabular cross-bedding and swaley cross stratification can be traced around cliffs. This is overlain by several metres of rippled very fine sandstones with bioturbated siltstone drapes. These beds contain *Rusophycus*, *Cruziana* and *Planolites* reflecting the deeper water, more diverse ichnofauna that is present in the Fucoid Beds Member in comparison with the Pipe Rock Member. The arthropod tracks (*Cruziana*) and resting traces (*Rusophycus*) are most likely to have been made by trilobites and represent a variety of feeding and walking activity. On the wave-cut platform below the cliff a bedding surface displaying excellent interference ripples can be observed.

Looking south, the boundary with the overlying Salterella Grit Member climbs down the cliff and can be observed on the shore at [NC 4401 5806]. The upper part of the Fucoid Beds Member is marked by a very light grey-green, silty mudstone overlain by decimetre-scale to centimetre-scale beds of medium to coarse sandstone. The boundary to the Salterella Grit Member is marked by a change to metre-scale beds of cross-bedded, white quartz arenites with prominent *Skolithos* towards the top; phosphatic shell debris, *Salterella*, and mud clasts are also present.

At the top of this 6 m unit is a nodular weathering, dolomite-cemented, yellow brown sandstone, and the top of this bed marks the base of the Ghrudaidh Formation (Durness Group). The base is composed of dark grey dolomitic siltstone with locally abundant *Salterella*, a small cone-shaped shelly fossil, visible on bed surfaces. Just above this, beds of quartz sand-rich dolostones decrease in thickness and abundance. Burrow-mottling becomes common, and, at some levels, spar-filled vugs containing calcite may represent a replacement of evaporite nodules.

From the boundary walk up the dip slope and grassy bank, and follow the sheep path towards the south along the top of the cliffs. Passing crags of

Fig. 105 View of the southern end of the An t-Sròn section, Locality 15.1 [NC 439 578], looking southwards. Very light grey, fine grained dolostones, typical of the Eilean Dubh Formation display crinkly microbial lamination and small stromatolites. (Photograph: © R. J. Raine)

dark grey, coarsely crystalline dolostone with few sedimentary structures (typical of the Ghrudaidh Formation), descend to a small cove at [NC 439 579], where intervals of light grey, finer grained dolostone start to become apparent in the succession (Fig. 105). These beds reflect a progressive decrease in relative sea-level towards the top of the formation. Sedimentary structures indicative of deposition under intertidal to supratidal conditions include tepee structures and flat pebble conglomerates. The upper part of the conglomerate is conspicuous, with pale clasts reworked into a very dark grey dolomite matrix. A fault truncates beds at the southern end of the cove.

Exit the bay inland where the descent was made and continue southwards, past crags of highly vuggy dolomite. At [NC 4393 5787], access can be made to the beach, via a small gully. When on the beach, walk northwards to the contact between the Ghrudaidh and the Eilean Dubh formations [NC 4392 5790]. Some faulting of the section is observed, but very light grey, fine grained dolomites, typical of the Eilean Dubh Formation display crinkly microbial lamination and small stromatolites. Loose blocks on the beach commonly show a fenestral fabric and soft sediment deformation. At [NC 4393 5789] large nodules of calcite and dolomite are observed and beds containing small crystal shaped vugs can be seen. This provides further evidence of evaporate pseudomorphs within the succession and, together with the fenestrae and planar stromatolites, allows a supratidal evaporitic setting to be deduced.

Walk southwards to [NC 4380 5774], where parasequences can be seen; these are shallowing upward successions of sedimentary rock, marked by a base that displays evidence of rapid flooding. At least three metre-scale parasequences are visible within the low cliffs. These comprise mid- to dark grey dolostone at the base, with irregular black cherts, overlain by planar, crinkly laminated mid-grey dolostone and capped by low-domed stromatolites of 10–20cm wavelength and 5cm amplitude. The cherts contain rare ooids.

Walk back (north) along the beach to a small stream at [NC 4384 5775] and follow it inland until a grassy scree bank. At the top of the bank, follow the path northwards, contouring around the hill and up to the road before walking back northwards to the lay-by at the start.

Locality 15.2 [NC 4520 9990]

The viewpoint at Ard Neackie: Eriboll overview.

A lay-by [NC 452 599] on the A838 overlooking the Ard Neackie peninsula provides panoramic views down the loch to the mountain massif of Foinaven and thus gives a natural cross-section through the Moine Thrust Zone. To the south of Eriboll much of the Moine Thrust Zone is represented by imbricated quartz arenites, chiefly the Pipe Rock Member. The upper part of the thrust zone contains far-travelled sheets of Lewisian gneisses capped in turn by the Moine Thrust and its mylonites. This deceptively simple description forms a counterpoint to the apparently more complex structural geometries to be visited in this excursion. This lay-by also provides a convenient parking place for continuing to Heilam and Ben Arnaboll (Localities 15.3 and 15.4), although there are other parking places in the vicinity.

Locality 15.3 [NC 4568 6133]

Port an Altain: imbricated Cambrian strata.

The ground to the north of the A838, centred on Ben Heilam, offers a generally well-exposed and accessible experience of imbricate structures, developed in the Cambrian strata (Fig. 106). The well-differentiated succession, as seen at An t-Sròn, provides an ideal template for recognising thrust repetitions. This part of the thrust belt was most extensively studied by Coward (1984). Our route examines evidence for imbrication and how the structures can be traced out in the landscape. The strain state in the imbri-

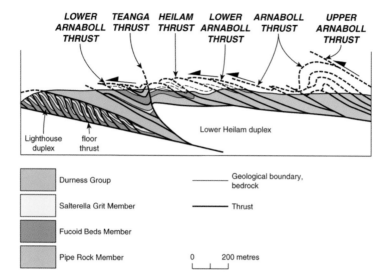

LOWER   TEANGA   HEILAM   LOWER   ARNABOLL   UPPER
ARNABOLL THRUST   THRUST   ARNABOLL   THRUST   ARNABOLL
THRUST   THRUST   THRUST

Lighthouse   floor
duplex   thrust

Lower Heilam duplex

Durness Group

Salterella Grit Member

Fucoid Beds Member

Pipe Rock Member

Geological boundary,
bedrock

Thrust

0   200 metres

Fig. 106 Cross-section through the Heilam area, after
Butler (2009), extending from the Lighthouse duplex in
the WNW (left) to Loch Hope in the ESE (right).

cate slices is also considered by examining the deformation of *Skolithos* in
the Pipe Rock Member.

From the lay-by (Locality 15.2), walk NNE along the road to where it
overlooks the Heilam area. Continue down the hillside to Loch Ach'an
Lochaidh and follow its SW shore to the outflow (Allt a'Mhuilleir). A
discontinuous path leads down to the coast at the rocky bay – Port an
Altain. The first stop lies at the northern end of the bay at a low headland
[NC 4568 6133].

These coastal outcrops consist of Fucoid Beds Member, Salterella Grit
Member and Durness Group carbonates. In general, bedding and unit
contacts are steeply dipping. These lie within the Lighthouse duplex of
Coward (1984) and the outcrops give insight into the imbricate structure.
This can be studied by working across strike, starting at the coast. Skerries
(accessible below mid-tide) are made of Durness Group carbonates that dip
at *c.*60 ESE. They are overlain by Fucoid Beds Member that dips more
steeply and which is in turn overlain by Salterella Grit Member. Thus the
contact between the Fucoid Beds Member and the Durness Group is a
thrust. Another thrust lies above the Salterella Grit Member, repeating it
and carrying a thin (50cm) slice of Fucoid Beds Member. The steep attitude

189

of bedding and the thrusts here is believed to be due to further imbricate thrusting at depth that has back-rotated these structures (Coward, 1984).

The lateral continuity of the imbricate slices can be followed by walking north along the coast for 500m to the skeletal lighthouse. The general trend of the imbricates is picked out by ridges of Salterella Grit Member. In general the imbricate slices incorporate increasing amounts of Durness Group carbonate and lose Fucoid Beds Member, implying that the imbricate thrusts climb gradually up stratigraphic section to the north-east.

Locality 15.4 [NC 4586 1779]

Lighthouse.

At the lighthouse, the gently overhanging sea-cliff (with prominent white-wash stain) is formed by a bedding plane of the Salterella Grit Member. Durness Group carbonates lie on either side of the thin sheet of these quartz arenites. Forty metres north of the lighthouse, a steep gully into the sea reveals a slice of Fucoid Beds Member thrust onto Salterella Grit Member. Collectively these outcrops display the architectural elements of imbricate thrusting, leading to repetitions of the stratigraphy, in this case on a detailed scale. Continuing NNE along the coast from the lighthouse, the imbricate structures become increasingly dominated by Durness Group carbonates. The thrust repetition of the carbonates is reflected in the landscape immediately inland as a series of NNE–SSW-trending ridges.

From the low knolls overlooking the lighthouse [NC 4595 6185] walk across strike inland. By way of diversion, the ridges of Durness carbonate may be counted as a proxy for imbricate slices. A change in vegetation to dominantly heather-cover marks the upper edge of Coward's (1984) Lighthouse duplex and the lower part of the main Heilam imbricate system, chiefly composed of Pipe Rock Member quartz arenites.

Locality 15.5 [NC 4604 6160]

Loch na Cathrach Duibhe.

Outcrops of the Pipe Rock Member may be examined on the low ridge near pt. 54m [NC 4606 6160], overlooking the northern edge of Loch na

Cathrach Duibhe. Bedding here dips gently ESE. The *Skolithos* burrows may be observed, nearly orthogonal to bedding (implying little bed-parallel shearing). On bedding planes, however, they show elliptical sections (ratios of up to 2:1), with long axes trending along strike, implying significant layer parallel shortening strains. There are also exposures of cataclasites, marked by strong blue/green mottling and pasty yellow seams that represent zones of intense grain fracturing. Thus the quartz arenites have experienced significant deformation as they have become incorporated into the thrust belt.

From the loch, an optional diversion up to the north coast of Heilam can be made to see further examples of deformed Pipe Rock Member. Photogenic examples of elliptical bed-sections of *Monocraterion* burrows (implying layer-parallel shortening strains) may be found in the small cove [NC 4645 6220]. At 300m ESE of this site, in outcrops in a grassy amphitheatre [NC 468 619], there are spectacular exposures of cataclasites (with the characteristic glassy-blue appearance and pasty yellow seams) that were described by White (1979). Nearby [NC 467 620] there are also 10m-scale folds within the imbricated Pipe Rock Member in a gully – with deflected *Skolithos* indicating flexural flow associated with the prominent synform. These northern exposures also provide good views out towards Whiten Head, the northernmost extension of the Moine Thrust Zone on mainland Scotland. To rejoin the main itinerary, follow the fence line SSE and hence reach Locality 15.6.

If a shorter route is required, from Locality 15.5 cross the boggy ground north of Loch na Cathrach Duibhe and ascend the steep slope on its eastern side, to the plateau above. This ascent crosses a sheet of Pipe Rock Member, which is probably internally imbricated. This ascent arises on the shore of an unnamed lochan. From here follow the upper edge of the escarpment for about 200m to a prominent square-cut glacial erratic.

Locality 15.6 [NC 4639 6180]

The bedrock here is Fucoid Beds Member, indicating that the main Heilam imbricates contain, at the current exposure level, both the Pipe Rock and Fucoid Beds members. The location provides good views down onto the Lighthouse duplex along the west coast of Heilam. Looking east reveals a landscape dominated by stacked up Pipe Rock Member, with rare exposures of Fucoid Beds Member.

The route now lies east, across a boggy area with sparse outcrop. Cross the fence with care and follow the northern shore of Loch a'Choire, ascending a 10m escarpment to a ridge overlooking the Hope valley.

Locality 15.7 [NC 4685 6124]

Folded Pipe Rock Member.

Locality 15.7 is a rocky tor composed of Pipe Rock Member. The structure it contains is a spectacular example of folding associated with a thrust ramp (Fig. 107). The fold lies on a plinth of sub-horizontal Pipe Rock Member. The outcrop can be explored to find examples of deformed *Skolithos* burrows that reveal shearing associated with this fold structure.

From Locality 15.7, the excursion now returns SSE to the A838, a hike of about 1200m over rough ground. In general the route follows ridge-lines that track the general trend of the imbricated Pipe Rock Member. Before reaching the road it is worth stopping at the vantage point at [NC 4655 6065], a site marked by several large glacial erratics of Lewisian gneiss and pegmatites. This gives good views onto the next localities on the excursion, the classic thrust terrain of Ben Arnaboll (Fig. 108). Suitably inspired, continue to the A838 near the road cutting [NC 464 601].

Locality 15.8 [NC 4615 5958]

Ben Arnaboll: major thrusts and associated structures.

The outcrops on the north side of Ben Arnaboll are amongst the most important in global geology. They inspired Geikie (1884) to coin the term 'thrust', apparently adopting the term from the colloquial, unpublished usage of Lapworth. They are also generally considered to be the type area for Lapworth's (1885) description of mylonites (White 1998).

To access the classic exposures of the Arnaboll Thrust ascend the hillside south of the A838, from the area of the cutting [NC 464 601], to a prominent heathery spur above a west-facing cliff of Pipe Rock Member. This is

Fig. 107 Spectacular folding in Pipe Rock Member associated with a thrust ramp, Locality 15.7. (Photograph: © R. W. H. Butler)

Fig. 108 (below) Annotated panorama of the north side of Ben Arnaboll from around [NC 465 606]. (Photograph: © R. W. H. Butler)

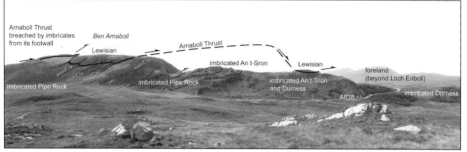

Locality 15.8 [NC 4615 5958], the type locality for the Arnaboll Thrust. Here Lewisian gneisses lie in tectonic contact upon Pipe Rock Member (Fig. 109). These quartz arenites are in their correct stratigraphic orientation, as indicated by the right way-up conical burrow tops of *Monocraterion*, which can be found at the western end of the section. These burrows are sheared but the depositional lamination is still evident. The more common *Skolithos* can be found in the Pipe Rock Member below the main part of the out-crop. Here too they are deformed, forming an angle of about 45° to bedding (imply-ing a shear strain of 1). A weak grain alignment defines a weak cleavage in the quartz arenites here. Both pipes and cleavage

Fig. 109 The type locality of the Arnaboll Thrust, Locality 15.8. Lewisian gneisses thrust over quartz arenites of the Pipe Rock Member. (BGS photo-graph, © NERC)

193

verge to the WNW, indicative of this shear sense on the thrust. The Lewisian gneisses above the thrust plane show varying deformation states. Two metres above the thrust plane the Lewisian Gneiss Complex retains amphibolite-facies metamorphic assemblages and coarse pegmatites, and they are only reworked and modified close to the thrust.

From its type location, it is instructive to walk out the Arnaboll Thrust, heading eastwards around the escarpment. Although the thrust plane dips eastwards here, it is repeatedly offset up the hillside so that for the most part the route contours the hillside. These offsets are achieved by small thrusts that re-imbricate the Arnaboll Thrust plane – a geometry described as 'breaching'. It is likely that these are parts of the same structure of imbricates as on Ben Heilam and indicate that at least some of this imbrication followed the emplacement of the Arnaboll Thrust Sheet. The best examples are found at the eastern edge of a rocky amphitheatre [NC 4629 5951]. From here, continue following the Arnaboll Thrust eastwards. At [NC 4641 5943] the thrust turns up and its outcrop trace heads southwards. It can be followed easily by keeping Pipe Rock exposures on the left and gneisses on the right. Bedding in the Pipe Rock Member is generally subvertical, parallel to the inferred thrust plane. At a few locations *Monocraterion* in the Pipe Rock Member shows the younging direction of these strata westwards, towards the Arnaboll Thrust. Traditional interpretations (e.g. Butler *et al.*, 2006) show the Arnaboll Thrust sheet to be folded. However, modern mapping by Wibberley and Butler (2010) shows no such fold in the thrust sheet itself. The contact between Pipe Rock and Lewisian gneisses is another breaching thrust.

Locality 15.9 [NC 4620 5910]

Unnamed lochan.

Continue along the trace of the thrust to the unnamed lochan on Ben Arnaboll, reaching it at NC 4620 5910. The outcrops on the eastern side of the lochan contain further exposures of Lewisian rocks resting tectonically upon Pipe Rock Member. These are most plausibly interpreted as representing again the Arnaboll Thrust, here dipping eastwards. Thus there is an antiform, cored by Pipe Rock, carried by a thrust that breaches and repeats the Arnaboll Thrust.

The detailed structure around Locality 15.9 is complex, consisting of imbricated alternations, on the metre-scale, of Pipe Rock Member and Lewisian basement. Both units are strongly sheared. The alternations are plausibly the result of a breaching imbrication process, albeit on a finer scale than seen further west along the trace of the Arnaboll Thrust. Unlike the outcrops at the type area of the Arnaboll Thrust, the Lewisian gneiss to the east of the unnamed lochan is strongly modified from its foreland state. This has led various workers to suggest that at this locality it is not the Arnaboll Thrust at all, but a higher, more ductile structure. The interpretation here (following Butler 1988; Butler *et al.*, 2006) is that it is indeed the Arnaboll Thrust, but that the site lies near its trailing edge. In these situations, where thrusts are closely spaced, rocks can become intensely sheared (e.g. Boyer and Elliott, 1982), a feature of these outcrops.

If time is limited, it is advisable to return to the A838. Navigationally the simplest way to achieve this is to walk north to the edge of the Heilam area. There are routes to the west, but these demand special care to find the correct way down the cliffs on the west slopes of Ben Arnaboll.

To continue the excursion, the plan now is to walk along strike within the mylonitic upper part of the Moine Thrust Zone. Outcrops are sparse, but can include spectacular deformation fabrics and folds. The protoliths to these are generally Lewisian gneisses. However, there is a narrow tract of mylonitic quartz arenite that continues southward from the unnamed lochan – plausibly interpreted as representing a strongly attenuated crest of the antiform that folds the Arnaboll Thrust. In this interpretation these quartz arenites are derived from the footwall to the Arnaboll Thrust. However, as will be evident later, not all the quartz arenites found within the mylonite belt are derived from this structural position.

Continue SSE across the open moorland from Ben Arnaboll, cross the wall and the head of a valley leading down to Kempie Bay to reach Locality 15.10.

Locality 15.10 [NC 4487 5726]

Upper Kempie: the mylonites.

The easiest place from which to explore the outcrops on the plateau is a small knoll (213m OD) at [NC 4487 5726]. These outcrops are quartzo-feldspathic mylonites plausibly derived from Moine metasedimentary rocks. They contain a strong ESE-plunging stretching lineation. These outcrops contain dramatic folds of the mylonitic foliation, traditionally interpreted as forming during progressive shearing within the ductile thrust zone.

The Moine mylonites represent the strongly sheared rocks derived from the hangingwall of the Moine Thrust. They overlie a thin (*c.* 1 m) strip of dark, phyllonitic rocks most plausibly derived from Lewisian gneisses. The original character of the rocks is completely obliterated as the associated dynamic metamorphism has thoroughly recrystallized the original amphibolite-facies mineral assemblages leaving a chloritic phyllonite. It is unclear whether these strongly sheared rocks were once the basement to the Moine (and therefore form the hangingwall to the Moine Thrust) or were derived from the foreland. However, other tracts of strongly sheared Lewisian gneisses can be found in the vicinity.

Walk about 100 m NW onto the plateau where alternations of foliated (locally mylonitic) quartzites and sheared gneisses and pegmatites crop out [NC 4491 5735]. These tracts broaden along strike to the north, back towards Ben Arnaboll, and the deformation state decreases. In these lower strain sites the depositional lamination can be found in the quartz arenites, which are part of the Basal Quartzite Member of the Eriboll Formation. Cross-bedding may be used to prove that the Lewisian–Eriboll Formation interleavings are here generated by folding. The ductile deformation fabrics relate to the folding, thus there is substantial ductile deformation in the footwall to the Moine Thrust. It is therefore probably of only semantic importance where the original discrete contact between the Moine Thrust Sheet and its 'foreland' footwall lies: the Moine Thrust here at Eriboll is a ductile shear zone.

The outcrops at Upper Kempie provide an interesting contrast to those farther north on Ben Arnaboll (Locality 15.8). Both sites contain repetitions of Eriboll Formation and Lewisian basement. At Upper Kempie the repetitions represent highly sheared folds, with the original unconformity between basement and Cambrian cover marking the contact between the units (Fig. 110). At Ben Arnaboll the alternations result from breaching imbrication, such that the Lewisian was tectonically emplaced onto the Eriboll Formation before the interleaving happened. In this case all contacts are tectonic. The two sites visited on the excursion have been chosen because it is possible to deduce these differences. In more strongly sheared and dismembered settings, such distinctions are increasingly problematic.

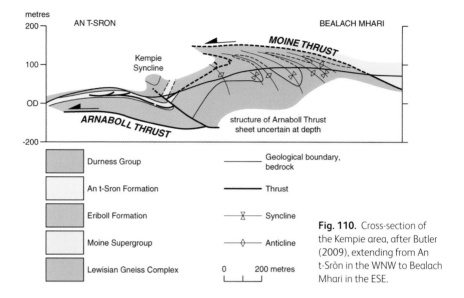

Fig. 110. Cross-section of the Kempie area, after Butler (2009), extending from An t-Sròn in the WNW to Bealach Mhari in the ESE.

Legend:
- Durness Group
- An t-Sron Formation
- Eriboll Formation
- Moine Supergroup
- Lewisian Gneiss Complex
- Geological boundary, bedrock
- Thrust
- Syncline
- Anticline
- 0   200 metres

From the mylonites the route now lies down to Kempie Bay. This descent down topography is also down structural level and provides an excellent example of a deformation gradient. The quartz arenites away from the Moine Thrust preserve good cross-bedding and depositional lamination. Folding is still evident but more open.

Continue down the steep slopes with outcrops of steeply-dipping Basal Quartzite and Pipe Rock members. Keep out of the narrow ravine at the foot of the slope (Fucoid Beds Member) and follow the north-running strip of more open ground that heads down to the road. The road sections are in the eastern (steep) limb of the Kempie Syncline (complementary to the An t-Sròn anticline, Locality 15.1). The road cuttings show overturned beds of Pipe Rock Member. These contain sheared *Skolithos* that display an easterly vergence. Deformation here presumably relates to the development of the Kempie Syncline, rather than to the general westward shearing that is typically displayed, for example on Heilam. Follow the road back to the car-park at Heilam Cottage. As the road climbs away from the coast at Ard Neackie the inferred position of the Arnaboll Thrust is crossed, so that, at the car-park, the rocks lie in the footwall. The road leads back to the parking sites.

197

Excursion 16

Roadside Stops around the North-west Highlands

Maarten Krabbendam

Purpose: This excursion provides details of a number of individual, roadside stops which do not fall easily into any one excursion, but which nonetheless are of signifi-cant interest geologically. These localities could be visited in a single day's road trip, or many of them could be taken in whilst driving to or from the main excursions. Road-side localities which fall in the main excursions, but which could also be visited as part of a road trip across the area, are mentioned briefly. These localities do not provide a full overview of the geology of the area, and for those with only a day to spare, the first halves of Excur-sions 1 and 6 are more suitable as an introduction.

Aspects covered: Classic exposures in the Lewisian Gneiss Complex, the Cambro-Ordovician succession, and the Moine Thrust Zone.

Maps: OS: 1:50,000 Landranger sheet 15 Loch Assynt and 9 Cape Wrath. BGS: 1:50,000 special sheet, Assynt district and 1:50,000 sheet 101E, Ullapool.

Terrain: These outcrops are all close to the road.

Time: Most of these localities would take less than an hour to visit. They could be treated as an excursion on their own and visited as part of a day's road trip.

Access: There are no access con-straints for this excursion, although great care should be taken at road-side stops.

Locality 16.1 [NC 1770 0279]

The Moine Thrust at Langwell.

This stop requires a short walk of about *c.*1km round trip on a good track, but the outcrop itself is somewhat slippery. The locality, which is not parti-cularly well known, provides an excellent exposure of the Moine Thrust.

Take the A835 road north from Ullapool. Approximately 10 km north of Ullapool, turn off to the right at Strathcanaird and drive towards Langwell Lodge. Do not drive as far as the lodge but park at a small parking place on the left, *c*.500 m before the lodge at [NC 167 028]. Walk along the track past the lodge to a bridge over a side stream. The Moine Thrust is exposed above a small waterfall in the River Canaird at [NC 1770 0279] (Fig. 111).

This is a very complicated outcrop of the Moine Thrust, which here overlies a small culmination – the Langwell Culmination (Elliott and Johnson, 1980). The Langwell Culmination is cut by a NNE–SSE-trending fault that occurs in the gorge of the stream to the north; this partially allowed the excellent outcrop to develop. The Moine Thrust here overlies dark-pink granitic to syenitic Ullapool Gneiss, part of the Lewisian Gneiss Complex that occurs within the Ullapool Thrust sheet (see Excursion 5), but a complex sequence of deformed rocks is associated with the thrust. In detail, the following sequence can be seen. The River Canaird flows over pink to green, densely fractured Ullapool Gneiss. Above this is *c*.0.5 m of fractured quartz arenite, which locally contains pink feldspar and is thought to be Basal Quartzite Member. Above this is a 10–30 cm thick layer of white mylonitic carbonate, with anastomosing contacts with another layer of fractured quartz arenite. This is followed by a 10–50 cm thick layer of pale green phyllonitic rock with strong anastomosing mylonitic fabric, not unlike the Oystershell Rock seen at Sango Bay (Excursion 14). The protolith of this rock is unclear. Above this is a brittle fault, with locally clayey fault gouge, marking the brittle Moine Thrust. Above the thrust is fractured mylonitic Moine psammite.

Fig. 111 The Moine Thrust, well exposed and picked out by the River Canaird, east of Langwell Lodge. Above the stream is psammitic mylonite; below is granitic Ullapool Gneiss. The thrust plane itself contains slivers of different rocks. View to the east. (BGS photograph P595958, © NERC)

199

Locality 16.2 [NC 169 056]

Moine mylonites.

Between Strathcanaird and Knockan, there are good exposures of Moine mylonites in roadside cuttings along the A835 at [NC 169 056]. The exposures are 500m NNE of the turn-off to Achiltibuie; there is a large lay-by on the east side of the road. The road cuts stretch for c.200m and are all composed of psammitic mylonite, becoming more mylonitic towards the west. At the south-western end of the cuttings there are small outcrops of the Salterella Grit and Fucoid Beds members, indicating that the Moine Thrust occurs near the corner; the thrust itself is not exposed.

Locality 16.3 [NC 208 104]

Elphin: extensional faults above the Sole Thrust.

Park at a large lay-by on the A835 in the village of Knockan [NC 212 106]. Walk south along the road for c.500m, passing a bed & breakfast, to the road cut at [NC 208 104]. This road cut contains Eilean Dubh Formation dolostones, cut by a thin sill, and shows a number of west-dipping extensional faults, with the bedding in the individual fault blocks dipping fairly steeply eastwards (Coward 1982). This zone of extensional faults overlies the Sole Thrust, which may be represented by a fault breccia at the western end of the road cut. Coward (1982) interpreted the extensional faults as part of a small-scale 'surge zone', where one part of the thrust zone moved farther onto the foreland than adjacent parts, by gravitational spreading of the thickened thrust mass.

Locality 16.4 [NC 287 096]

Allt a'Mhuillin Quarry.

Disused quarry just north of the A 837, 2.5km ESE of the Altnacealgach Motel. This location contains some of the best exposures of the rock-type 'borolanite' (pseudoleucite-syenite) in the Loch Borralan Pluton. It is fully described in Locality 10.6.

Locality 16.5 [NC 250 157]

Loch Awe Quarry.

This small, intermittently active quarry lies 3.5km north from Ledmore Junction on the A837. The quarry contains excellent exposures of the Fucoid Beds Member, and a variety of trilobites have been found here. The rock splits more easily than at most outcrops of the Fucoid Beds Member, partly because of the quarried nature and partly because it is locally metamorphosed; this also renders the siltstones very splintery and great care should be taken when hammering. The most common species is *Olenellus reticulatus* Peach, 1894, but *O. intermedius* Peach, 1894, *O. lapworthi* Peach and Horne, 1892, and *O. hamoculus* Cowie and McNamara, 1978, have also been found here; this is the type locality for the latter. Other, very rare, components of the fauna include *Salterella*, hyolithids, gastropods, echinoderm fragments and non-articulate brachiopods (Cowie and McNamara, 1978; Prigmore and Rushton, 1999).

Locality 16.6 [NC 248 200]

Stronchrubie cliffs.

Park at the large lay-by at [NC 248 200], 2km south of Inchnadamph, and look up at the cliffs to the north-east.

Along the road are outcrops of Pipe Rock Member, which dips some 10° to the east and is part of the foreland. In the rough ground east of the road, scattered outcrops of Fucoid Beds and Salterella Grit members are seen. The lower part of the cliffs to the east consists of dark grey dolostone of the Ghrudaidh Formation, cut by a prominent pale grey sill of vogesite. Above are pale grey banded dolostones of the Eilean Dubh Formation. The dolostones in the lower and middle parts of the cliff dip gently to the east, but steeply dipping slices of pale grey Eilean Dubh dolostone can be seen in the uppermost part of the cliffs to the north-east (Fig. 112). These are the Stronchrubie imbricate thrust slices which root into a floor thrust (Stronchrubie Thrust) that runs along the upper part of the cliff, separating gently dipping strata below from deformed, steeper strata above. Further to the east, the Stronchrubie Thrust links with the Traligill Thrust (Excursion 7). Below the Stronchrubie Thrust, the Sole Thrust lies roughly at the base of the cliffs. Here there has only been relatively minor displacement along the Sole Thrust.

201

Fig. 112 The imbricate thrust stack in Eilean Dubh Formation dolostones in the Stronchrubie cliffs, viewed from the lay-by to the south-west. (BGS photograph P667674, © NERC)

Locality 16.7 [NC 248 222]

Peach and Horne Monument at Inchnadamph.

On a hillock just west of Inchnadamph, overlooking both Loch Assynt and the Assynt Culmination, is a monument to Benjamin Peach and John Horne, the Geological Survey geologists who were instrumental in the mapping of the Moine Thrust Zone at the end of the 19th century. In 1912 they organised a field-trip to Assynt to summarise their results, and a page of the visitors book, showing the international flavour of this trip, is exhibited in Inchnadamph. The monument was erected in 1930 and the opening ceremony was attended by H. M. Cadell, by then the only surviving member of the original Geological Survey team that mapped the North-west Highlands.

Locality 16.8 [NC 210 250] to [NC 240 240]

Loch Assynt to Skiag Bridge section.

Exposures along the A837 near Skiag Bridge, 3km NNW of Inchnadamph [NC 235 244], provide the classic section through the foreland, introducing the different rock types of the area. This section is described in full in Excursion 1.

Locality 16.9 [NC 234 248]

Cnoc Breac: viewpoint for the double unconformity.

A large lay-by on the west side of the A894, some 500m north from Skiag Bridge, provides a good viewpoint of the famed 'double unconformity'. Being on a north facing slope, the view is best photographed early or late in the day

On the south side of Loch Assynt is the hill of Beinn Garbh (539m). At the base is hummocky ground, underlain by rocks of the Lewisian Gneiss Complex (Fig. 113). Above this, much of the north face of the hill is formed of flat-lying layers of Torridon Group sandstone (mainly Applecross Formation). The eastern side of Beinn Garbh is a dipslope of Basal Quartzite Member (Eriboll Formation), dipping some 10–15° to the east, capping the eastern slopes and giving Beinn Garbh its roughly triangular shape.

The formation of the double unconformity requires the following sequence: (1) deposition of Torridon Group on Lewisian Gneiss Complex, forming the first, Neoproterozoic unconformity; (2) westward tilting (c.10–15°) and erosion to form a flat peneplain by Cambrian times; (3) deposition of the Eriboll Formation; (4) eastward tilting of c.10–15°.

The double unconformity can be regarded as the intersection of two approximately planar surfaces. On the southern shore of Loch Assynt, this intersection is positioned c.100m above loch level. In contrast, on the

Fig. 113 The double unconformity on the north-facing slopes of Beinn Garbh, with Loch Assynt in the foreground. View southwards from the north side of Loch Assynt. (BGS Photograph P527482, © NERC)

203

northern shore of Loch Assynt, the double unconformity lies some 10–20m below loch level, some 500m west of Skiag Bridge. The double unconformity can thus be used to accurately constrain the displacement along the Loch Assynt Fault (Krabbendam and Leslie, 2010), which records both pre- and post-thrust movement.

Locality 16.10 [NC 236 321]

Loch Glencoul.

A viewpoint on the A894 at Unapool with an SNH interpretative panel offers one of the classical geological views (Fig. 114). On the hill north of Loch Glencoul, the easterly-dipping Glencoul Thrust emplaces rocks of the Lewisian Gneiss Complex (forming the hummocky topography on the upper slopes of Beinn Aird da Loch) over cliffs of pink Cambrian quartz arenite of the Eriboll Formation, which in turn rests unconformably upon Lewisian gneiss of the foreland. Note that Krabbendam and Leslie (2004) argue that the Glencoul Thrust Sheet terminates against a lateral ramp along Loch Glencoul, and that the Lewisian gneiss to the north of Loch Glencoul is continuous with that forming the Ben More Thrust Sheet farther south-east.

Further to the east, the Stack of Glencoul is visible. This hill is composed of mylonites of the Moine Supergroup and Eriboll Formation. The Moine Thrust is exposed at the base of the west face of the Stack (see Excursion 9).

Fig. 114 The Glencoul Thrust from Unapool. Lewisian gneiss, characterised by rather hummocky topography, forms the upper slopes of the hill; this has been thrust over the Eriboll Formation quartz arenites that form the prominent cliff line. (BGS photograph P500377, © NERC)

Locality 16.11 [NC 232 486]

Loch na Fiacaill – the 'multicoloured rock stop'.

Some 2.5 km north of Laxford Bridge, on the A838, is a large lay-by with an interpretational panel. Road cuts opposite the lay-by give a good introduction to the complexities of the Lewisian Gneiss Complex, and three main elements can be seen (Fig. 115). Grey quartzo-feldspathic gneisses show a well developed gneissosity, dipping gently to the south. Dark-green to black amphibolite-bearing basic sheets also dip gently south and are approximately parallel to the gneissosity. However, detailed examination along the contacts shows that the basic sheets have cross-cutting relationships with the gneiss. The basic sheets are probably Scourie Dykes, but have been deformed and generally contain a fabric. Clearly, the Scourie Dykes intruded the gneisses at a relatively high angle and have been deformed into sub-parallelism to the gneissosity by later deformation. Both the gneisses and the basic sheets are cut by a swarm of pegmatitic granite sheets, some of which show boudinage. One of these granite sheets has been dated at $c.1855$ Ma (Friend and Kinny, 2001); these are Laxfordian granites, similar to those seen on the south side of the Laxford Shear Zone at Tarbet (Excursion 13). However, this locality lies to the north of the Laxford Shear Zone, in the Rhiconich Terrane.

Fig. 115 Road cuttings in the Rhiconich Terrane of the Lewisian Gneiss Complex, showing grey tonalitic gneisses cut by black Scourie Dykes and pink Laxfordian granite. (Photograph: © K. M. Goodenough)

205

References

AMOR, K., HESSELBO, S. P., PORCELLI, D., THACKREY, S. and PARNELL, J. (2008): A Precambrian proximal ejecta blanket from Scotland, *Geology*, **36**, pp. 303–306.

ATTFIELD, P. (1987): The Structural History of the Canisp Shear Zone, in PARK, R. G. and TARNEY, J. (eds): *Evolution of the Lewisian and Comparable Precambrian High Grade Terranes*, Geological Society Special Publication, **27** (London: The Geological Society), pp. 165–73.

BAILEY, E. B. (1935): The Glencoul Nappe and the Assynt Culmination, *Geological Magazine*, **72**, pp. 151–65.

BARBER, A. J., BEACH, A., PARK, R. G., TARNEY, J. and STEWART, A. D. (1978): The Lewisian and Torridonian Rocks of North-west Scotland, *Geologists' Association Field Guide*, no. 21.

BARBER, A. J. and SOPER, N. J. (1973): Summer field meeting in the North-West of Scotland, *Proceedings of the Geologists Association*, **84**, pp. 207–35.

BARNICOAT, A. C. and O'HARA, M. J. (1979): High temperature pyroxenes from an ironstone at Scourie, *Mineralogical Magazine*, **43**, pp. 371–75.

BEACH, A. (1973): The mineralogy of high temperature shear zones at Scourie, NW Scotland, *Journal of Petrology*, **14**, pp. 231–48.

BEACH, A. (1978): The Scourie–Laxford Region (Lewisian), in BARBER, A. J., BEACH, A., PARK, R. G., TARNEY, J. and STEWART, A. D. (eds): The Lewisian and Torridonian Rocks of North-West Scotland, *Geologists' Association Field Guide*, no. 21, pp. 14–27.

BEACH, A., COWARD, M. P. and GRAHAM, R. H. (1974): An interpretation of the structural evolution of the Laxford Front, north-west Scotland, *Scottish Journal of Geology*, **9**, pp. 297–308.

BEACOM, L. E. (1999): *The kinematic evolution of reactivated and non-reactivated faults in basement rocks, NW Scotland*. Unpub. PhD Thesis, Queen's University of Belfast.

BEACOM, L. E., ANDERSON, T. B. and HOLDSWORTH, R. E. (1999): Using basement-hosted clastic dykes as syn-rifting palaeostress indicators; an example from the basal Stoer Group, Northwest Scotland, *Geological Magazine*, **136**, pp. 301–310.

BEACOM, L. E., HOLDSWORTH, R. E., McCAFFREY, K. J. W. and ANDERSON, T. B. (2001): A quantitative study of the influence of pre-existing compositional and fabric heterogeneities upon fracture zone development during reactivation, in HOLDSWORTH, R. E., STRACHAN, R., MAGLOUGHLIN, J. F. and KNIPE, R. J. (eds): *The nature and tectonic significance of fault zone weakening*, Geological Society Special Publication, **186** (London: The Geological Society), pp. 195–211.

BOYER, S. E. and ELLIOTT, D. (1982): Thrust systems, *Bulletin of the American Association of Petroleum Geologists*, **66**, pp. 1196–230.

BRITISH GEOLOGICAL SURVEY (1998): Summer Isles, Scotland Sheet 101W, Solid and Drift geology, 1:50,000 (Keyworth, Nottingham: British Geological Survey).

BRITISH GEOLOGICAL SURVEY (2002a): Loch Eriboll, Scotland Sheet 114W, 1:50,000 (Keyworth, Nottingham: British Geological Survey).

BRITISH GEOLOGICAL SURVEY (2002b): Point of Stoer. Scotland Sheet 107W, Solid and Drift Geology, 1:50,000 (Keyworth, Nottingham: British Geological Survey).

BRITISH GEOLOGICAL SURVEY (2007): Assynt, Scotland Special Sheet, Bedrock, 1:50,000, Geology Series (Keyworth, Nottingham: British Geological Survey).

BRITISH GEOLOGICAL SURVEY (2008): Scotland Sheet 101E Ullapool, Bedrock. 1:50,000 (Keyworth, Nottingham: British Geological Survey).

BURTON, K. W., CAPMAS, F., BIRCK, J.-L.,

ALLEGRE, C. J. and COHEN, A. S. (2000): Resolving crystallisation ages of Archaean mafic-ultramafic rocks using the Re-Os isotope system, *Earth and Planetary Science Letters*, **179**, pp. 453–67.

BUTLER, R. W. H. (1982): A structural analysis of the Moine Thrust Zone between Loch Eriboll and Foinaven, NW Scotland, *Journal of Structural Geology*, **4**, pp. 19–29.

BUTLER, R. W. H. (1987): Thrust Sequences, *Journal of the Geological Society of London*, **144**, pp. 619–34.

BUTLER, R. W. H. (1988): The Moine Thrust Belt at Loch Eriboll, in ALLISON, I., MAY, F. and STRACHAN, R. (eds): *An Excursion Guide to the Moine Geology of the Scottish Highlands* (Edinburgh: Scottish Academic Press), pp. 195–215.

BUTLER, R. W. H. (1997): Late Proterozoic rift faults and basement-cover relationships within the Ben More thrust sheet, NW Scotland, *Journal of the Geological Society of London*, **154**, pp. 761–64.

BUTLER, R. W. H. (2004): The nature of 'roof thrusts' in the Moine Thrust Belt, NW Scotland: implications for the structural evolution of thrust belts, *Journal of the Geological Society of London*, **161**, pp. 849–60.

BUTLER, R. W. H. (2007): Peach and Horne – the memoir at 100, *Geoscientist*, **17**, pp. 20–25.

BUTLER, R. W. H. (2009): Moine Thrust Belt, in MENDUM, J. R., BARBER, A. J., BUTLER, R. W. H., FLINN, D., GOODENOUGH, K. M., KRABBENDAM, M., PARK, R. G. and STEWART, A. D. (eds): Lewisian, Torridonian and Moine Rocks of Scotland, *Geological Conservation Review Series*, vol. 34, pp. 229–348 (Peterborough: Joint Nature Conservation Committee)

BUTLER, R. W. H., HOLDSWORTH, R. E. and MATTHEWS, S. J. (2006): Styles of basement involvement in the Moine Thrust Belt, NW Scotland, in MAZZOLI, S. and BUTLER, R. W. H. (eds): Styles of continental contraction, Special Paper of the Geological Society of America, **414**.

CADELL, H. M. (1888): Experimental researches in mountain building, *Transactions of the Royal Society of Edinburgh*, **35**, pp. 337–57.

CALLAWAY, C. (1884): Notes on progressive metamorphism, *Geological Magazine*, **1**, pp. 218–24.

CARTWRIGHT, I. and BARNICOAT, A. C. (1987): Petrology of Scourian supra-crustal rocks and orthogneisses from Stoer, NW Scotland: implications for the geological evolution of the Lewisian complex, in PARK, R. G. and TARNEY, J. (eds): *Evolution of the Lewisian and comparable Precambrian high-grade terrains*, Geological Society Special Publication, **27** (London: The Geological Society), pp. 93–107.

CAWOOD, P. A., NEMCHIN, A. A., STRACHAN, R. A., KINNY, P. D. and LOEWY, S. (2004): Laurentian provenance and an intracratonic tectonic setting for the Moine Supergroup, Scotland, constrained by detrital zircons from the Loch Eil and Glen Urquhart successions, *Journal of the Geological Society of London*, **161**, pp. 861–74.

CHAPMAN, H. J. (1979): 2390 Myr Rb-Sr whole-rock age for the Scourie dykes of north-west Scotland, *Nature*, **277**, pp. 652–43.

CHOWDHARY, P. K. and BOWES, D. R. (1972): Structure of Lewisian rocks between Loch Inchard and Loch Laxford, Sutherland, Scotland, *Krystalinikum*, **9**, pp. 21–51.

CHRISTIE, J. M. (1956): *The post-Cambrian thrusts of the Assynt region*, Unpublished PhD Thesis, University of Edinburgh.

CHRISTIE, J. M. (1960): Mylonitic rocks of the Moine thrust zone in the Assynt region, northwest Scotland, *Transactions of the Edinburgh Geological Society*, **18**, pp. 79–93.

CHRISTIE, J. M. (1963): The Moine thrust zone in the Assynt region, Northwest Scotland, *University of California Publications in Geological Sciences*, **40**, pp. 345–440.

CHRISTIE, J. M. (1965): The Moine thrust zone in the Assynt region, northwest Scotland (discussion), *Journal of Geology*, **73**, pp. 672–81.

CORFU, F., HEAMAN, L. M. and ROGERS, G. (1994): Polymetamorphic evolution of the Lewisian complex, NW Scotland, as recorded by U-Pb isotopic compositions of zircon, titanite and rutile, *Contributions to Mineralogy and Petrology*, **117**, pp. 215–28.

COWARD, M. P. (1980): The Caledonian

thrust and shear zones of NW Scotland, *Journal of Structural Geology*, **2**, pp. 11–17.

COWARD, M. P. (1982): Surge zones in the Moine Thrust Zone of NW Scotland, *Journal of Structural Geology*, **4**, pp. 247–56.

COWARD, M. P. (1983): The thrust and shear zones of the Moine Thrust Zone of NW Scotland, *Journal of the Geological Society of London*, **140**, pp. 795–811.

COWARD, M. P. (1984): A geometrical study of the Arnaboll and Heilam thrust sheets, NW of Ben Arnaboll, Sutherland, *Scottish Journal of Geology*, **20**, pp. 87–106.

COWARD, M. P. (1985): The thrust structures of southern Assynt, Moine thrust zone, *Geological Magazine*, **122**, pp. 596–607.

COWARD, M. P. (1988): The Moine Thrust and the Scottish Caledonides, in MITRA, G. and WOJTAL, S. (eds): *Geometries and Mechanics of Thrusting, with special reference to the Appalachians*, Geological Society of America Special Paper, **222**, pp. 1–16.

COWARD, M. P. and ENDFIELD, M. A. (1987): The structure of the West Orkney and adjacent basins, in BROOKS, J. and GLENNIE, K. (eds): *The Petroleum Geology of NW Europe* (Graham and Trotman), pp. 687–96.

COWARD, M. P. and KIM, J. H. (1981): Strain within thrust sheets, in McCLAY, K. R. and PRICE, N. J. (eds): *Thrust and Nappe Tectonics*, Geological Society Special Publication, **9** (London: The Geological Society), pp. 275–92.

COWIE, J. W. and McNAMARA, K. J. (1978): Olenellus (Trilobita) from the Lower Cambrian strata of northwest Scotland, *Palaeontology*, **21**, pp. 615–34.

DALLMEYER, R. D., STRACHAN, R. A., ROGERS, G., WATT, G. R. and FRIEND, C. R. L. (2001): Dating deformation and cooling in the Caledonian thrust nappes of north Sutherland, Scotland: insights from ^{40}Ar/^{39}Ar and Rb-Sr chronology, *Journal of the Geological Society of London*, **158**, pp. 501–12.

DAVIES, F. B. (1974): A layered basic complex in the Lewisian, south of Loch Laxford, Sutherland, *Journal of the Geological Society of London*, **130**, pp. 279–84.

DAVISON, S. and HAMBREY, M. J. (1996): Indications of glaciation at the base of the Proterozoic Stoer Group (Torridonian), NW Scotland, *Journal of the Geological Society of London*, **153**, pp. 139–49.

DAVISON, S. and HAMBREY, M. J. (1997): Discussion on indications of glaciation at the base of the Proterozoic Stoer Group (Torridonian), NW Scotland, *Journal of the Geological Society of London*, **154**, pp. 1087–88.

ELLIOTT, D. and JOHNSON, M. R. W. (1980): Structural evolution in the northern part of the Moine thrust belt, NW Scotland, *Transactions of the Royal Society of Edinburgh: Earth Sciences*, **71**, pp. 69–96.

EVANS, C. R. (1965): Geochronology of the Lewisian basement near Lochinver, Sutherland, *Nature*, **204**, pp. 638–41.

EVANS, D. J. and WHITE, S. H. (1984): Microstructural and fabric studies from the rocks of the Moine nappe, Eriboll, NW Scotland, *Journal of Structural Geology*, **6**, pp. 369–90.

FISCHER, M. W. and COWARD, M. P. (1982): Strains and folds within thrust sheets: the Heilam sheet NW Scotland, *Tectonophysics*, **88**, pp. 291–312.

FREEMAN, S. R., BUTLER, R. W. H., CLIFF, R. A. and REX, D. C. (1998): Direct dating of mylonite evolution; a multi-disciplinary geochronological study from the Moine thrust zone, NW Scotland, *Journal of the Geological Society of London*, **155**, pp. 745–58.

FRIEND, C. R. L., JONES, K. A. and BURNS, I. M. (2000): New high-pressure granulite event in the Moine Supergroup, northern Scotland: implications for Taconic (early Caledonian) crustal evolution, *Geology*, **28**, pp. 543–46.

FRIEND, C. R. L. and KINNY, P. D. (1995): New evidence for protolith ages of Lewisian granulites, northwest Scotland, *Geology*, **23**, pp. 1027–1030.

FRIEND, C. R. L. and KINNY, P. D. (2001): A reappraisal of the Lewisian Gneiss Complex: geochronological evidence for its tectonic assembly from disparate terranes in the Proterozoic, *Contributions to Mineralogy and Petrology*, **142**, pp. 198–218.

FRIEND, C. R. L., KINNY, P. D., ROGERS, G., STRACHAN, R. A. and PATTERSON, B. A. (1997): U-Pb zircon geo-chronological evidence for Neoproterozoic events in the Glenfinnan Group (Moine Supergroup): the formation of the Ardgour granite gneiss, north-west Scotland, *Contributions to Mineralogy and Petrology*, **128**, pp. 101–13.

FRIEND, C. R. L., STRACHAN, R. A., KINNY, P. D. and WATT, G. R. (2003): Provenance of the Moine Supergroup of NW Scotland; evidence from geochronology of detrital and inherited zircons from (meta)-sedimentary rocks, granites and migmatites, *Journal of the Geological Society of London*, **160**, pp. 247–57.

GEIKIE, A. (1884): The crystalline schists of the Scottish Highlands, *Nature*, **31**, pp. 29–31.

GLENDINNING, N. R. W. (1988): Sedimentary structures and sequences within a late Proterozoic tidal shelf deposit; the upper Morar Psammite Formation of north-western Scotland, in WINCHESTER, J. A. (eds): *Later Proterozoic stratigraphy of the Northern Atlantic Regions* (Glasgow and London: Blackie), pp. 17–31.

GOODENOUGH, K. M., EVANS, J. A. and KRABBENDAM, M. (2006): Constraining the maximum age of movements in the Moine Thrust Belt: dating the Canisp Porphyry, *Scottish Journal of Geology*, **42**, pp. 77–82.

GOODENOUGH, K. M., MILLAR, I. L., STRACHAN, R., KRABBENDAM, M. and EVANS, J. A. (2011): Timing of regional deformation and development of the Moine Thrust Zone in the Scottish Caledonides: constraints from the U-Pb geochronology of alkaline intrusions, *Journal of the Geological Society of London*, **168**, pp. 99–114.

GOODENOUGH, K. M., PARK, R. G., KRABBENDAM, M., MYERS, J. S., WHEELER, J., LOUGHLIN, S., CROWLEY, Q., L, F. C. R., BEACH, A., KINNY, P. D. and GRAHAM, R. (2010): The Laxford Shear Zone: an end-Archaean terrane boundary?, in LAW, R., BUTLER, R. W. H., HOLDSWORTH, R. E., KRABBENDAM, M. and STRACHAN, R. (eds): *Continental Tectonics and Mountain Building*, Geological Society Special Publication, **335** (London: The Geological Society), pp. 101–118.

GOODENOUGH, K. M., YOUNG, B. N. and PARSONS, I. (2004): The minor intrusions

of Assynt, NW Scotland: early development of magmatism along the Caledonian Front, *Mineralogical Magazine*, **68**, pp. 541–60.

GRACIE, A. J. and STEWART, A. D. (1967): Torridonian sediments at Enard Bay, Ross-shire, *Scottish Journal of Geology*, **3**, pp. 181–94.

HALLIDAY, A. N., AFTALION, M., PARSONS, I., DICKIN, A. P. and JOHNSON, M. R. W. (1987): Syn-orogenic alkaline magmatism and its relationship to the Moine Thrust Zone and the thermal state of the lithosphere in NW Scotland, *Journal of the Geological Society of London*, **144**, pp. 611–17.

HAQ, B. U. and SCHUTTER, S. R. (2009): A chronology of Palaeozoic sea-level changes, *Science*, **322**, pp. 64–68.

HEAMAN, L. and TARNEY, J. (1989): U-Pb baddeleyite ages for the Scourie dyke swarm, Scotland: evidence for two distinct intrusion events, *Nature*, **340**, pp. 705–708.

HIGGINS, A. K., SMITH, M. P., SOPER, N. J., LESLIE, A. G., RASMUSSEN, J. A. and SONDERHOLM, M. (2001): The Neoproterozoic Hekla Sund Basin, Eastern North Greenland: a pre-Iapetan extensional sequence thrust across its rift shoulders during the Caledonian orogeny, *Journal of the Geological Society of London*, **158**, pp. 487–99.

HIPPLER, S. J. and KNIPE, R. J. (1990): The evolution of cataclastic fault rocks from a pre-existing mylonite, in KNIPE, R. J. and RUTTER, E. H. (eds): *Deformation Mechanisms, Rheology and Tectonics*, Geological Society Special Publication, **54** (London: the Geological Society), pp. 71–79.

HOLDSWORTH, R. E., ALSOP, G. I. and STRACHAN, R. A. (2007): Tectonic stratigraphy and structural continuity of the northernmost Moine Thrust Zone and Moine Nappe, Scottish Caledonides, in RIES, A. C., BUTLER, R. W. H. and GRAHAM, R. H. (eds): *Deformation of the Continental Crust: the Legacy of Mike Coward*, Geological Society Special Publication, **272** (London: The Geological Society), pp. 121–42.

HOLDSWORTH, R. E., STRACHAN, R. and ALSOP, G. I. (2001): Geology of the Tongue District, *Memoir of the British Geological Survey* (London: HMSO).

HOLDSWORTH, R. E., STRACHAN, R. A., ALSOP, G. I., GRANT, C. J. and WILSON, R. W. (2006): Thrust sequences and the significance of low-angle, out-of-sequence faults in the northernmost Moine Nappe and Moine Thrust Zone, NW Scotland, *Journal of the Geological Society of London*, **163**, pp. 801–814.

HUSELBEE, M. Y. and THOMAS, A. T. (1998): Olenellus and conodonts from the Durness Group, NW Scotland, and the correlation of the Durness succession, *Scottish Journal of Geology*, **34**, pp. 83–88.

JOHNSON, M. R. W. (1965): The Moine Thrust: a discussion, *Journal of Geology*, **73**, pp. 672–75.

JOHNSON, M. R. W. (1967): Mylonite zones and mylonite banding, *Nature*, **213**, pp. 246–47.

JOHNSON, M. R. W. and PARSONS, I. (1979): *Geological Excursion Guide to the Assynt District of Sutherland* (Edinburgh: Edinburgh Geological Society).

KELLEY, S. P. (1988): The relationship between K-Ar mineral ages, mica grain sizes and movement on the Moine Thrust Zone, NW Highlands, Scotland, *Journal of the Geological Society of London*, **145**, pp. 1–10.

KINNAIRD, T. C., PRAVE, A., KIRKLAND, C. L., HORSTWOOD, M., PARRISH, R. and BATCHELOR, R. A. (2007): The late Mesoproterozoic–early Neoproterozoic tectonostratigraphic evolution of NW Scotland: the Torridonian revisited, *Journal of the Geological Society of London*, **164**, pp. 541–51.

KINNY, P. and FRIEND, C. (1997): U-Pb isotopic evidence for the accretion of different crustal blocks to form the Lewisian Complex of Northwest Scotland, *Contributions to Mineralogy and Petrology*, pp. 326–40.

KINNY, P. D., FRIEND, C. R. L. and LOVE, G. J. (2005): Proposal for a terrane-based nomenclature for the Lewisian Complex of NW Scotland, *Journal of the Geological Society of London*, **162**, pp. 175–86.

KINNY, P. D., FRIEND, C. R. L., STRACHAN, R. A., WATT, G. R. and BURNS, I. M. (1999): U-Pb geochronology of regional migmatites in East Sutherland, Scotland; evidence for crustal melting during the Caledonian Orogeny, *Journal of the Geological Society of London*, 156, pp. 1143–52.

KINNY, P. D., STRACHAN, R. A., FRIEND, C. R. L., KOCKS, H., ROGERS, G. and PATERSON, B. A. (2003): U-Pb geochronology of deformed metagranites in central Sutherland, Scotland; evidence for widespread late Silurian metamorphism and ductile deformation of the Moine Supergroup during the Caledonian orogeny, *Journal of the Geological Society of London*, **160**, pp. 259–69.

KNIGHT, I. and JAMES, N. P. (1987): Stratigraphy of the St George Group (Lower Ordovician), western Newfoundland: the interaction between eustasy and tectonics, *Canadian Journal of Earth Sciences*, **24**, pp. 1927–52.

KRABBENDAM, M. and LESLIE, A. G. (2004): Lateral ramps and thrust terminations: an example from the Moine Thrust Zone, NW Scotland, *Journal of the Geological Society of London*, **161**, pp. 551–54.

KRABBENDAM, M. and LESLIE, A. G. (2010): Lateral variations and linkages in thrust geometry: the Traligill Transverse Zone, Assynt Culmination, Moine Thrust Belt, NW Scotland, in LAW, R., BUTLER, R. W. H., HOLDSWORTH, R. E., KRABBENDAM, M. and STRACHAN, R. (eds): *Continental Tectonics and Mountain Building*, Geological Society Special Publication, **335** (London: The Geological Society of London), pp. 333–56.

KRABBENDAM, M., PRAVE, A. P. and CHEER, D. (2008): A fluvial origin for the Neoproterozoic Morar Group, NW Scotland; implications for Torridon–Morar Group correlation and the Grenville Orogen Foreland Basin, *Journal of the Geological Society of London*, **165**, pp. 379–94.

LAPWORTH, C. (1883): On the structure and metamorphism of the rocks of the Durness–Eriboll district, *Proceedings of the Geological Association*, **8**, pp. 438–42.

LAPWORTH, C. (1885): The Highland Controversy in British geology: its causes, course and consequence, *Nature*, **32**, pp. 558–59.

LAW, R. D. (1987): Heterogeneous deformation and quartz crystallographic fabric transitions; natural examples from the Moine thrust zone at the Stack of Glencoul, northern

Assynt, *Journal of Structural Geology*, **9**, pp. 819–33.

LAW, R. D. (1998): Quartz mylonites from the Moine thrust zone at the Stack of Glencoul, NW Scotland, in SNOKE, A. W., TULLIS, J. and TODD, V. R. (eds): *Fault-Related Rocks: a Photographic Atlas* (Princeton, New Jersey: Princeton University Press), pp. 490–93.

LAW, R. D. (2010): Moine thrust zone mylonites at the Stack of Glencoul: II – results of vorticity analyses and their tectonic significance, in LAW, R. D., BUTLER, R. W. H., HOLDSWORTH, R., KRABBENDAM, M. and STRACHAN, R. A. (eds): *Continental Tectonics and Mountain Building – The Legacy of Peach and Horne*, Geological Society Special Publication (London: The Geological Society), **335**, 579–602.

LAW, R. D., BUTLER, R. W. H., HOLDSWORTH, R., KRABBENDAM, M. and STRACHAN, R. A. (eds) (2010a): *Continental Tectonics and Mountain Building – The Legacy of Peach and Horne*, Geological Society Special Publication (London: The Geological Society), **335**.

LAW, R. D., CASEY, M. and KNIPE, R. J. (1986): Kinematic and tectonic significance of microstructural and crystallographic fabrics within quartz mylonites from the Assynt and Eriboll regions of the Moine thrust zone, NW Scotland, *Transactions of the Royal Society of Edinburgh, Earth Sciences*, **77**, pp. 99–126.

LAW, R. D., MAINPRICE, D., CASEY, M., LLOYD, G. E., KNIPE, R. J., COOK, B. and THIGPEN, J. R. (2010b): Moine thrust zone mylonites at the Stack of Glencoul: I – microstructures, strain and influence of recrystallization on quartz crystal fabric development, in LAW, R. D., BUTLER, R. W. H., HOLDSWORTH, R., KRABBEN-DAM, M. and STRACHAN, R. A. (eds): *Continental Tectonics and Mountain Building – The Legacy of Peach and Horne*, Geological Society Special Publication (London: The Geological Society), **335**, 543–57.

LAWSON, D. E. (1972): Torridonian volcanic sediments, *Scottish Journal of Geology*, **8**, pp. 345–62.

McCLAY, K. R. and COWARD, M. P. (1981): The Moine Thrust Zone: an overview, in

McCLAY, K. R. and PRICE, N. J. (eds): *Thrust and Nappe Tectonics*, Geological Society Special Publication, **9** (London: The Geological Society), pp. 241–60.

MacGREGOR, M. and PHEMISTER, J. (1937): *Geological Excursion Guide to the Assynt District of Sutherland* (Edinburgh: Edinburgh Geological Society).

McKIE, T. (1990): Tidal and storm influenced sedimentation from a Cambrian transgressive passive margin sequence, *Journal of the Geological Society of London*, **147**, pp. 785–94.

McKIE, T. (1993): Relative sea-level changes and the development of a Cambrian transgression, *Geological Magazine*, **130**, pp. 245–56.

McKIE, T. and DONOVAN, S. K. (1992): Lower Cambrian echinoderm ossicles from the Fucoid Beds, northwest Scotland, *Scottish Journal of Geology*, **28**, pp. 49–53.

McLEISH, A. J. (1971): Strain analysis of deformed pipe rock in the Moine Thrust Zone, northwest Scotland, *Tectonophysics*, **12**, pp. 469–503.

MENDUM, J. R., BARBER, A. J., BUTLER, R. W. H., FLINN, D., GOODENOUGH, K. M., KRABBENDAM, M., PARK, R. G. and STEWART, A. D. (2009): *Lewisian, Torridonian and Moine rocks of Scotland*, Geological Conservation Review Series, **34** (Peterborough: Joint Nature Conservation Committee).

MILLAR, I. L. (1999): Neoproterozoic extensional basic magmatism associated with emplacement of the West Highland granite gneiss in the Moine Supergroup of NW Scotland, *Journal of the Geological Society of London*, **156**, pp. 1153–62.

MILNE, K. P. (1978): Folding and thrusting in the upper Glen Oykel area, Assynt, *Scottish Journal of Geology*, **14**, pp. 141–46.

MORROW, D. W. (1978): Dolomitisation of Lower Palaeozoic burrow-fillings, *Journal of Sedimentary Petrology*, **48**, pp. 295–305.

NICHOLAS, C. J. (1994): New stratigraphical constraints on the Durness Group of NW Scotland, *Scottish Journal of Geology*, **30**, pp. 73–85.

NICHOLSON, P. G. (1993): *A basin reappraisal of the Proterozoic Torridon Group, northwest Scotland*, Special

Publication of the International Association of Sedimentologists, **20**, pp. 183–202.

NIELSEN, A.-T. (2004): Ordovician sea level changes: a Baltoscandian perspective, in WEBBY, B. D., PARIS, F., DROSER, M. L. and PERCIVAL, I. G. (eds): *The Great Ordovician Biodiversification Event* (New York: Columbia University Press), pp. 84–93.

O'HARA, M. J. (1960): *The metamorphic petrology of the Scourie district, Sutherland,* unpub. PhD Thesis, University of Cambridge.

O'HARA, M. J. (1961a): Zoned ultrabasic and basic gneiss masses in the early Lewisian metamorphic complex at Scourie, Sutherland, *Journal of Petrology,* **2**, pp. 248–76.

O'HARA, M. J. (1961b): Petrology of the Scourie dyke, Sutherland, *Mineralogy Magazine,* **32**, pp. 848–65.

OLDROYD, D. R. (1990): *The Highlands Controversy: Constructing Geological Knowledge through Fieldwork in Nineteenth-Century Britain* (Chicago: University of Chicago Press).

PALMER, T. J., McKERROW, W. S. and COWIE, J. W. (1980): Sedimentological evidence for a stratigraphical break in the Durness Group, *Nature,* **287**, pp. 721-22.

PARK, R. G., CLIFF, R. A., FETTES, D. J. and STEWART, A. D. (1994): Precambrian rocks in northwest Scotland west of the Moine Thrust, in GIBBONS, W. and HARRIS, A. L. (eds): *A Revised Correlation of Precambrian Rocks in the British Isles,* Geological Society Special Report 22 (London: The Geological Society), pp. 6–22.

PARK, R. G. and TARNEY, J. (1987): The Lewisian complex: a typical Precambrian high-grade terrain?, in PARK, R. G. and TARNEY, J. (eds): *Evolution of the Lewisian and comparable Precambrian high-grade terrains,* Geological Society Special Publication, **27** (London: The Geological Society of London), pp. 13-25.

PARSONS, I. (1965a): The feldspathic syenites of the Loch Ailsh intrusion, Assynt, Scotland, *Journal of Petrology,* **6**, pp. 365–94.

PARSONS, I. (1965b): The sub-surface shape of the Loch Ailsh intrusion, Assynt, as deduced from magnetic anomalies across the contact, with a note on traverses across the Loch Borrolan Complex, *Geological Magazine,* **102**, pp. 46–58.

PARSONS, I. (1999): Late Ordovician to mid-Silurian alkaline intrusions of the North-west Highlands of Scotland, in STEPHENSON, D., BEVINS, R. E., MILLWARD, D., HIGHTON, A. J., PARSONS, I., STONE, P. and WADSWORTH, W. J. (eds): Caledonian Igneous Rocks of Great Britain, Geological Conservation Review Series, **17** (Peterborough: Joint Nature Conservation Committee), pp. 345–93.

PARSONS, I. and McKIRDY, A. P. (1983): The interrelationship of igneous activity and thrusting in Assynt: excavations at Loch Borralan, *Scottish Journal of Geology,* **19**, pp. 59–67.

PEACH, B. N. (1894): Additions to the Fauna of the Olenellus-zone of the North-West Highlands, *Quarterly Journal of the Geological Society of London,* **50**, pp. 661.

PEACH, B. N. and HORNE, J. (1892): The Olenellus zone in the North-West Highlands of Scotland, *Quarterly Journal of the Geological Society of London,* **48**, pp. 227.

PEACH, B. N., HORNE, J., GUNN, W., CLOUGH, C. T., HINXMAN, L. W. and TEALL, J. J. H. (1907): *The geological structure of the North-West Highlands of Scotland,* Memoir of the Geological Society of Great Britain.

PHEMISTER, J. (1926): The alkaline igneous rocks of the Loch Ailsh District, in READ, H. H., PHEMISTER, J. and ROSS, G. (eds): The Geology of Strath Oykell and Lower Loch Shin. Memoir of the Geological Survey of Great Britain, Sheet 102 (Scotland), pp. 22–111.

PIDGEON, R. T. and BOWES, D. R. (1972): Zircon U-Pb ages of granulites from the central region of the Lewisian of north-western Scotland, *Geological Magazine,* **109**, pp. 247–58.

PRIGMORE, J. K. and RUSHTON, A. W. A. (1999): Scotland: Cambrian and Ordovician of the Hebridean Terrane, in RUSHTON, A. W. A., OWEN, A. W., OWENS, R. M. and PRIGMORE, J. K. (eds): British Cambrian to Ordovician Stratigraphy, *Geological Conservation Review Series,* **18**, pp. 295–315 (Chapman & Hall).

RAINBIRD, R. H., HAMILTON, M. A. and YOUNG, G. M. (2001): Detrital zircon geo-chronology and provenance of the

Torridonian, NW Scotland, *Journal of the Geological Society of London*, **158**, pp. 15–27.

RAMSAY, J. G. and GRAHAM, R. (1970): Strain variation in shear belts, *Canadian Journal of Earth Sciences*, **7**, pp. 786–813.

RIDER, M. H. (2005): *Hutton's Arse* (Rogart: Rider-French Consulting).

ROGERS, G., HYSLOP, E. K., STRACHAN, R., PATERSON, B. A. and HOLDSWORTH, R. E. (1998): The structural setting and U-Pb geochronology of Knoydartian pegmatites in Invernessshire: evidence for Neoproterozoic tectono-thermal events in the Moine of NW Scotland, *Journal of the Geological Society of London*, **155**, pp. 685–96.

ROGERS, G., KINNY, P. D., STRACHAN, R. A., FRIEND, C. R. L. and PATTERSON, B. A. (2001): U-Pb geochronology of the Fort Augustus granite gneiss, constraints on the timing of Neoproterozoic and Paleozoic tectonothermal events in the NW Highlands of Scotland, *Journal of the Geological Society of London*, **158**, pp. 7–14.

ROLLINSON, H. R. (1981): Garnet-pyroxene thermometry and barometry in the Scourie granulites, *Lithos*, 14, pp. 225–38.

SABINE, P. A. (1953): The petrography and geological significance of the post-Cambrian minor intrusions of Assynt and the adjoining districts of north-west Scotland, *Quarterly Journal of the Geological Society of London*, 109, pp. 137–71.

SANDERS, I. S. and JOHNSTON, J. D. (1989): The Torridonian Stac Fada Member: an extrusion of fluidized peperite?, *Transactions of the Royal Society of Edinburgh, Earth Sciences*, **80**, pp. 1–4.

SANDERS, I. S. and JOHNSTON, J. D. (1990): Reply to: The Torridonian Stac Fada Member: a discussion, *Transactions of the Royal Society of Edinburgh, Earth Sciences*, **81**, pp. 249–50.

SAVAGE, D. and SILLS, J. D. (1980): High pressure metamorphism in the Scourian of NW Scotland: evidence from granet granulites, *Contributions to Mineralogy and Petrology*, **74**, pp. 153–63.

SEARLE, M. P., LAW, R. D., DEWEY, J. F. and STREULE, M. J. (2010): Relationships between the Loch Ailsh and Borralan alkaline intrusions and thrusting in the Moine Thrust zone, southern Assynt Culmination, NW Scotland, in LAW, R., BUTLER, R. W. H., HOLDSWORTH, R. E., KRABBENDAM, M. and STRACHAN, R. (eds): *Continental Tectonics and Mountain Building: The Legacy of Peach and Horne*, Geological Society Special Publication, **335** (London: Geological Society of London).

SHERATON, J. W., SKINNER, A. C. and TARNEY, J. (1973): The geochemistry of the Scourian gneisses of the Assynt district, in PARK, R. G. and TARNEY, J. (eds): *The early Precambrian of Scotland and related rocks of Greenland* (Keele: University of Keele), pp. 31–43.

SILLS, J. D., SAVAGE, D., WATSON, J. V. and WINDLEY, B. F. (1982): Layered ultramafic-gabbro bodies in the Lewisian of northwest Scotland: geochemistry and petrogenesis, *Earth and Planetary Science Letters*, **58**, pp. 345–60.

SMITH, R. L., STEARN, J. E. F. and PIPER, J. D. A. (1983): Paleomagnetic studies of the Torridonian sediments, NW Scotland, *Scottish Journal of Geology*, **19**, pp. 29–45.

SNOKE, A. W. and TULLIS, J. (1998): An overview of fault rocks, in SNOKE, A. W., TULLIS, J. and TODD, V. R. (eds): *Fault-related rocks: a photographic atlas* (Princeton, New Jersey: Princeton University Press), pp. 3–18.

SOPER, N. J. and WILKINSON, P. (1975): The Moine thrust and the Moine nappe at Loch Eriboll, Scotland, *Scottish Journal of Geology*, **11**, pp. 339–59.

STEWART, A. D. (1978): Stoer and Loch Assynt (Torridonian) in BARBER, A. J., BEACH, A., PARK, R. G., TARNEY, J. and STEWART, A. D. (eds): The Lewisian and Torridonian rocks of North-West Scotland, *Geologists' Association Guide*, No. 21, pp. 27–35.

STEWART, A. D. (1982): Late Proterozoic rifting in NW Scotland: the genesis of the 'Torridonian', *Journal of the Geological Society of London*, **139**, pp. 413–20.

STEWART, A. D. (1990): The Torridonian Stac Fada Member: a discussion, *Transactions of the Royal Society of Edinburgh, Earth Sciences*, **81**, p. 247.

STEWART, A. D. (1997): Discussion on indications of glaciation at the base of the

Proterozoic Stoer Group of Scotland, *Journal of the Geological Society of London*, **154**, pp. 373–76.

STEWART, A. D. (2002): The later Proterozoic Torridonian rocks of Scotland: their sedimentology, geochemistry and origin, *Geological Society Memoir*, **24** (London: The Geological Society).

STEWART, A. D. and IRVING, E. (1974): Palaeomagnetism of Precambrian sedimentary rocks from NW Scotland and the apparent polar wandering path of Laurentia, *Geophysical Journal of the Royal Astronomical Society*, **37**, pp. 51–72.

STRACHAN, R. A. (1986): Shallow-marine sedimentation in the Proterozoic Moine Succession, Northern Scotland, *Precambrian Research*, **32**, pp. 17–33.

STRACHAN, R. A., FRIEND, C., ALSOP, G. I. and MILLER, S. (2010): *A Geological Excursion Guide to the Moine Geology of the Northern Highlands of Scotland* (Edinburgh: Edinburgh Geological Society and Geological Society of Glasgow, with NMS Enterprises Limited Publishing).

SUTTON, J. and WATSON, J. V. (1951): The pre-Torridonian metamorphic history of the Loch Torridon and Scourie areas in the northwest Highlands, and its bearing on the chronological classification of the Lewisian, *Quarterly Journal of the Geological Society of London*, **106**, pp. 241–307.

SWETT, K. and SMIT, D. E. (1972): Cambro-Ordovician shelf sedimentation of western Newfoundland, north west Scotland and central east Greenland, *Proceedings of the 24th International Geological Congress*.

TANNER, P. W. G. and EVANS, J. A. (2003): Late Precambrian U-Pb age for peak regional metamorphism and deformation (Knoydartian orogeny) in the western Moine, Scotland, *Journal of the Geological Society of London*, **160**, pp. 555–64.

TARNEY, J. (1973): The Scourie dyke suite and the nature of the Inverian event in Assynt, in PARK, R. G. and TARNEY, J. (eds): *The early Precambrian of Scotland and related rocks of Greenland* (Keele: University of Keele.), pp. 105–118.

TARNEY, J. and WEAVER, B. L. (1987): Mineralogy, petrology and geochemistry of the Scourie dykes: petrogenesis and crystal-

lisation processes in dykes intruded at depth, in PARK, R. G. and TARNEY, J. (eds): *Evolution of the Lewisian and comparable Precambrian high grade terrains*, Geological Society Special Publication, **27**, pp. 217–33.

TEALL, J. J. H. (1885): The metamorphosis of dolerite into hornblende-schist, *Quarterly Journal of the Geological Society of London*, **41**, pp. 133–45.

THIRLWALL, M. F. and BURNARD, P. (1990): Pb-Sr-Nd isotope and chemical study of the origin of undersaturated and oversaturated shoshonitic magmas from the Borralan pluton, Assynt, NW Scotland, *Journal of the Geological Society of London*, **147**, pp. 259–69.

THOMPSON, R. N. and FOWLER, M. B. (1986): Subduction-related shoshonitic and ultrapotassic magmatism: a study of Siluro-Ordovician syenites from the Scottish Caledonides, *Contributions to Mineralogy and Petrology*, **94**, pp. 507–522.

TORSVIK, T. and STURT, B. A. (1987): On the origin and stability of remanence and the magnetic fabric of the Torridonian Red Beds, NW Scotland, *Scottish Journal of Geology*, **23**, pp. 23–38.

TREWIN, N. H. (ed.) (2002): *The Geology of Scotland* (London: The Geological Society).

TURNBULL, M. J. M., WHITEHOUSE, M. J. and MOORBATH, S. (1996): New isotopic age determinations for the Torridonian, NW Scotland, *Journal of the Geological Society of London*, **153**, pp. 955–64.

VAN BREEMEN, O., AFTALION, M. and JOHNSON, M. R. (1979a): Age of the Loch Borrolan complex, Assynt and late movements along the Moine Thrust Zone, Journal of the *Geological Society of London*, **16**, pp. 489–95.

VAN BREEMEN, O., AFTALION, M., PANKHURST, R. J. and RICHARDSON, S. W. (1979b): Age of the Glen Dessarry syenite, Inverness-shire: diachronous Palaeozoic metamorphism across the Great Glen, *Scottish Journal of Geology*, **15**, pp. 49–62.

VANCE, D., STRACHAN, R. A. and JONES, K. A. (1998): Extensional versus compressional settings for metamorphism: garnet chronometry and pressure-temperature-time

histories in the Moine Supergroup, north-
west Scotland, *Geology*, **26**, pp. 927–30.
WHITE, S. H. (1979): Grain and sub-grain size
variations across a mylonite zone, *Contri-
butions to Mineralogy and Petrology*, **70**,
pp. 193–202.
WHITE, S. H. (1980): On mylonites in ductile
shear zones, *Journal of Structural Geology*,
2, pp. 175–87.
WHITE, S. H. (1998): Fault rocks from Ben
Arnaboll, Moine Thrust Zone, Northwest
Scotland, in SNOKE, A. W., TULLIS, J. and
TODD, V. R. (eds): *Fault-related rocks: a
photographic atlas* (Princeton, New Jersey:
Princeton University Press), pp. 382–91.
WHITE, S. H., EVANS, D. J. and ZHONG, D.
L. (1982): Fault rock in the Moine Thrust
Zone: microstructures and textures of
selected mylonites, *Textures and Micro-
structures*, **5**, pp. 33–61.
WHITEHOUSE, M. J. (1989): Sm-Nd evidence
for the diachronous crustal accretion of the
Lewisian complex of northwest Scotland,
Tectonophysics, **161**, pp. 245–56.
WIBBERLEY, C. A. J. (2005): Initiation of
basement thrust detachments by fault-zone
reaction weakening, in BRUHN, D. and
BURLINI, L. (eds): High-Strain Zones:
Structure and Physical Properties, Geological
Society Special Publication, **245** (London),
pp. 347–72.
WIBBERLEY, C. A. J. and BUTLER, R. W. H.
(2010): Structure and internal deformation
of the Arnaboll Thrust Sheet, NW Scotland:
implications for strain localization in thrust
belts, in LAW, R., BUTLER, R. W. H.,
HOLDSWORTH, R. E., KRABBENDAM,
M. and STRACHAN, R. (eds): *Continental
Tectonics and Mountain Building*, Geological
Society Special Publication, **335** (London),
pp. 319–22.
WILKINSON, P., SOPER, N. J. and BELL,
A. N. (1975): Skolithus pipes as strain
markers in mylonites, *Tectonophysics*, **28**,
pp. 143–57.
WILLIAMS, G. E. (1969): Petrography and
origin of pebbles from Torridonian strata
(late Precambrian), northwest Scotland, in
KAY, M. (eds): North Atlantic – geology and
continental drift: a symposium, pp. 609–29.

WILLIAMS, G. E. (2001): Neoproterozoic
(Torridonian) alluvial fan succession,
Northwest Scotland, and its tectonic setting
and provenance, *Geological Magazine*,
138, pp. 471–94.
WILSON, R. W., HOLDSWORTH, R. E.,
WILD, L. E., McCAFFREY, K. J. W.,
ENGLAND, R. W., IMBER, J. and
STRACHAN, R. (2010): Basement-
influenced rifting and basin development: a
reappraisal of post-Caledonian faulting
patterns in the North Coast Transfer Zone,
Scotland, in LAW, R., BUTLER, R. W. H.,
HOLDSWORTH, R. E., KRABBENDAM,
M. and STRACHAN, R. (eds): *Continental
Tectonics and Mountain Building*,
Geological Society Special Publication,
335 (London), pp. 785–816.
WOODCOCK, N. and STRACHAN, R. (eds)
(2000): *Geological History of Britain and
Ireland* (Oxford: Blackwell Science).
WOOLLEY, A. R. (1970): The structural
relationships of the Loch Borrolan complex,
Scotland, *Geological Journal*, **7**, pp. 171–
82.
WRIGHT and KNIGHT (1995): A revised
chronostratigraphy for the lower Durness
group, *Scottish Journal of Geology*, **31**, pp.
11–22.
YOUNG, B. N., PARSONS, I. and THREAD-
GOULD, R. (1994): Carbonatite near the
Loch Borralan Intrusion, Assynt, *Journal of
the Geological Society of London*, **150**, pp.
945–54.
YOUNG, G. M. (1999): Some aspects of the
geochemistry, provenance and palaeo-
climatology of the Torridonian of NW
Scotland, *Journal of the Geological Society
of London*, **156**, pp. 1097–1113.
YOUNG, G. M. (2002): Stratigraphy and
geo-chemistry of volcanic mass flows in the
Stac Fada Member of the Stoer group,
Torridonian, NW Scotland, *Transactions
of the Royal Society of Edinburgh*, **93**, pp.
1–16.
ZHU, X. K., O' NIONS, R. K., BELSHAW, N.
S. and GIBB, A. J. (1997): Lewisian crustal
history from in situ SIMS mineral chronometry and related metamorphic textures,
Chemical Geology, **136**, pp. 205–18.

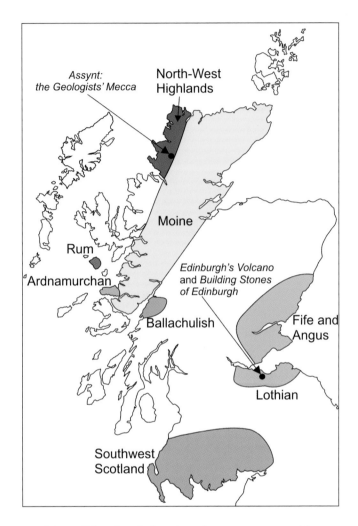

Map of Scotland showing the areas covered by
Excursion Guides of the Edinburgh Geological Society.
Leaflets are indicated in italics. For more information:

www.edinburghgeolsoc.org

1. SW Scotland is published jointly with the British Geological Survey;
2. Fife and Angus is published by the Pentland Press
with financial support from the Society.